Exotic Herbs

Henry Holt and Company • New York

Exotic Herbs

A COMPENDIUM OF EXCEPTIONAL CULINARY HERBS

Carole Saville

Photographs by Rosalind Creasy

Henry Holt and Company, Inc.
Publishers since 1866
115 West 18th Street
New York, New York 10011

Henry Holt® is a registered trademark
of Henry Holt and Company, Inc.

Published in Canada by Fitzhenry & Whiteside Ltd.,
195 Allstate Parkway, Markham, Ontario L3R 4T8

Library of Congress Cataloging-in-Publication Data
Saville, Carole.
Exotic herbs : a compendium of exceptional culinary herbs /
Carole Saville; photographs by Rosalind Creasy.—1st ed.
p.   cm.
Includes bibliographical references (p. 289) and index.
1. Herb gardening.   2. Herbs.   3. Cookery (Herbs) I. Title.
SB351.H5S28   1997   96-23418
641.3'57—dc20   CIP

ISBN 0-8050-4073-0

Henry Holt books are available for special promotions
and premiums. For details contact: Director, Special Markets.

First Edition: 1997

Designed by Betty Lew

Photographs on pages 144 and 258 courtesy of Michael H. Dodge.

Printed in the United States of America
All first editions are printed on acid-free paper. ∞

10   9   8   7   6   5   4   3   2   1

Important Notice on Consumption of Edible Plants
This book contains information on a wide range of culinary herbs available from specialty seed catalogs. The author and the publishers accept no liability for any harm, damage, or illness arising from the misuse of the plants described in this book. The advice this book contains is general, and not specific to individuals and their particular circumstances. Any plant substance used internally as food or handled externally can cause an allergic reaction in some people. During pregnancy, avoid taking any new or unknown substances without first consulting a physician. Neither the author nor the publishers can be held responsible for claims arising from mistaking the identity of any herb or using it inappropriately. Neither the author nor the publishers can be held responsible for any adverse reaction to the recipes, recommendations, or instructions contained herein. The use of any herb is entirely at the reader's own risk.

To B, and my family,

and the happy memories of Blue Mill Road,

Primrose Brook Farm, and Briar Knoll

Contents

Acknowledgments

My thanks go first of all to talented photographer, author, gardener, and friend Rosalind Creasy; and to artful editor Ray Roberts, in whose company I am pleased to be. My gratitude goes to the hardest-working agents in the publishing business, Betsy Amster and Angela Miller; and to Joan DeFato, Librarian of the Plant Science Library at the Los Angeles County Arboretum, for her knowledgeable and cheerful assistance. Equal thanks are extended to Renée Shepherd, Beth Benjamin, and Wendy Krupnick formerly of Shepherd's Garden Seeds; Brian Hauck of the Biology Department's Botanical Garden at California State University, Northridge; Sally at Thanh My restaurant; and Molly Kellogg, my Southeast Asian connection.

Part I 🍀

A Practical Guide to Cultivation and Use of a World of Herbs

INTRODUCTION

My beginner's herb garden wasn't planted with basic basil, sage, marjoram, and thyme, but rather with the more exotic sweet cicely, blue borage, angelica, hyssop, lovage, salad burnet, and costmary. They formed a so-called "friendship garden," because the plants grew from slips of herbs given to me by a friend from the abundance of her Colonial period garden. Growing herbs became my lifelong passion. Perhaps the learning experience of planting that first fragrant herb bed twenty-five years ago inclined me and my garden senses to continue to seek out the unusual and more exotic culinary herbs to plant among the traditional herb garden basics: parsley, oregano, thyme, sage, mint, and rosemary. I learned to treasure the time-honored standards as much as the exotics; many of the standards are exotic in themselves, with their multiple flavors ranging from the perfumed English lavender and sweet marjoram to musky sage and clove-scented basil, and continue to give us their descendants in the form of cultivated varieties.

The culinary herbs of antiquity have always held for me a particular fascination. I am continually awed that so many of the treasured culinary herbs grown in ancient times for their beauty and taste—bay, fennel, dill, coriander, anise, purslane, onions (including shallots), saffron, savory, garden cress, and garlic, in addition to the other herb basics mentioned above—are the very same herbs that we, too, cherish in our gardens, both for their ornamental qualities and for flavoring our contemporary cooking. Many of these were included in the list of herbs for "the spice rack" recommended to be kept on hand in the Roman house so that there may be "nothing wanting," as proclaimed by the first-century Roman gastronome and cookbook author Apicius. Salads were as popular in Roman days as they are in today's salad bars with their endless choices of ingredients residing behind glass counters. The Romans often used a heavy hand with herbs in their salads, some of them of the everything-but-the-kitchen-sink variety, using herb leaves, seeds, and roots with assorted

vegetables. But they were also discriminating in their choice of herbs: combining herbs and spices to give dishes a unique taste was considered a fine art. One ancient epicurean counseled the cook to season food with a harmony of flavors, "like a man who tunes a lyre until it rightly sounds." Some things never change. The romance of the herb garden with its myriad colors, textures, shapes, and scents is as appreciated by our senses today as it was in ancient times. The sensual experience of the fragrance released by scented herbs when brushed against in the garden—

whether by the folds of Roman togas or gowns, billowing medieval skirts, Renaissance silks, Early American cotton aprons, or the down-to-earth utilitarian garden garb of today's blue jean generation—remains the same.

Still waters run deep, for these seemingly unassuming plants in reality have subtle power. The flavorful herbs that form a bouquet garni—parsley, thyme, and bay—or fines herbes—chervil, chives, parsley, and tarragon—undoubtedly need no introduction. But consider the basis of numerous ethnic regional dishes that makes them national treasures: the basil in Italian pesto, the sauce for *pasta al pesto* that seems to belong to America; the oregano in Greek *souvlakia*, succulent skewered meats roasted over an open fire; the garlic in French aioli, the pungent mayonnaise sauce for vegetables, fish, and meat known as "the butter of Provence"; the parsley in *jambon persille de Bourgogne*, the Burgundian ham specialty that is de rigueur for Easter Sunday; the lemongrass in the Thai signature dish *tom kha gai*, a silken chicken and coconut milk soup; and of course, the mint in a julep for two.

A rich tapestry of history and a world of colorful legend and charming folklore surround the culinary herbs. In olden times, an innocent herb like savory, which we so freely sprinkle over a mundane plate of green beans, was considered an aphrodisiac, as it "arouses the passions in which desire enters as well," stated the Italian writer Platina, the author of *De Honesta Voluptate*, published in 1475. Another aphrodisiac was coriander, which makes us think not of passionate love but of how nice a pinch would be in a jar of pickles. That is not far off the mark, for the seeds, lightly crushed and combined with caraway, were used as a preservative for meat in the early Roman days of nonrefrigeration. The recipe for using it as an aphrodisiac to make a partner willing was to pound fresh coriander leaves (also called cilantro) with garlic and drop the muddle into a glass of wine—I assume this garlic-scented love potion was designed to be drunk by two. Now, if you begin to read many old herbals, you'll discover that every other herb in your garden is noted somewhere as an aphrodisiac, which may not be true, but the fragrance of certain herbs is surely sweet enough to put one in the mood for love. In the first century, Roman gardeners—the unscientific ones—when sowing and tending basil, believed the herb would grow more abundantly if verbally abused. The early Greeks felt likewise, believing it would not grow unless it were denounced as it was planted. Supposedly the practice was to shout curses and stomp violently on the ground while sowing the poor little seeds—oh, and yes, basil was considered a powerful love charm. However, a late fifteenth-century Italian cookbook author firmly stated that "man does not lose his reason by smelling it, and, mixed with wine and vinegar, it heals stings of scorpions—either the land or sea varieties."

Another popular use of herbs was to drive away witches. Dill was thought to have this power, but its other reputation, for inducing a good evening's sleep if one drank a steaming, hot cup of dill tea just before bedtime, may be more accurate, as its name is derived from the Norse word *dillan*, meaning "to lull." Oregano, thyme, rosemary, roses, and saffron were used not only to flavor foods but to perfume the body with sweet and savory scents. A person drenched in beneficially fragrant lavender advertised his or her wealth, so expensive was the essential oil. At other times in herbal history women have perfumed their hair by combining lavender with sweet basil in a pomade and combing it through their tresses. Lemon balm, a nectar-favorite herb of bees, was considered a citrus-scented beacon to guide the way home to the hive for lost honeybees. The herb is evidently helpful for all types of harrowing trips: prominent on the label of a popular French cordial made with lemon balm, Eau de Melisse, is the claim for its soothing effects on those with motion sickness. An 1819 "receipt book" combined lemon balm with sage and lavender in a recipe for a cordial—an unusual trio. If all three herbs grow in your garden, it's easy to test such curious recipes found in cherished old cookbooks; you may rediscover an excellent one to include in your contemporary repertoire of cookery, or add a few of the latest herb discoveries.

The romance and the delights of the herb garden are never-ending. Whether you have a kitchen garden planted with just culinary herbs or have herbs planted in among your ornamentals, taking an evening stroll in the garden just before preparing dinner is rewarding even if you don't pick any herbs. But most likely you will, for gathering a sprig of this, then that, and perhaps a handful of herb flowers with their soft-hued colors, inspires one to be creative in the kitchen and removes the chore from cooking. The same inspirational stroll can be taken in the morning before breakfast to gather a little handful of fraises des bois for cereal, or a leaf or two of sage to make fresh savory biscuits, or perhaps for sage butter to brush on top of the store-bought kind. Another stroll at lunchtime could produce a delicious sorrel soup, and one more in the late afternoon could result in a refreshing cold or hot mint tea, or the aforementioned icy mint julep. Perhaps the most subtle gift a garden of culinary herbs gives, which seems to occur without your being aware of it, is the way its bounty enhances your cooking. Even in winter you needn't be without your flavoring herbs, for the essence of the little workhorse plants can be captured in vinegars and oils, sugars and salts, and honeys and butters, all put up in one fashion or another. This was well known to keepers of seventeenth- and eighteenth-century "still rooms," where such specialties were stored.

As if the flavor-giving qualities of herbs weren't enough, the other pleasurable aspect of growing a garden of culinary herbs is the design process. The heritage seed-saving movement, along with the idea of the edible/ornamental landscape popular in the last decade, has created new interest in the culinary herbs, because we realize that instead of the *one* rosemary bush or the *one* sage in the kitchen garden, we can plant an entire *row* of them to form a beautiful edible and ornamental tapestry hedge, or interplant them in a perennial or flower border. We can use herbs like thyme, hyssop, and miniature sage to create a historical knot garden; or make an inviting theme garden of fragrant herbs like scented geraniums, lavender, and chamomile, planted in containers if necessary, where space is minimal. In my longtime involvement in growing herbs, one of the good things I have discovered about them is their versatility. Theme gardens can be designed with them ad infinitum: you can create beds devoted solely to white, pink, purple, yellow, or blue-flowering herbs, or to those with silver and gray foliage; a literary garden (the writings of Shakespeare remain an excellent source); an eighteenth-century parlor or "dooryard" garden close by the house planted with herbs, perennials, roses, and annual flowers surrounded by a rustic paling or picket fence; an Elizabethan knot garden; a rose garden underplanted with herbs; a shade herb garden; an herbal rock garden; a Native American herb garden; a tea garden; a garden of seed-producing herbs (dill, fennel, caraway, anise, cilantro, ajwain, etc.); and for those with patience, an herb topiary garden in pots, so unique and decorative on a patio or balcony where there is no room for a large garden.

The choice in accoutrements available today in garden stores and catalogs to make the landscape even more beautiful is staggering. There are artful elements to complement any style of herb garden the designer wishes, from romantic, formal, and elegant to traditional, cottage, and cute. There are beautiful pale blue-green glass cloches to place over and protect budding herbs in cold climates, or to use as garden art in both cold and warm climates; there are authentic English love-knot benches for sitting and for creating a restful focal point in the garden—the ideal adornment for the aforementioned knot garden. Available are fanciful trellises for herbs like ground cherries and climbing roses to scamper up; "horizontal trellises," which

are lacy cast stepping stones through which creeping thymes and chamomile peek through and emit their special scents under footfalls; movable stone water bowls to be set down in a bed of moisture-loving herbs like mint, bee balm, and lemon balm to form a miniature oasis in the garden; and elegant sundials and birdbaths of all sorts around the bases of which pinks and violets can grow. These garden ornaments are complemented by the beauty of all manner of herbs.

This book celebrates sixty of the exotic culinary herbs that I have planted in my gardens over the years, which I consider to be extraordinary—beautiful in the garden, and delicious in the kitchen. The word "exotic" in this book has many meanings, reflecting not only proper horticultural parlance and the dictionary's first meaning of the word, "from another part of the world; not indigenous; foreign," but also its second meaning, "having the charm of the unfamiliar; strikingly and intriguingly unusual or beautiful." And of course these herbs all possess exceptional culinary attributes. "Exotic" here also refers to plants that are generally considered ornamental only but that in fact also have special culinary qualities. Silene has a delightful "toothy" texture when mixed with radicchio and tender salad greens; it's also a terrific substitute for escarole in a rich beef consommé. The pungent, pebbly, gray suede leaves of Cleveland sage, native to California, make an aromatic substitute for garden sage. Violets not only make a royal posy, but with their leaves full of vitamin C and their flowers full of fragrance, they also make a lovely, refreshing spring salad. Dianthus, the darling of the cottage garden and the dependable pink that creates a clove-perfumed sea of colorful spring and summer bloom, also makes a heady sorbet or sweetly scented syrup to pour over pancakes, crepes, or Belgian waffles.

A new world of exotic ethnic herbs has recently reached our shores with the influx to the United States of people from many diverse cultures who have brought with them the fascinating herbs traditionally used to flavor their foods. These herbs have unusual and exciting tastes most certainly foreign to our palates, so I have included a number of the intriguing "new" herbs that I now snip from the garden for cooking as casually as I do thyme. For example, rau ram adds zip to a salad of fresh bean sprouts, shredded carrots, and roasted peanuts, and it also makes a lovely ground cover in the garden for a semishaded area. Roselle, known as "jamaica" in the Caribbean, is a tart and tangy flavoring that makes terrific cerise-colored sauces, jellies, and beverages. Curry leaf from India enriches vegetable curries with its unique musky flavor and makes a graceful focal point in the garden with its frondlike branches.

Equally exotic are the intriguing hybrids, cultivars, and varieties of the traditional culinary herbs, among them 'African Blue' basil, 'Majorca Pink' rosemary, 'Orange Balsam' thyme scented with just a hint of orange, and white-flowering and pink-flowering English lavender.

Languishing between the lines in nursery catalogs, herbs with exotic attributes go unnoticed year after year as gardeners continue to order only the tried and true or the yearly new introductions—showy winners of garden trials announced annually with great fervor. The 'Échalote de Jersey' onion, or "Jersey shallot," might be passed over as just another French import, but this small, mild onion is identical in flavor to true shallots, and is grown from seed in just one year. Leaf celery is a lush green-on-green herb, and a cook's secret, for its slender stems impart a more pungent celery flavor to foods than celery itself. The cilantro-mimic herb papaloquelite is popular in Bolivia and parts of the Southwest and Mexico, where its pungent flavor enhances chile salsas. Fraises des bois, or alpine strawberries, are now available with perfumed *white* berries, plus in a variegated-leaf form with the familiar rich red fruit. In a way, all culinary herbs are "exotic," in the everyday use of the word, simply because of the myriad of tastes and scents with which they flavor foods.

Most of the herbs discussed here are not available as cut herbs in the marketplace, but all of them are available either in seed or plant form from specialty mail order nurseries, which makes a case for growing your own. New gardeners can begin to tuck in an exotic herb or two between the parsley and sage in the beginner's garden and can add several new plants a season, and longtime gardeners who enjoy knowing about the latest imports and new cultivars can interweave them into their established gardens to create new color and design schemes—and both will reap the culinary benefits. Chefs can expand their repertoire of kitchen herbs and have the latest in their production gardens. We all know that even parsley tastes better when grown in a garden, no matter how large or small—in pots on a balcony or patio, in an apartment window box, in a roof garden or in an allotment in the neighborhood community garden. I have never been without my kitchen garden, whether it was the first victory-style garden hodgepodge in the ruins of an old dairy barn or the "dooryard garden" viewed from the window of a eighteenth-century farmhouse on the East Coast. I have grown my "potager" in as many pots as I could fit onto a tiny balcony adjacent to a cardboard-box apartment facing the Pacific Ocean in Venice, California, and now I garden on one third of an acre on a mountaintop in Los Angeles that I share with the deer and squirrels.

My gardening friend and the photographer for this book, Rosalind Creasy, calls me an herb maven. I admit it's true, for after gardening and cooking with herbs for twenty-five years, I am still enthralled with the discovery of a new herb. Since I know firsthand the positive difference that fresh herbs play in cooking, I am particularly excited about experimenting in the kitchen with the expanding new treasure trove of unfamiliar, exotic, ethnic herbs and the ever-increasing number of alluring new cultivars of the traditionals. I want to share the enthusiasm I feel for these culinary herbs, the creativity  that cooking with them inspires, and the pleasure and satisfaction to be gained from gardening with them and watching them grow. This book is for those gardeners and cooks who consider both arts—gardening and cooking—pleasurable, creative, calming, and rewarding work, instead of a chore. I hope that curious cooks will find these newly discovered exotic herbs with their unique flavors exciting to add to their repertoire of creative cooking, and that curious gardeners will discover delicious new edible ornamentals with unusual leaf forms and shapes to create new design plans for their gardens.

GROWING HERBS IN THE GARDEN

One of the criteria for defining herbs is culinary usage; other criteria are a plant's use historically or in modern times for fragrance, medicinal, household, or economic purposes. A further way of describing culinary herbs is "non-woody plants whose leaves, stems, flowers, and roots are those parts used in food." As always, there are exceptions to the rule. For example, sage, rosemary, lavender, and thyme, four of the most respected culinary herbs, do have woody stems; and some herbs, like cilantro and fennel, double as spices, for the seeds that are collected from them are considered spices. A general distinction between herbs and spices is that herbs are grown in temperate regions, and spices, from which are collected culinary roots, bark, fruit, buds, and seeds, are grown in the tropics.

The technical distinctions between herbs and spices are less important than the culinary riches there are to explore and experiment with, and the vast variety of these edible plants seems to increase as the world gets smaller. In this book are culinary herbs as annuals, perennials, biennials, herbal trees and shrubs, ground covers, and edible flowers. Fortunately, herbs are easy to grow when planted in situations that suit their needs, and there are herbs that thrive in every growing situation, whether it be sunny, shady, part sun and part shade, wet, or dry.

ZONE INFORMATION

The U.S. Department of Agriculture has created the USDA Plant Hardiness Map, depicting the average annual minimum temperatures for the eleven geographical zones of the United States based on validated meteorological data from 14,500 government stations in the United States, Canada, and Mexico. The records used included the annual low temperatures recorded from 1974 to 1986 for the United States and Canada, and 1971 to 1984 for Mexico.

The herb entries contain information on the range of climate zones where the plants grow best, and many may survive in warmer or colder zones, but survival does not necessarily represent satisfactory performance. Therefore, other factors should be taken into consideration such as soil, moisture, exposure, and day and nighttime temperatures, as well as the individual practice of maintaining plants. Even within a certain zone, there are subtle and not-so-subtle differences between microclimates, and these affect the growth of the herbs. There are microclimates in your home vicinity and even on your own property. Given the right care or under the right micro-conditions, many of the herbs could conceivably survive— and thrive—in colder or warmer zones than those indicated. Often, determined gardeners succeed in growing plants that aren't supposed to grow in a particular zone, motivated by the challenge or sheer desire of having them in the garden. Longtime gardeners in your area and the local agricultural cooperative extension office can be quite helpful regarding what will grow where in your particular climate.

A NOTE ON PLANT NAMES

The many common names for herbs and other plants are at once charming, curious, poetic, imaginative, and cognate, according to familiar root words. Add to the various common names of plants the latinized botanical family name and scientific name, variety names, cultivar names, hybrid names—and confusion sets in.

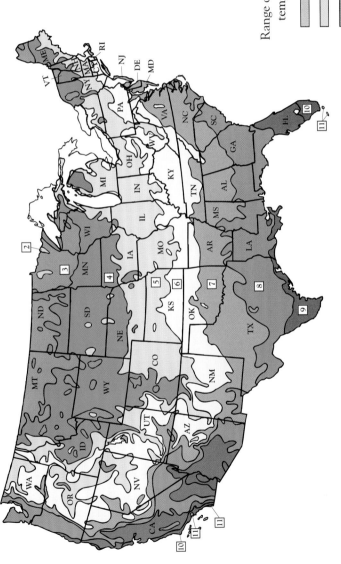

Range of average annual minimum
temperatures for each Zone.

Zone 1   below −50°F
Zone 2   −50° to −40°
Zone 3   −40° to −30°
Zone 4   −30° to −20°
Zone 5   −20° to −10°
Zone 6   −10° to   0°
Zone 7   0° to 10°
Zone 8   10° to 20°
Zone 9   20° to 30°
Zone 10   30° to 40°
Zone 11 above 40°

Understanding the nomenclature of plants may seem daunting, but knowledge of the scientific name of a plant is a must in order to know what to ask for either in the local nursery or from a mail-order seed catalog so you can acquire exactly the plant you have in mind. Choosing plants by their common names can be confusing and not necessarily reliable. For instance, *Dianthus superbus*, discussed in this book, is listed in garden catalogs and garden books by the various names of cupid's lace, lilac pink, rainbow loveliness, and superb pink; another herb, *Chenopodium gigantea*, is listed among several catalogs as purple goosefoot, tree spinach, magentaspreen lamb's-quarter, and magenta lamb's-quarter. While I chose the most common name of herbs listed in the different seed catalogs for inclusion in this book, it is generally best to order plants by their scientific Latin names. The following is an aid to navigating through the plant name maze.

The plant naming system begins with a family name that includes plants with the same structure such as the Rosaceae or rose family. The family names usually end in *-aceae*. The plants within the family are generally referred to by two scientific names. The first part states the plant's genus, which is the group to which it belongs, as it shares many features and similar flower structure. The second part of the name states its species, which denotes different growth habits or special characteristics that distinguish it from other plants in the genus. For example, plants with wrinkled leaves are called *rugosa*, as in *Rosa rugosa*, the wonderful old Turkestan rose with rough, crinkled leaves. The second name sometimes describes the color of plants, as in *alba* (white) or *purpurascens* (purple); or a pattern, as in *variegata* (variegated). The second name can also describe a plant's form or habit, such as *spicata*, meaning spiked, as in *Thymbra spicata*; or stature, such as *nobilis*, meaning noble, as in *Laurus nobilis*, or *Thymus vulgaris*, meaning common. The second name of many herbs is *officinalis*, as in *Rosmarinus officinalis*, meaning a noted herb "of the workshop," in allusion to the apothecary of bygone days. Plants are also named after people, as in *Salvia clevelandii* or Cleveland sage, named after the botanist Daniel Cleveland. They can also be named after legendary people, as in *Mentha*, the genus named after Menthe, the lovely Greek nymph who was turned into her namesake plant by the jealous wife of Pluto. When an herb is discovered either in the wild or in the garden that is not sufficiently different from its species to be a separate one, and produces seedlings of the same kind, it is known as a natural variety or subspecies, and a third name is added to the scientific name, as in *Porophyllum ruderale* subspecies *macrocephalum* or papaloquelite. A cultivated variety or cultivar is one that has been selected from the wild or from gardens and grown under controlled cultivation, such as *Thymus vulgaris* 'Orange Balsam'. Hybrids are the offspring resulting from a cross between two species, subspecies, varieties, and even between two plants from different genera. Hybrids are generally written with an 'x' between the names of the two parent species, such as in *Ocimum kilimandscharicum* x *Ocimum purpurascens*, or 'African Blue' basil.

With scientific plant names demystified, garden catalogs and books become more enjoyable to read and understand, rather than just words and pretty pictures. In turn, our gardens become bountiful with informed plant choices, as the acquired knowledge of the language of botanical nomenclature becomes second nature.

ANNUALS, PERENNIALS, AND BIENNIALS

An annual is a plant that germinates, blooms, sets seed, then dies in one growing season, having completed its life cycle. Seed must be collected for propagation. Hardy annuals are those that will survive some frost, and can be seeded directly in the ground where they are to flower. Many hardy annuals will self-seed after fall bloom, and some, such as nigella, are purposely sown in the fall so they can develop good root growth and bloom with large flowers the following spring. Half-hardy annuals are those that survive no frost; they are sown in the garden when all danger of frost is past, or sown indoors in early winter for transplanting when the soil has warmed. Tender annuals are plants that don't survive even the slightest nip in the air.

Perennials are plants that survive the cold winter, returning each season from the same root system. Some need winter protection such as a mulch of pine branches to keep them from heaving out of the ground with repeated thaw-and-freeze conditions, or must be sited in an area that is protected from cold winter winds. When sown indoors in early winter, many perennials will flower the first year. Tender perennials are those that will not survive frost or freezing. Sometimes they will survive with winter protection.

Biennials are plants that germinate in the spring, put on leaf growth in the summer, over-winter, and bloom the following spring. Some biennials can self-sow after flowering.

SOWING SEED INDOORS AND OUTDOORS

Most of the herbs in this book are best obtained as plants from specialty nurseries because seed is not widely available. However, about one third of the herbs are available in seed form, and if you enjoy the "birth process" of growing herbs from scratch, or would like a large plantation of a certain herb for an edging or ground cover, or if you want to set up shop as a pro-

duction gardener catering to local restaurants, propagating herbs from seed is the most economical way to grow them. It is also the best method for getting a jump on the growing season for planting annuals that will already be off to a good start come warm weather. Those perennials that can bloom in their first season, such as 'Lady' lavender, are good bets for planting the seeds of indoors. Starting seed indoors in a more controlled environment than the great outdoors is more desirable when collected seeds are treasured such as those of white borage, white fraises des bois, or 'Échalote de Jersey,' which is available only from a foreign seed house, and you want assured germination. These days, in many parts of the country, seeds can be sown in the "second" gardening season, mid- to late summer; this is the ideal time to sow seeds for late harvests for herbs such as garland chrysanthemum, broadleaf cress, and miner's lettuce for cool weather salads or herbs that winter over for healthy spring harvests.

Don't try and get too early a jump on the growing season by planting too early indoors, or the plants will be weak and spindly. To sow seeds eight weeks before the last date of frost is a good rule of thumb for healthy seedlings. Use clean pots or plastic flats filled with sterile potting soil, or the lightweight commercial soilless mixes. The three necessities for growing seeds indoors are attention to watering, nutrients, and proper light. A greenhouse obviously provides the best conditions for the latter, but a diligent gardener can grow seedlings in a sunny window that faces south or southeast with no obstruction from the outside. Artificial light stands are the other option. Plant seeds at the depth indicated in the package directions, and label each row of seeds with the names of the herbs and the date of sowing. Water the container by placing it in a pan with about two inches of water and remove it when the soil has become moist; or water from above with a fine spray. When two true leaves appear, which are the second set of leaves to grow, the seedlings can be transplanted from flats to small pots. When they are ready to be planted outdoors, they will first need to be "hardened off," meaning gradually acclimatized to their new environment. Place the herbs outside in a spot that is sheltered from sun and wind. For the first several days, bring them indoors for the night. After their first night outdoors, gradually expose them to full sun.

Herb seeds that are directly sown in the ground tend to produce the healthiest herbs. This method is especially recommended for annual herbs that grow quickly like lamb's-quarter, purslane, and African valerian. After all danger of frost is past in your area, sow herb seeds in prepared soil at a depth indicated by the package directions. Very small seeds can be broadcast on top of the soil, then covered with finely sifted soil. Herb seeds can also be sown in rows or a little patch. Tamp the soil and moisten with a fine spray of water, preferably from a "rose" or flat nozzle attachment at the end of a wand that is fitted onto the garden hose. When the two true leaves develop, thin the seedlings so each one has healthy room to grow.

PROPAGATION BY STEM CUTTINGS, DIVISION, AND LAYERING

Stem cuttings are an easy way to share with a fellow gardener an herb that he or she secretly, or not so secretly, covets. Cuttings are an excellent way to obtain a variety of herbs in case the garden shoe is on the other foot and you happen to be the one envious of an herb in a friend's garden. During the spring or summer take cuttings from the young, leafy tips of the herbs just below a node, the point where a leaf joins the stem, using sharp scissors or pruning shears. The cuttings should be about 6 inches long and contain several nodes. Place them in a glass of water in a bright area, but not in direct sun. Change the water daily. As soon as the expected roots are about ¼ inch long, pot them up in sterile potting soil and water gently. Place them in a box or other container and cover with plastic. Then place them in an area with bright, not direct, light, or on an artificial-light stand. As soon as new topgrowth appears, remove the pot from the container and harden off the plant in a shady, protected spot for several days before putting it in full sun. Ginger mint, rau ram, and rice paddy herb are good candidates for this method of propagation.

Stem cuttings can also be grown in a pot of perlite, vermiculite, or coarse sand. White lavender, 'Golden Rain' and 'Majorca Pink' rosemary, and 'Mabel Grey' scented geranium are good choices for this method, because they take longer to root. Dip the stems in the commercial hormone preparation RooTone powder, and without knocking the substance off the stems, stick the cutting in the pot. Water it thoroughly. Place the pot in a box and cover with plastic. Then place it in an area with bright, not direct, light, or on an artificial-light stand. Open the plastic cover regularly to provide air circulation and mist the plants and water the soil. Eventually when you gently tug at the stems you will feel resistance; then you will know you have succeeded, and the cuttings have rooted.

A quick and easy method of propagation is root division, most often used with perennial herbs. Divide the root mass either by teasing apart its dense root system into several pieces or by cutting and lifting a portion of the clump of roots with a sharp slicing spade. Replant in freshly prepared soil, or if the clump is going to a friend's garden, wrap it in wet newspaper and suggest planting as soon as possible. This operation is best undertaken either in the early spring or at the end of the growing season.

Layering is the lazy way to propagate herbs. Sage, rosemary, and thyme benefit from this method of encouraging stems to root while they are still attached to the parent plant. Select a vigorous branch growing close to the ground, or one flexible enough to be bent down without snapping, and bury a central portion of the stem after scraping the outer layer of the surface. Use a hairpin to hold the stem down. Bend the growing tip vertically and support it with a small stake. When the stem has rooted, sever it from the plant, then carefully dig it up and transplant it.

An excellent book with detailed information on propagating herbs that is easy to read and understand is *Growing Herbs from Seed, Cutting and Root: An Adventure in Small Miracles*, by Thomas DeBaggio (Interweave Press).

SOIL PREPARATION, FERTILIZERS, AND MULCHES

If you have the luxury of long-range planning for your herb garden, ideally the soil is prepared in the fall and planting done in the spring so the prepared bed has time to stabilize and settle. If you cannot wait a whole season to plant your herbs, do wait two weeks after tilling the soil; at this time the soil amendments are added. Choose a location for the herb garden that gets five to six hours of direct unobstructed sun a day. Some herbs need part sun or part shade, which generally means an area that receives a few hours of full sun and is shaded for the remainder of the day. Part shade also refers to dappled light created by trees or foliage with open branching. Shade means little or no direct exposure to the sun.

Well-drained, moderately fertile soil combined ("amended") with a good amount of organic matter that helps retain nutrients and moisture and keeps the soil well aerated is a basic necessity for growing healthy herbs. An evaluation must be made to determine what type of soil you have so you will know what you need to improve it. Your county agriculture extension office can guide you regarding the type of native soil in the area, or you can have your soil tested by sending samples to a local soil testing lab. To prepare the bed, loosen the soil to one foot, using one of the excellent garden forks with four square tines or a spade available from specialty gardening stores. If your soil is of poor quality or cannot be worked, raised-bed planting is an alternative, as the beds can be filled with suitable soil to provide excellent drainage and air circulation. A raised bed contains soil that is above the general ground level and whose sides are supported by a suitable material such as nontoxic treated wood. Stone and brick also make handsome borders for raised beds. The beds can be as low as one foot above the ground. Higher raised beds can be designed with walls of stacked wood or stone to contain the soil, and they are especially effective with cascading herbs. Raised bed planting can be a lovely design feature, allowing the gardener to get closer to those fragrant herbs.

The three basic types of soil are clay, sand, and loam. Clay soil is rich in nutrients but is not porous. Sandy soil is porous, but is unable to hold nutrients and water for long. The most desirable soil, loam, is a mix of clay, silt, and sand, and is considered friable, which means easily pulverized and sufficiently dry to crumble between your hands rather than forming a wet ball. Organic matter can be added to clay soils and coarse sand or gravel, and composted bark can be added to provide good drainage. To improve sandy soils, copious amounts of organic matter and lime need to be added. Loamy soil can be amended with lesser amounts of organic matter. Lime is commonly added to acid soils to improve soil productivity. Organic amendments to improve soil include your own homemade garden compost pile, which is the most economical, and/or pulverized bark, leaf mold, peat, well-rotted animal manures, mushroom compost, and seaweed. Herbs that like well-drained, moist soil benefit from a layer of organic mulch such as cocoa hulls, rice hulls, buckwheat, chipped bark, and chopped straw; as the mulch gradually decomposes it will add to the enrichment of the soil. In the humid south, two or three inches of pea gravel aid in keeping plant roots cool and helps protect the herbs from soil-borne diseases.

Many herb gardeners prefer to rely on a properly amended soil to grow healthy herbs instead of depending on fertilizer, but herbs do appreciate a well-balanced fertilizer in moderation. A happy medium needs to be struck, for a soil that is too poor will produce sparse herbs with little flavor in the leaves, and a soil too richly fertilized will generate a lush, leafy growth with a small concentration of the plant's essential oils. Heavily harvested herbs benefit from fertilizing often. Generally, native soil contains enough nutrients to grow herbs, but not necessarily enough nutrients to produce tasty leaves filled with rich essential oils. Organic fertilizers, which are preferable, include dry fish fertilizer and liquid fish emulsion (dry fish fertilizer has a higher nitrogen content than liquid fish emulsion, and is not as smelly), seaweed extracts, bonemeal, bloodmeal, soybean or cottonseed meal, rock phosphate, greensand, worm castings, bird or bat guano, "zoo doo," (aged fertilizer provided by zoo animals), and compost, which is both fertilizer and soil conditioner. The quick-acting inorganic fertilizers are usually a combination of the three essential nutrients—nitrogen, phosphorous, and potassium—and come in granulated, soluble, and timed-release pellets. The formula consists of three numbers indicating the proportion of the three nutrients. Herbs grown in beds benefit from two or three applications each year of a complete granular fertilizer high in phosphorous—say, 15-30-15. Timed-release pellets are designed to distribute nutrients gradually over a period of months and are worked into the soil during planting. Liquid fertilizer can be used every three weeks during the growing season, either poured into the soil around the plants or used to foliar feed the herbs. It can also be mixed at half strength and used more often. An old method that is still viable is to crush eggshells and scratch them into the surface around lavender, rosemary, and thyme to sweeten the soil with calcium, which aids in the development of strong roots.

GROWING HERBS IN CONTAINERS

The main consideration when you grow herbs in pots is that you as the gardener are responsible for *all* the plants' needs, for they can't forage for nutrients or water as they do in the ground. Plant the herbs in commercial soilless mixes that are formulated to drain quickly yet retain moisture and nutrients long enough for the herbs to use them. These usually contain peat mixed with sharp sand and perlite and/or vermiculite, with a little lime added to neu-

tralize the acidic peat. The plants should be fed every ten days to two weeks with fish emulsion, liquid seaweed, or a 20-20-20 soluble fertilizer at half strength. Herbs in containers also
have increased water needs. Herbs with roots firmly situated in the ground can miss a watering and survive, but not those in containers, where the soil warms up quicker and dries out

faster. Polymer granules, which
absorb and store water, then
slowly release it as it's needed, are
helpful in supplying moisture to
potted herbs and can be mixed
into the soil at planting time.
Soluble salts from fertilizers build
up in container-grown herbs, and
the soil should be flushed out
periodically. Thorough watering,
instead of just a dollop of water,
will help leach out these salts.
Antique urns; ceramic pottery in
bright primary colors; whimsical
clay or stone pots fashioned as
animals; stone, terra-cotta, or

cast-iron containers with classic reliefs; wine crates and whiskey barrels; redwood planter
boxes; woven baskets; architectural clay drain tiles; large tin cans with colorful graphics; the
ever-popular strawberry jar, which is rarely seen planted with strawberries, as herbs are more
interesting; and the "fake" English stone sinks made of hypertufa (or the grand real thing)—
all are choices for containers that will make a definite design statement when overflowing
with herbs.

Large pots of herbs can herald an entry, and march the visitor right up to the front door
in a charming, welcoming manner. They can reappear again in the backyard in the form of
several mini garden respites, created with just a few well-placed pots. There are many reasons for growing a container garden. Some gardeners who have had plenty of land or a large
backyard move to smaller homes or apartments, but the herb garden still remains de rigueur.
Perhaps the gardener has no land or backyard, but does have a balcony or patio or sunny
front or back porch. Or perhaps the enthusiasm for growing herbs is so great (as in my case)
that there is not one inch left in the herb garden, so containers come to the rescue.

WATERING

The proper amount of water is important to the health of herbs, and good drainage is an essential requirement. Most herbs are drought-tolerant, but they do have specific watering needs. Generally they should be watered infrequently but thoroughly, to a depth of six inches. Herbs will send down their roots as deeply as water is available to them, so deep watering produces well-anchored plants that are less susceptible to wilting when the soil dries out. Generally, allow the soil around the herbs to approach the dry state between waterings.

In the humid South, watering practices differ because of the hot, steamy weather. In general, water herbs between rains in hot weather, and as a rule, water in the evening to allow the ground around the plants to soak up moisture. Never water in the hot sunshine. An excellent book on growing herbs in the South is *Southern Herb Growing,* by Madalene Hill and Gwen Barclay (see Bibliography, page 289).

OVERWINTERING HERBS INDOORS

Certain herbs can be brought indoors for the winter. You may choose to overwinter those herbs you just can't bear to lose over the long, cold winter, or those whose fresh leaves you want to continue to savor. Many herbs can weather a winter indoors, but there is a difference

between growing and flourishing, and those that do survive the indoor desert will be relieved to be back outside again come spring. Ideal situations for overwintering herbs indoors are a greenhouse or an artificial-light stand. Give the herbs a light pruning and plant them in a commercial soil mix specified for indoor use in containers slightly larger than the root mass of each herb. Leave a little of the garden soil attached to the roots of the herb so the plant won't go into greater shock than it needs to when you replant it to bring it indoors. Cuttings may also be taken of certain herbs like 'Frieda Dixon' pineapple sage. The herbs that are to be brought indoors need hardening off just as those do that are going out the door the following spring. Place the pots under the shade of a tall tree, then in an area with low light such as the north side of the house. When the weather gets chilly, let them spend the night indoors and return them to the north side of the house during the day. When frost warnings are noted, give them a good drenching with insecticidal or Ivory soap, to eliminate any pests living on them, then bring the herbs indoors for the duration. Place them in the window that receives the most constant bright light and even temperature without drafts. Give the herbs a quarter turn every few days so they grow evenly all around. Herbs grown indoors don't tolerate over-heated houses, so provide high humidity for them if possible, and spray their leaves with water often, best done in the morning or evening, not when the herb is in full light. Line a tray with a layer of pebbles, and set the pots on top. The tray will catch any excess water and will provide some humidity. When watering, make sure the pots don't sit continually in the collected water. Rosemary can be watered by standing the pot in a container of water for a few hours.

Indoor plants need very light feeding during their sojourn indoors; use fish emulsion fertilizer at half strength formulated for indoor plants, and water the herbs only when the soil is approaching the dry state. The exception is basil, which needs constant moisture. Watch for aphids, spider mites, and whiteflies—which are inevitable—and spray with insecticidal soap. When spring arrives, to begin hardening off, put them outdoors on the east side of the house on warm, sunny days, and bring them in at night. After the last frost, move them once again to their outdoor environment.

PESTS

A healthy herb is the most pest-free herb. Ironically, the very aromas that attract us to these culinary plants are offensive to many insects and animals—but not all. Ants, aphids, spider mites, whiteflies, scale, and spittlebugs are insects you can see; nematodes are those you can't. In addition there are snails, rust, and mildew. The one creature, mentioned in the bronze fennel entry, that should be allowed to stay in the herb garden is the swallowtail caterpillar/butterfly; it doesn't eat too much compared to the colorful beauty it brings to the garden. The other pests can be controlled with insecticidal soap, and the snails can best be removed by hand; ideally do this at night, guided by a flashlight. I bought a long coil of copper wire at a plumbing supply house and lined the inside of the brick edging in my garden where the snails were most active, and they do not cross that line. Agricultural-grade diatomaceous earth is another substance snails won't crawl over, and it can be used to deter other pests as well.

Integrated pest management is a logical method of insect control that does not endanger the environment with dangerous chemicals. Two excellent recent books on the subject are *Good Bugs for Your Garden*, by Allison Mia Starcher (Algonquin Books, Chapel Hill, North Carolina) and *Rebugging Your Home Garden: A Step by Step Guide to Modern Pest Control*, by Ruth Troetschler (PTF Press, Los Altos, California).

IMPORTANT NOTICE ON CONSUMPTION OF EDIBLE PLANTS

The philosopher Lucretius in his work *De Rerum Natura,* or *The Nature of Things*, wrote, wisely, "What is food to one man may be a fierce poison to another." The chemical components of edible plants are often very powerful, even though the plants are considered culinary. Different parts of the plants produce different compounds, some safe, some toxic. One familiar example is rhubarb, found in every supermarket across the country, also known as "pie plant," whose stems are the only edible part; its leaves are toxic because of their high oxalic acid content. We enjoy sorrel soup and spinach, but both sorrel and spinach, not generally thought of as poisonous foods, contain oxalic acid as well and can be harmful if taken in large quantity, especially for those with kidney stones or arthritis. Many herbs that are generally considered safe to eat in small amounts can have distressing or dangerous side effects if taken in quantity. That one individual can enjoy a certain culinary herb without reaction is no guarantee that another individual won't have an allergic or toxic reaction, for tolerance varies from person to person. Consider chamomile. It is widely marketed as a soothing, calming tea, which it is, but it is a member of the ragweed family, and has the potential for producing allergies in sensitive individuals. Sometimes an herb may initially appear harmless, but taken constantly over a long period of time, it will produce a toxic reaction; if the herb contains toxic compounds they accumulate in the body. Comfrey tea used to be recommended as a comforting drink but is no longer because of toxic alkaloids found in its leaves that may cause liver damage.

Toxicity is related to dosage. Culinary herbs are generally considered safe if used in moderation for flavoring foods. Excessive consumption of familiar plants such as *Allium cepa*—onions—can cause anemia. The leaves of epazote are widely used in Mexican cuisine as a flavoring herb. However, the potent oil derived from its seeds has also been used through the ages to treat parasites, and according to well-known herbal authority Dr. James A. Duke, formerly with the U.S. Department of Agriculture, the therapeutic dose is close to the minimum toxic levels. Sage contains the compound thujone, which can be toxic. According to Dr. Varro Tyler, the author of *The Honest Herbal*, using sage leaves for flavoring cooked foods is probably not critical since heating the food apparently drives off most of the volatile thujone, but to be absolutely safe, he suggests not consuming too much, especially when its essential oils are at their peak, in spring—or in any other month. We know that it is wise to consume alcoholic beverages in moderation, and in fact it is generally considered best to consume most things in moderation—including culinary herbs.

FROM GARDEN TO KITCHEN:

Cooking with Herbs in the Kitchen—Herb Gathering, Harvesting, Storing, and Preserving

When you begin cooking with herbs from your own garden you will become aware of the zest they add to all manner of food. The experience of walking to your garden during the cool of the morning to gather the herbs for the day is a serene pleasure. They should be gathered after the dew has evaporated, but before the sun becomes hot, which causes the aromatic and flavorful essential oils in the leaves to escape into the atmosphere. Of course, you can dash to the garden any hour of the twenty-four to snip a sprig or two for your cooking, but this time of day is when herbs are at their peak of flavor, and if you are collecting herbs for drying, this is the only time they should be harvested. Most herbs can be harvested several times a season. They may be cut back by one third during midseason when their growth is exuberant. In cold-winter areas where it freezes, the last harvest of perennial herbs should be done no later than one month before the first frost so that the herb is not weakened and lost over the winter. After a heavy harvest the herbs can be side-dressed with compost and fertilizer (placed near the roots) to ensure a healthy second growth. Annual herbs can simply be cut to the ground at the end of the growing season, or pulled up.

In the southern states, harvesting should be treated somewhat differently. Mint can be hard-pruned (cut way back), but hard-pruning should not be attempted on sages and thyme because it will weaken the plant and make it unable to withstand extremes of temperature.

For cooking or for use in salad, gather two or three inches of the young tips as well as older and larger leaves on the stems. Plucking and pruning your herbs in this manner encourages the herb's fuller growth. As the season lengthens and the herbs show promise of flowering is the optimum time to gather them for cooking and to harvest them for preserving (with the exception of ginger mint, which should be picked for optimum flavor when the herb is in flower). The basils and papaloquelite will keep in a glass of water placed in a sunny window for a week or more, and are nice decor on the kitchen counter. Most of the other herbs will stay fresh for a week if wrapped in damp paper towels and then placed in a sealed plastic bag and refrigerated.

A cache of dried green herbs in small glass bottles is convenient to have on the cupboard shelf when running to the garden is inconvenient or when your herb garden is under a blanket of snow. Now that microwave ovens seem to be regular fixtures in kitchens, herbs can be dried to crisp bright green in minutes. Quickly rinse freshly cut herbs and pat them thoroughly dry with paper towels. Place them in a single layer between two sheets of paper towels in the microwave oven. Heat on high power in increments of one minute until the herbs are parchment dry. Strip the dried leaves from the stems and place them whole in a small airtight jar. Label, date, and store on a cool, dark shelf. They will keep for one year, by which time another harvest can be made, and the process repeated.

Herbs can also be dried in three time-honored ways. First, they may be crisped in a warm (150-degree) oven in a single layer on a cookie sheet. This takes fifteen to twenty minutes for some herbs, and those with thicker leaves will take longer. Second, stems of herbs can be laid on screens in a warm, dark, well-ventilated spot such as an attic where it is not over 90 degrees. It usually takes about one week for the leaves to dry. The third way is to hang dried herb stems in small bunches and place bouquet end down in a brown paper bag tied with a string. Hang the bag(s), clothesline fashion, on a cord in a dry room or attic. Drying in this manner takes about a week.

Dried herbs can be reconstituted in wines and fortified wines, chicken or beef stock, beer, and brandy, depending on the nature of the dish you are preparing.

PREPARING HERB VINEGARS

Herbs complement many types of vinegar. White wine vinegar, rice vinegar, red wine vinegar, sherry vinegar, and apple cider and fruit vinegars are excellent carriers to be transformed into a variety of pungent to delicate herb vinegars by the addition of 'Golden Rain' rosemary, 'Bronze' perilla, oregano and Mexican oregano, 'Cinnamon' basil, lemon grass, and 'Mabel Grey' scented geranium. A shelf lined with homemade vinegar creations is a rewarding sight to the gardener—and the people who sit at her/his table. These herb-flavored vinegars find the greatest use in salad dressings, but they are also excellent for savory marinades, sauces, and for bringing out the flavor of soups, fruits, and cooked vegetables, as well as for deglazing sautéed chicken, fish, or meat.

The recipe for herbed vinegar is simple. Gather a bunch of herb stems and leaves as directed above. Two cups of one of the aforementioned fresh herbs to 2 cups of vinegar is a

good ratio. Three to four leaves of 'Bronze' perilla is all that is needed to color two cups of rice vinegar with a rosy hue and spicy flavor. Wash the herbs and pat them dry with paper towels. Place them in a sterilized glass jar with a nonreactive lid. Bruise them with the back of a spoon if you wish. Fill the jar with the vinegar of your choice, making sure the herbs are totally submerged. Cover tightly and place the jar in a cool, dark place. Taste in one week, and if the flavor suits you, strain the vinegar through a fine sieve lined with cheesecloth. Pour the strained vinegar into a sterilized glass jar with a nonreactive top. Cover tightly. It will keep for up to one year. As pretty as these personal treasures are, they should not be on display in a sunny window, for the light quickly dissipates the flavor. Keep them under wraps on a cool, dark shelf in the kitchen cabinet.

HERB-INFUSED OILS

The best time to create herb-flavored oils is at the height of the season, when the herb's leaves are full of fragrant essential oils. These intensely pungent infusions used in the winter kitchen will bring back the flavor of the summer garden. Bronze fennel with a pinch of fennel seed; oregano, culantro, Mexican tarragon, and curry leaf—all can permeate oils with their unique flavors. Their taste lends unique character to vinaigrettes and salads of sliced tomatoes. Pour a small amount in a ramekin and let crusty slices of bread soak up the fragrant oil. Sautéeing and stir-frying take on a different air when herb oils are used. Oils can be gingerly poured over cooked vegetables to bring out their flavor, and big portobello mushrooms glistening with herb-scented oil are unforgettable.

Two cups of one of the above herbs to 2 cups extra virgin olive oil is a good ratio to use. Quickly rinse the herbs. Place them in a sieve and pour boiling water over them. Drain them, then pat them *thoroughly* dry with paper towels. In a food processor fitted with the metal blade, combine the herbs with 2 teaspoons lemon juice and about ¼ cup of the olive oil. Process until the herbs are finely chopped, then pour in the remaining olive oil in a thin stream until the mixture is emulsified. Pour into a sterilized jar with a nonreactive lid. Cover tightly and place in the refrigerator for one week. Bring the oil to room temperature and strain through a fine-mesh sieve lined with cheesecloth. Return the strained oil to the same jar and cover tightly. The oil can be stored in the refrigerator for up to two weeks. The oil will solidify again but will liquefy

at room temperature after a few minutes, or if the jar is run under hot water.

Unlike herb vinegars, herb oils have a short life and must be refrigerated to prevent harmful bacteria and mold from forming. It is important to add the lemon juice, which acidifies the mixture, as the key factors in the prevention of botulism are the acidity of the mixture, the amount of moisture in the herbs (which is why you pat them thoroughly dry), and the temperature at which the product is stored.

HERB PERSONALITIES

When cooking with herbs, use them judiciously until you have become familiar with their strength. For subtly flavored herbs, in general, use one third the amount of dried herb as fresh. When using herbs with assertive flavors such as lavender, rosemary, the oreganos, and sage, the ratio of dried to fresh would be about 1:6.

The flavor of most herbs is lost in long cooking. Add the sturdy-flavored herbs about forty-five minutes before soups and stews are done, and the milder ones fifteen minutes before the dish is done. For food served cold or at room temperature the herbs should be allowed to infuse several hours or overnight.

An excellent way to become familiar with the taste of an herb is to chop it finely and combine it with softened butter or natural cream cheese (*fromage blanc*) and let the flavor infuse for one hour. Spread the mixture on a plain melba toast, and then pass judgment.

When cooking vegetables, toss fresh herb sprigs into the boiling water, then sprinkle the same herb over the vegetables just before serving for an extra herb punch.

All the taste requirements for a perfect mesclun salad can be prepared from the list of exotic herbs.

Sweet:	'Cinnamon' basil
Tart:	sorrel
Smooth:	purslane
Textured:	samphire
Colorful:	violets, superb pink
Delicate:	miner's lettuce
Cucumber-y:	borage blossoms
Nutty:	broadleaf cress

Part II

60 Exotic Herbs
and Recipes

The Alliums

Alliums are the enormous onion genus of over four hundred species of herbs that grow in bulb or rhizome form and are widely distributed throughout the world. Onions are one of the oldest cultivated vegetables, having existed since ancient history. The origins of the cultivated onion were in central Asia, ranging from Iran to Pakistan and north to Afghanistan, but the mystery of its wild ancestors has never been solved.

Myths and colorful folklore surround the onion. During Christmas holiday celebrations in olden times, as the yule log blazed, a jolly fellow representing Saint Thomas, to whom the onion was considered sacred, would give the young ladies present an onion, to which each would whisper the name of the man she wanted for her husband. In bed by midnight, she waved the onion over her head, and if the fates were with her she would dream of her intended. The onion was also a dubious cure-all: onion juice applied in full sunlight to a bald head would cause the hair to speedily return; after a bite from a hateful dog, onion juice mixed with honey, salt, and rue from the garden would cure the wound; and onions beautified complexions, making them porcelain clear. As with our apple-a-day rhyme, an onion eaten daily was considered to promote good health. The New England colonists hung a string of onions over their homestead doorways to absorb disease; thus they thought to protect those inside. One remedy probably best to remain in folklore was the use of onion juice placed in the eye to cure dim vision. And of course onions, like so many other culinary herbs, were considered aphrodisiacs. One truth, however, has endured through the ages, spoken by the sixteenth-century botanist John Gerard: "The Onion requireth a fat ground well digged and dunged. . . . It is cherished every where in kitchen gardens."

The useful alliums grown to flavor foods include onions, leeks, garlic, shallots, chives, garlic chives, and scallions, also called green or spring onions. Hundreds of more exotic, ornamental alliums—gigantic, tall, medium, and small—beautify wild gardens and grace domestic flower borders and rock gardens.

'ÉCHALOTE DE JERSEY'

(Allium cepa 'Échalote de Jersey') (Jersey shallot)

Annual
Native habitat   Thought to be Jersey Island in the Channel Islands

An avid self-taught gentleman gardener in Illinois who specializes in growing many varieties of alliums discovered a company in Bordeaux, France, that offered an interesting shallot that was grown from seed, not sets, and could be planted and harvested in one year. The gardener had great success with his shallot seeds. It was discovered that the shallot was a very old allium mentioned both in Fearing Burr's 1865 book, *Field and Garden Vegetables of America*, and in an 1885 edition of the French gardening book *Les Plantes Potagères,* or *The Vegetable Garden*, written by members of the Vilmorin family, which founded an esteemed French seed company. It seems that the 'Échalote de Jersey' or Jersey shallot is an onion masquerading as a shallot, for it produces only one bulb per plant; the bulbs do not multiply like a true shallot. Although the Vilmorin catalog lists this unique allium in the shallot category, calling it 'Échalote de Jersey', it is also listed as false shallot. Onion or shallot, its taste is identical to a shallot's: sweet and mild and oh, so much easier to peel than a shallot. The French seed company that offers the seed for this, Graines Baumaux, state in their description that they feel it is neither an onion nor a shallot but an as yet unnamed category of allium. 'Échalote de Jersey' by any name would taste as sweet. The rediscovery of this unique cultivar has saved from extinction one more seed worth growing, the result of the diligence and sleuthing of an avid gardener.

GROWING YOUR OWN

Seeds of 'Échalote de Jersey' can be started in the early winter in the greenhouse and the seedlings transplanted to the garden when the ground can be worked. Seeds can also be direct sown in early spring. 'Échalote de Jersey' is not hardy, so fall planting is not recommended. Plant seeds ¼ inch deep in well-drained, richly amended soil. Keep the soil moist during germination as well as during the growing season. Thin the seedlings to 8 to 12 inches apart. Grow them in single rows, or interplanted in groups to nestle in among other herbs. They are delicious to eat, but not ornamental enough to be featured in a spot in the garden. Their whitish leaves grow to about 1 foot tall. The bulbs are irregular, some short and rounded, others long and slender, but generally 'Échalote de Jersey' bulbs are about 3 inches long and 2 inches in diameter with reddish-tan skins, flushed with a rose-violet tint. It is usually harvested in August or September, but it is not a good onion for storing over the winter. Although it is a long-day onion—it prefers northern regions where the summer days are long—it is more adaptable than other onions to different growing areas. For example, in Zone 10, seed started in the greenhouse in early February and transplanted outdoors in early April yields fully grown shallots in early August.

CULINARY USES

'Échalote de Jersey' can be used just like a true shallot; there is no taste difference. To make a tantalizing sauce for either filet mignon or lean hamburgers, combine its minced bulbs with red wine and a little beef bouillon, reduce the mixture by half, and stir in fresh parsley and thyme. The addition of the finely chopped bulbs makes a tasty difference when used in recipes for eggless mayonnaise. 'Échalote de Jersey' is large enough to slice with ease to be used in place of onions in individual creamy shallot tarts flavored with French thyme. Add the chopped bulbs to a golden saffron risotto. Sweet pink peppercorns combined with finely minced 'Échalote de Jersey' in a tart vinaigrette poured over a salad of warm sliced red potato salad are a trio of good tastes.

Braised Portobello Mushrooms with Ginger Mint and 'Échalote de Jersey'

Mint with meaty portobello mushrooms is a classic combination, and the mild, sweet taste of 'Échalote de Jersey' rounds out the flavors. This dish makes a perfect vegetable accompaniment to rabbit or game dishes.

For another recipe using 'Échalote de Jersey', see page 204, Fragrant Fish Soup.

1 pound fresh portobello mushrooms or brown cremini mushrooms

2 tablespoons fruity olive oil

4 tablespoons coarsely chopped 'Échalote de Jersey'

1 tablespoon chopped garlic

3 four-inch sprigs ginger mint or other mild mint

1 cup chopped fresh Italian plum tomatoes

½ cup chicken stock

1 teaspoon chopped fresh lemon thyme

Sea salt and freshly ground black pepper to taste

1 tablespoon finely chopped ginger mint or other mild mint

Pinch cayenne pepper

Pinch nutmeg

Remove the stems from the mushrooms and save them for another purpose. Slice the mushrooms ½ inch thick. Heat the olive oil in a large skillet. Add the 'Échalote de Jersey', garlic, and mushrooms. Nestle the 3 sprigs of ginger mint with the mushrooms, then add the tomatoes, chicken stock, thyme, salt, and black pepper to taste. Cover the skillet and simmer over low heat for 15 to 20 minutes. Remove the ginger mint sprigs, then add the remaining tablespoon of the chopped mint, the cayenne, and nutmeg. Stir mixture well. Remove from heat and serve immediately.

Serves 4.

EGYPTIAN ONION

(*Allium cepa,* Proliferum group)

Hardy Perennial   Zones 4–9

The Egyptian onion is curiously unique. It grows bulbs underground, and it also grows "upside down," tree fashion, to 2 or 3 feet tall, with a topknot of small shiny, copper-green bulb sets at the tips of its flower stalks, hence its second common name, tree onion. Its mature stalks then bend to the ground and "walk" some distance away from the parent plant, where its crown of onion bulbs takes root, to form yet another colony—hence its third common name, walking onion—and the growth process begins anew. Here is the onion you never have to plant again.

"Top onion" and "multiplier onion" are other names for this unusual allium, known only in cultivation. Its origins are unknown, and despite its exotic-sounding but most often used common name, Egyptian onion, garden historians are divided on whether this allium species was indeed grown in Egypt. Written records show that onions were cultivated along the banks of the Nile River five thousand years ago, and other ancient records state that large sums of money were paid to supply workers on the Great Pyramid with onions, garlic, and radishes. During the First Dynasty, the onion shape was represented as a deity on monuments, and a Fifth Dynasty relief from a tomb in Memphis depicts onions being harvested. An author writing on the Holy Land in the mid-1800s rhapsodized, "Whoever has tasted of onions in Egypt, must allow that none could be had better in any part of the universe. Here, they are sweet . . . here, they are soft. . . . Hence they cannot in any place be eaten with less prejudice and more satisfaction than in Egypt."

The Egyptian onion was grown in both English and American gardens in the seventeenth and eighteenth centuries, and the horticulturist Thomas Jefferson listed "Tree Onion" in his garden diary. Today it is grown in home gardens in North America and is naturalized around old homesteads. Perhaps the reason Egyptian onion endures is its versatility. Both its ground and "air" bulbs can be used, in addition to its tender, new green growth in the spring for chives—strong chives. Its bulbs can be picked and used fresh like garlic or shallots, or pickled, although they have a strong flavor, and a little goes a long way. It is a hardy perennial, and arrives early, allowing the cooking gardener to have fresh onions to season foods long before the other onions are ready to dig. Egyptian onions are strange in behavior, but what a unique edible ornamental for the culinary herb garden.

GROWING YOUR OWN

Throughout the country, fall is the best time of the year to plant Egyptian onions, although they can also be planted in the spring. They are probably the hardiest and easiest to care for of all the onions. Planted in early autumn, the onions produce fresh, slender green shoots for chopping and sprinkling over Christmas holiday vegetables and salads. In cold growing zones, if the tops die back in the cold winter weather, the established root systems will again send up new green shoots in early spring to be eaten as green onions, or scallions. Order bulbs of Egyptian onions from specialty plant nurseries; it is not grown from seed. The bulbs you receive will be summer harvested topsets, or bulbs, in cluster form. If the bulbs are ½ inch in diameter, separate them and plant them 6 to 12 inches apart and 1 inch deep. If they are smaller, plant the whole cluster without dividing them. Egyptian onions like rich, well-drained, moist soil. At planting time add well-rotted manure with a little bone- and blood-meal. They do best in full sun but will tolerate partial shade.

In subsequent seasons, you can produce your own Egyptian onions in several ways. The first is the carefree way: allow them to "walk" where they want to and root where they please, to create their own undisturbed, serendipitous little plantation. Or, when harvesting the topsets in midsummer for culinary use, save a few bulbs to plant in the fall for next year's crop. Another method is to harvest only three or four bulbs from the cluster in the ground and leave one in place to multiply. Established clumps should be routinely divided in the spring every three or four years. Harvested bulbs may be dried for keeping by braiding their flower stalks and hanging them upside down in a dark, dry place like a basement or garage that doesn't have extremes of temperature. When harvesting them for culinary use, pick the bulbs after they develop but before they sprout. Likewise, the onion shoots are best eaten young, before they age and become fibrous.

Egyptian onions can be planted in sentried rows in a vegetable garden, but because of their unusual appearance, they pique attention not only in the herb garden, but in flower gardens and borders. They do not grow well in containers.

CULINARY USES

The new green, hollow shoots of Egyptian onions can be used as chives, and as the stalks grow in diameter they can be used as scallions. When mature, the stalks become too fibrous to be eaten raw, but they can still be used in vegetable soup or stock, to which they will impart a nice onion flavor. The small bulbs can be used fresh in stir-fried dishes. The larger ones can be sliced into salads, and they are perfect for giving herb vinegars such as tarragon or rosemary vinegars just the ideal hint of onion flavor. Parboiled, they can be alternated on skewers with marinated chicken, red and green sweet peppers, and mushrooms and grilled. An Egyptian onion and saffron "marmalade" is an exotic chutney condiment made with a large handful of the boiled bulbs, dark currants, and yellow raisins.

Petits Pois with Purslane and Egyptian Onions

Petits pois à la française is the French manner of cooking sweet tiny peas in a small amount of chicken stock combined only with the liquid that water-filled lettuce leaves release. In this recipe, vitamin- and water-rich purslane replaces the lettuce, producing a delicate vegetable accompaniment that is the essence of early summer.

For another recipe using Egyptian onions, see page 143, Steamed Magenta Lamb's-quarter with Bronze Fennel.

2 tablespoons unsalted butter

4 cups fresh young green peas

6 to 8 Egyptian onion bulbs, halved

2 teaspoons lemon juice

¼ cup chicken stock

1 teaspoon sugar

Sea salt and freshly ground white pepper to taste

Bouquet garni consisting of 2 fresh sprigs each of parsley and thyme

2 cups green purslane leaves, washed, drained, and seeds removed

Heat butter in a medium saucepan with a tight-fitting lid. Add peas, onions, lemon juice, chicken stock, sugar, salt, pepper, and bouquet garni. (If using frozen peas follow package directions for cooking. Cook the onions in ⅔ cup water for 5 minutes before adding them to frozen peas). Stir to combine, then cover with the purslane. Cover the pan and simmer for approximately 30 minutes, or until vegetables are tender. Remove bouquet garni. Taste for seasoning, then cover pan and cook 2 to 3 minutes longer. Serve immediately.

Serves 6

ALLSPICE

(Pimenta dioica)

Tender Perennial   Zones 10–11
Native Habitat   West Indies, southern Mexico, Central and South America

From the garden at Festival Hill, Round Top Texas

The spice called allspice, from the plant's berries, is common on grocery shelves, but not the herb allspice *leaf*, which is finely flavored and delicately scented with the same clove-cinnamon-nutmeg combination as the berries. The unripe fruit of the allspice tree is dried and used commercially to flavor many foods we routinely consume in baked goods and confectionery, soft drinks and alcoholic beverages (Benedictine and Chartreuse among them), sauces, pickles, and condiments. The oil from allspice leaves flavors many of the same commercially produced foods. The oil content is higher in the leaves of the male allspice trees, probably because they do not have to put energy into fruiting. (The active ingredient in allspice, eugenol, also found in cloves, cinnamon, and nutmeg, causes contact dermatitis in some people.) Allspice is cultivated for export primarily in Jamaica. Its Spanish name is *pimienta* (Anglicized as "pimento"), meaning pepper, as that is what Christopher Columbus mistook it for; it is also known as clove spice and Jamaica allspice.

In its native habitat the handsome allspice tree grows to 8 to 20 feet or taller, with long, shiny, pointed oval leaves and powder-white flowers. Whereas a group of geese is called a "gaggle," and a bunch of sheep a "flock," an orchard of allspice trees is poetically called a "walk." In most parts of the United States it is doubtful that allspice will produce a lovely walk, but that doesn't inhibit the gardener from growing this spice as an herbal shrub or small container tree to collect its scented leaves for cooking.

GROWING YOUR OWN

Allspice is evergreen in Zones 10 and 11. It is tolerant of temperatures down to 27 degrees and can be grown in certain parts of Zone 9. It can be planted in the ground, or it makes a lovely container-grown specimen. In the ground, allspice should be planted in rich, loamy soil that is on the acid side. A handful of 14-14-14 timed-release fertilizer pellets can be added at planting time. Although the tree can tolerate alkaline soil, its leaves will sometimes acquire salt burn. Drainage is key to the good health of allspice. It grows best in full sun, although it will tolerate afternoon shade. Feed regularly with fish emulsion mixed at half strength through October or November, then stop feeding during the winter months. Resume the fertilizing schedule again in February. Do not feed with a fertilizer high in nitrogen.

In cold-winter areas, allspice can be container-grown outdoors in the summer, and brought indoors for the winter. It can spend many years in its pot, and while it is slow-growing, it can eventually reach 5 to 8 feet, but can be kept pruned to a more manageable 5 feet. Indoors, place allspice in the sunniest window of the house. Providing this subtropical with high humidity is beneficial.

Planted in the ground in Zones 10 and 11, allspice can grow to 15 to 25 feet (there are two this size at the San Diego Zoo); eventually it will produce allspice berries, although it takes 5 to 11 years to flower. Unfortunately, it is difficult to identify male and female plants, so even if you plant two, you are not assured of getting fruit.

CULINARY USES

An allspice leaf is a fragrant addition to smothered chicken, and is also excellent with veal and fish. In Jamaica, a local mullet is sautéed with onions and red peppers, and flavored with allspice and a dash of vinegar. This dish can be easily re-created by using several allspice leaves in place of the berries with any nonoily fish. Jamaican jerk pork is a popular tourist dish that uses both allspice berries and leaves. Put one allspice leaf in the pot when making a beef stew, or in a saucepan of applesauce for that fragrant clove flavor. Allspice leaves make a spicy marinade for game or chicken. One 4-inch allspice leaf and a stick of cinnamon in the yearly standard-recipe Thanksgiving cranberry sauce makes a hit. Infuse a simple syrup with allspice leaves for pouring over poached fruit, or add a leaf to the water when poaching peaches or other fruits. In Mexico and Cuba, the leaves are steeped for a fragrant tea. Add a leaf to a cup of orange pekoe tea leaves for a fragrantly bracing taste and aroma. The Aztecs used allspice to flavor chocolate, and the marshmallow garnish in a steaming cup of hot chocolate could just as well be replaced with an aromatic allspice leaf scented with its blend of nutmeg, cinnamon, and clove.

Braised Pork Loin with Gilded Apples and Allspice Leaves

2 to 2½ pounds pork loin
Sea salt and freshly ground pepper to taste
1 tablespoon olive oil
2 cups coarsely chopped onions
2 four-inch-long fresh allspice leaves, chopped

1 teaspoon grated orange zest
1 cup dry vermouth
2 tablespoons butter
2 apples (Rome or Granny Smith), cored, seeded, and sliced

Season the pork loin with salt and pepper. In a straight-sided skillet or Dutch oven, heat the olive oil. Add the pork loin and brown well on all sides, about 15 minutes. Remove the pork and reserve. Add the onions to the skillet and sauté in the remaining oil over low heat until they begin to soften. Stir in the allspice leaves and the orange zest. Return the pork to the skillet and add the vermouth. Quickly bring to a boil over high heat, then reduce the heat to low. Cook the pork loin, covered, for 30 to 40 minutes, or until a meat thermometer registers 155 degrees.

Meanwhile, heat the butter in a large skillet. Add the apple slices, and sauté until they are golden ("gilded"). Remove to a warm platter and reserve.

Transfer the cooked pork loin to a cutting board and slice into slices 1 inch thick. Place on a warmed platter and cover to keep warm. Reduce the sauce in the skillet for 3 to 4 minutes, then add salt and pepper to taste. Place the gilded apples on the platter with the pork, then spoon the sauce over pork. Serve immediately.

Serves 4

ANISE HYSSOP
(Agastache foeniculum)

Hardy Perennial   Zones 5–9
Native Habitat   Northern Central and North America

Few culinary herbs are more ornamental than anise hyssop. Its lavender-blue tubular flowers look like miniature bottle brushes, and its handsome serrated, pointy leaves have a pretty, pronounced pattern and soft, smooth texture. It grows in a lush upright manner, and the whole plant is aromatic of mint. Bees, hummingbirds, and butterflies flit around it when it blooms, and later, wild birds eat its black seeds. It readily self-sows. Both its leaves and flowers are edible and provide a strong anise-mint dose of aroma and flavor. Other members of the agastache genus bloom in white, raspberry pink, copper-orange, apricot, vivid red, violet blue, yellowish-green, and other showy colors.

As a plant of the prairies, anise hyssop was prized by American Indians for use as a tea beverage as well as a sweetener. It is widely grown as a honey plant, for it produces copious amounts of nectar, yielding it throughout the whole day, not only at certain periods. It makes a high-quality light honey with agastache's characteristic anise-mint taste. The herb's common name is curious, as it is associated with another culinary herb, hyssop (*Hyssopus officinalis*), a bitter herb (though tastily so) that has the exact opposite of the sweet flavor of anise hyssop. Perhaps the key lies in the similarity of the shape of both herbs' tubular flowers, which both have two pairs of stamens. Anise hyssop has a long blooming period and presents a fine show of color in late summer and early autumn.

GROWING YOUR OWN

Anise hyssop grows 3 to 5 feet tall, so it is a good back-of-the-border plant. If growing more than one, space the plants about 18 inches apart. A sheltered, south-facing site is an excellent environment. Anise hyssop's dense flower spikes grow 3 to 4 inches long. The herb grows in ordinary, well-drained soil. Take care that anise hyssop has good drainage, as it doesn't survive wet soil in rainy winters. It likes full sun, but in hot climate zones, provide it with afternoon shade. Seed sown indoors in late winter and planted outdoors when the soil has warmed will bloom the first season. Seed may also be sown in the fall. Once established, anise hyssop is drought-tolerant. It self-sows freely, but the little seedlings are easily removed where you don't want them. Anise hyssop is easily transplanted, and can be propagated by seed, stem cuttings, and root division in the early spring. It can also be grown in a pot.

The lilac-blue blossoms of anise hyssop look elegant in the herb garden when planted next to the alabaster-white-flowering anise hyssop (*Agastache foeniculum* 'Alba').

CULINARY USES

The tiny flowers of anise hyssop are so tasty that they give edible flowers a good name. With a flavor of anise, mint, and root beer combined, they are excellent in icy drinks, delicate desserts, and fancy tea breads. The plant's leaves make a licorice-tasting herb tea when used alone; combine with bergamot or mint for a tisane with fragrant punch. The leaves may be dried for winter use.

Anise hyssop leaves can be used to flavor baked chicken, or a stir-fry of succulent strips of beef mixed with chopped ginger. They make an aromatic marinade for white-fleshed fish.

Finely chopped, they flavor herb butter for braised celery, carrots, or fresh haricots verts. Anise hyssop shines in the dessert category. Infuse its chopped leaves in crème fraîche for a few days, then remove them and spoon the anise-mint-flavored sauce over fresh berries. Anise hyssop honey is a complement to fresh fruit salads or toasted bread. Its finely chopped flowers or leaves make wonderful old-fashioned sugar cookies to accompany anise hyssop ice cream for the kids (in all of us) or sorbets for the grown-ups as between-the-course palate refreshers.

Anise Hyssop Ice Cream

The Herbfarm in rural Fall City, Washington, is a celebration of the lush herbs grown on its beautiful grounds and in the many display gardens. The proprietor, Ron Zimmerman, shared his recipe for the elegant anise hyssop ice cream served at the farm's charming restaurant. This lovely delicate anise confection is excellent with fraises des bois or strawberries and a cool, mint-flavored sauce.

1⅓ cups half-and-half
2⅔ cups heavy cream
¾ cup plus 2 tablespoons sugar

20 anise hyssop leaves, minced
5 egg yolks

In a saucepan, combine the half-and-half, cream, and sugar. Over medium heat, bring the mixture to a slow boil, stirring to dissolve the sugar. Add the anise hyssop. Reduce the heat to the lowest setting and allow the mixture to steep for 25 to 40 minutes, or until the strength of the flavor suits your taste.

Place the egg yolks in a medium-sized bowl and whip with a whisk or fork until creamy. Slowly add a small amount of the warm cream mixture to the egg yolks, stirring constantly. When half of the cream mixture has been added, pour the contents of the bowl into the saucepan. Over medium heat, stir the mixture constantly until thickened, approximately 10 minutes. Strain the mixture and discard the leaves. Place the mixture in a metal bowl and allow to cool on a bed of ice.

Freeze the chilled mixture in an ice cream machine according to the manufacturer's instructions. Alternately, place the mixture in a bowl and freeze in the freezer. In a food processor fitted with the metal blade, chop the frozen mixture, then refreeze it until firm.

Makes 1 quart

The Basils

Since the time of the ancient Greeks, scores of words, both praises and curses, have been written about basil, the myths of its magical and utilitarian uses woven into the folklore of many cultures. *Ocimum*, basil's generic name, comes from the ancient Greek *okimon*, which derives its name from the meaning of the word, "smell." Basil's colorful legendry is set with intrigue and centers on its multiple meanings of fertility and expectancy, love and hate. The stories surrounding basil are erotic and sinister, sacred and royal, and denote strong emotions and passion. In Italian folklore, a young woman would tuck a sprig of basil in her lingerie to ensure chastity, and a perfumed sprig in the hair of a married woman was considered the proper come-hither ploy to arouse passion in her husband. Basil became entangled with associations surrounding the Latin word *basiliscus*, a mythical and fearful fire-breathing dragon-lizard that could kill with only a glance, and the Greek word *basilikon*, meaning "royal"—thus compounding the confusion and sense of intrigue surrounding this innocent, sweet-smelling herb.

Basil was on the list of herbs in the Doctrine of Signatures, the ancient document expressing the belief that each herb possesses a natural icon to identify its medicinal use: it was considered that basil's association with serpents and other vile crawly things made it an effective cure of scorpion and bee stings. In Greece, in a more logical custom, on the first day of the year, Saint Basil's Day, women traditionally carried basil with them to be blessed while attending church. Upon their return home the basil leaves were strewn on the floor for good fortune, then a delicious meal was made in which the herb was used, which ensured good health for the coming year. In India, tulasi, or holy basil, is sacred to the Hindu deities Vishnu and Krishna and is grown near temples and homes to ward off misfortune.

The stream of words about the fragrance and uses of this prized herb is bound to continue. There are upwards of 150 species of annual and perennial basils that are native to the temperate regions of Africa, Asia, and Central and South America. Recent basil introductions include 'Rubin', which holds its garnet color better than other purple-leaved basils; 'New Guinea', a variegated purple and green form; and the columnar-growing 'Aussie Sweetie', which requires no pinching or pruning, as it doesn't seem to flower in the growing zones of the United States. In addition, horticulturalists are so fascinated with the herb that exciting new culinary cultivars, the more ornamental the better, are on the gardener's horizon.

'AFRICAN BLUE' BASIL

(Ocimum kilimandscharicum x O. basilicum purpurescens)

Tender Perennial   Zone 10

'African Blue' basil keeps trying to set seed, but it's a sterile hybrid and can't. It does, however, flower profusely, seed or no seed, so you have to love this unique basil with its extraordinary grape juice and green variegated coloring, for in order to keep it looking tidy and lush and bushy from the bottom up, you must continually deadhead its flowers, which grow so profusely. It's worth every snip of the pruning shears, because 'African Blue' basil is a showstopping focal point in the herb garden. In areas with a long, warm growing season, 'African Blue' basil can be perennial, depending on individual microclimates; in areas with a short growing season, it can be a perennial of sorts—as a potted plant indoors.

'African Blue' basil originated in Athens, Ohio. In 1982, Peter Borchard, of Companion Plants, a specialty herb nursery, introduced to the public this natural hybrid, which he discovered in his production beds. It is a cross between opal basil and African camphor basil, which is native to East Africa. The camphorous quality in the latter basil is too overwhelming for culinary use, but it mellows in taste when mixed with the sweet and spicy flavor of opal basil in 'African Blue'. Thus a new culinary basil was born, as well as an intriguing edible ornamental.

'African Blue' basil grows up to 3 feet tall and as wide. Its blossoms are light pink, blooming on long dark purple flower spikes that can reach 7½ inches long, as they do in my garden if I neglect to deadhead them. When I prune the plant, I sometimes save the fragrant flower stalks to create a unique little bouquet to give as a host or hostess gift instead of a bunch of flowers or a bottle of wine. If you like delighted raves over a simple present, this is it.

The oval leaves of 'African Blue' grow in bouquetlike clusters on purple stems. Their new growth is dusted with purple on top and brushed with a deeper hue on the underside, eventually fading to garnet-veined green. 'African Blue' looks beautiful in the herb garden surrounded with the bright green of sweet or Genovese perfume basil, or herbs with the same wine coloration like 'Rubin', Dark Opal', and miniature purple 'Well-Sweep' basils. I grow 'New Guinea' basil near it, as it echoes the beautiful variegated coloration of 'African Blue' and grows only to 2 feet, with complementary, purple-veined, pointed leaves. Red-stemmed 'Cinnamon' basil is another color-coordinated companion. Italian parsley

A Study in Basils at the National Arboretum, Washington, D.C. (from bottom to top): 'African Blue' *basil, Lemon basil,* 'Opal' *basil,* 'Aussie Sweetie' *basil, and Tabasco pepper at right*

looks good as a camouflage at the front of the woody base of 'African Blue.' This unique basil also makes a nice canopy to shelter herbs that appreciate part shade such as the lemon balms, Vietnamese balm, 'Bronze' perilla, and potted ginger mint.

'African Blue' Basil Vinegar

The camphorous 'African Blue' basil results in an excellent herb vinegar good for making marinades, deglazing pans for sauces, and splashing over salads and vegetables. The purple of the herb's lovely variegated leaves colors the vinegar with a gemlike garnet hue.

2 cups 'African Blue' basil leaves and stems
2 cups white wine vinegar

Wash the basil, then pat it dry with paper towels. Place it in a wide-mouthed sterilized container with a nonreactive lid, then fill the jar with the wine vinegar, making sure all the leaves are submerged. Cover tightly and place in a cool, dark place for 1 week. Taste the vinegar, and if a stronger infusion is desired, allow to stand for 1 more week. When the basil has infused the vinegar to suit your taste, strain the vinegar through a fine sieve, discarding the basil. Pour the vinegar into a sterilized glass bottle and seal with a nonreactive lid. Fresh 'African Blue' basil sprigs may be added for visual effect. Use within 1 year.

Makes 2 cups

'MRS. BURNS' FAMOUS LEMON BASIL'

(*Ocimum basilicum* 'Mrs. Burns' Famous Lemon Basil'

Hardy Annual

from left to right: Thai basil, sweet basil, 'Mrs. Burns' Famous Lemon Basil', *sweet basil,* 'Mrs. Burns' Famous Lemon Basil' *with ornamental flowers*

'Mrs. Burns' Famous Lemon Basil' has been reseeding itself for the past sixty years in south-western New Mexico. A devoted gardener in Carlsbad, a Mrs. Clifton, who avidly planted according to *The Moon Book,* an astrological guide, had been growing this luscious lemon-scented basil for thirty years when she passed the seed on to another fine gardener, a Mrs. Burns, who continued to grow it for another thirty years. Mrs. Burns's son Barney, who grew up enjoying many herbs from his mother's garden, was a particular devotee of her delicious lemon basil and made tasty hamburgers with it during his college days. As word of his unique lemony creation spread, they became known as "Barney's Famous Basil Burgers." A seat at the dining table on his patio was a coveted one. Mrs. Burns was the founder of Native

Seed/SEARCH, a nonprofit native-seed conservation organization that offers the seed, as do a growing number of other specialty nurseries. Fortunately, 'Mrs. Burns' Famous Lemon Basil'—and Barney's burgers—live on.

'Mrs. Burns' Famous Lemon Basil' is quite distinct in growth habit from the lower-growing lemon basil (O. *citriodorum*) and forms a graceful pattern to 3 feet tall, with 1½- to 2-inch leaves that have a hint of clove mingled with their lemon scent. The pink- or white-flowering stalks take their time about flowering, so deadheading is easily managed to keep the plant looking and tasting its best. I grow this basil with its pointed light green leaves next to a sprawling stand of Roman mint (*Micromeria* sp.), which has rounded darker leaves, the two herbs perfectly complementing one another. The dark green of purslane and the yellow-green of golden purslane also look nice close by.

Carlo's Pesto with Haricots Verts and Potatoes

This recipe, Genoese in origin, combines potatoes and green beans with *pasta al pesto*. Not limited by tradition, I substituted 'Mrs. Burns' Famous Lemon Basil' for the typical sweet basil. Another nontypical flourish is the Italian garnish of fresh sweet marjoram, an herb that perfectly complements the basil. If using fresh sweet marjoram, make sure it is the true sweet marjoram, also known as knotted marjoram (*Origanum majorana*).

Prepare the pesto right before you serve the pasta, so the sauce stays bright green, as basil oxidizes quickly.

1 tablespoon coarsely chopped garlic

¼ cup toasted pine nuts

1 teaspoon sea salt

2 cups packed fresh leaves of 'Mrs. Burns' Famous Lemon Basil'

3 tablespoons coarsely chopped Italian parsley

½ cup extra virgin olive oil

½ cup grated Parmesan cheese

2 tablespoons freshly grated Romano pecorino cheese

2 Yellow Finn potatoes, cut into ½-inch cubes

4 ounces haricots verts, cut on the diagonal into 1-inch pieces

1 pound dried fettucine

1 tablespoon finely chopped fresh sweet marjoram, or 1 teaspoon dried

In a food processor fitted with the metal blade or in a blender, combine the garlic, pine nuts, and salt. Process until finely chopped, then add basil, parsley, and 2 tablespoons of the oil. Process until the ingredients are well blended. Scrape down the ingredients on the sides of the bowl, then slowly add the remaining oil until a smooth purée is formed. Transfer the mixture to a medium-sized bowl and beat in the cheeses with a whisk. Lay a sheet of plastic wrap directly on the pesto's surface, so the sauce remains bright green, and set aside.

Bring a large pot of salted water to a boil. Add the potatoes and cook for 5 minutes. Add the beans to the pot and cook for 5 minutes. With a slotted spoon, remove potatoes and beans to a warmed small bowl and reserve. Add the fettucine to the boiling water and boil for approximately 7 to 10 minutes; check the package directions for timing. When the pasta is almost cooked, add 1 or 2 tablespoons of the cooking water to the pesto to thin it. Thirty seconds before draining the fettucine, add the reserved potatoes and beans to the pot, then drain pasta and vegetables together immediately. Place in a large warmed serving bowl. Add the reserved pesto and quickly toss to coat the pasta evenly. Divide among 6 warmed plates and sprinkle each serving with the marjoram. Serve at once.

Serves 4

'CINNAMON' BASIL

(*Ocimum basilicum* 'Cinnamon')

Tender Annual

'Cinnamon' basil's sweet, true cinnamon bouquet qualifies it as one of the most unusual, delicately scented basils. In whatever country this basil cultivar is grown, its flavor is beguiling to the cook. At the southeast Asian and Oriental market where I shop, 'Cinnamon' basil is always nestled next to a cache of other fragrant herbs: *bai gaprow*, or holy basil; *bai horapa*, or Thai basil; Vietnamese balm; and lemon grass. Inventive American chefs create tantalizing dishes with this spice-in-an-herb basil, and domestic cooks and home gardeners will find it to be as easily at home in a perfumed arrangement of ornamental flowers as it is in the kitchen.

In the garden, 'Cinnamon' basil grows to about 2½ feet tall with medium purple stems, lavender-with-white blossoms, and smooth, 2-inch-long, pointed leaves with a matte finish, instead of the shiny one typical of basil; glandular hairs on the leaf surface hold its cinnamon-scented essential oils. When it begins to send up its flowering stalk, an intensely garnet-colored cluster in the center of its medium green leaves, the result is a startling contrast that is quite decorative. For a theme bed of basils, the redder-stemmed Thai basils are quite complementary, especially the new 'Siam Queen' Thai basil which looks like like a fancy relative of 'Cinnamon' basil, with abundant center flower clusters of intense royal purple. And the small pointy leaves of dwarf 'Minimum' basil or the large crinkly leaves of lettuce-leaved basil make an attractive contrast of leaf structure, all bordered by a minihedge of dwarf Greek basil.

Strawberry Vinegar with 'Cinnamon' Basil

This fruit vinegar is enlivened by the spicy taste of 'Cinnamon' basil. Prepare it during the season when strawberries are at their sweet and juicy height. It makes a wonderful variation for vinaigrettes. Combined with extra virgin olive oil it is delightful, and combined with nutty oils such as walnut and hazelnut, this rose-colored vinegar is sublime.

For other recipes using 'Cinnamon' basil, see page 105, Pink Superb Sorbet with 'Cinnamon' Basil, and page 83, Asian Pesto.

1 cup packed fresh 'Cinnamon' basil leaves and stems
1 pint fresh strawberries, stemmed and washed
2 cups white wine vinegar

Wash the 'Cinnamon' basil, then pat it dry with paper towels. Place it in a sterilized wide-mouth glass container with a nonreactive lid. Add the strawberries and mash them with the back of a spoon or a wooden pestle. Add the vinegar. Cover tightly and place in a cool, dark place for 1 week. Taste the vinegar, and if a stronger infusion is desired, add fresh 'Cinnamon' basil and strawberries to the strawberry vinegar, and allow to sit 1 more week. Strain the vinegar through a fine sieve, discarding the basil and strawberry pulp. Pour the vinegar into a sterilized glass bottle and seal with a nonreactive lid. Use within 2 months.

Makes 2 cups

EAST INDIAN BASIL

(Ocimum gratissimum)

Tender Perennial   Zone 10

Native Habitat   Tropical Africa

It is surprising to learn that East Indian basil is a member of the basil family, for it looks like
nothing associated with most culinary basils. Its other name, tree basil, is a more apt description, for it is a bushy shrub with a woody stem that can grow to 6 feet tall in its native tropics; it is the tallest of the cultivated basils. Its coarse, felty, forest-green serrated leaves grow
to about 4 inches long and 3 inches wide. It is widely cultivated in India, the West Indies,
and northern South America. In the United States, where it can grow to 4½ or 5 feet tall, it
is an excellent specimen for a large decorative container. In growing zones with no frost, it
may be planted in the ground. Camphor, anise, mint, citrus, and clove are flavors and scents
we associate with the other culinary basils, but East Indian basil smells only of clove; if there

are indeed other olfactory notes, they are overwhelmed by its bracing spiced scent. Because it exudes such a healthy fragrance, take advantage of it by placing the container on a patio where brushing against it will release its enlivening essential oils. In my Zone 10 garden, I grow it in a terra-cotta pot where it reaches about 3½ feet tall. Its flowering stalks are not decorative, like those of most other basils, but it doesn't need pinching back as often to stay looking full from bottom to top. My family discovered a very useful nonculinary application on the patio one hot summer evening: arms and legs can be dabbed with a leaf of East Indian basil when the mosquitoes are driving you to distraction, and—bug-be-gone. (Please make sure you are not allergic to the plant before you try our home remedy.)

Baked Apples à la Gratissimum

For another recipe using East Indian basil see page 257, Four Herb Honeys for Berries.

4 Golden Delicious apples
½ cup maple syrup
1 tablespoon finely minced East Indian basil
½ teaspoon ground cinnamon

¼ teaspoon lemon zest
1 tablespoon butter
1 cup apple juice

Preheat the oven to 350 degrees. Prepare the apples. With a melon baller core each apple, taking care not to cut through to the blossom end. With a sharp knife score evenly around each apple ⅛ inch deep about one third of the way down from the stem end. Place the apples in a Pyrex baking dish or pie pan and pour in water to reach ½ inch up the side of the pan.

In a medium bowl, whisk together the maple syrup, East Indian basil, cinnamon, and lemon zest. Pour equal amounts of the mixture into the cavity of each apple. Dot each apple with the butter. Bake the apples, basting them every 10 minutes with the apple juice until they are tender when pierced with a skewer, about 40 minutes. Place the apples on 4 small dessert plates or bowls, and serve immediately.

Serves 4

GROWING YOUR OWN

'Cinnamon' basil and 'Mrs. Burns' Famous Lemon Basil' may be started from seed, either directly sown in well-amended soil, or started indoors 6 to 8 weeks before the last frost, then transplanted outdoors as soon as the soil has thoroughly warmed and night temperatures are above 55 degrees. Basils are very frost-sensitive and will blacken at the very breath of cold weather. Thin seedlings to about 2 feet apart. Obtain 'African Blue' basil and East Indian basil as potted plants from specialty seed nurseries. In regions where no frost occurs, these two varieties may be perennial, depending upon gardens' microclimates. 'African Blue' and East Indian basils may be propagated from stem cuttings.

Basils thrive in full sun or a light amount of shade, and need well-draining, evenly moist soil. Mulching will help to keep the soil moist, but wait until the ground has thoroughly warmed to at least 60 degrees before you apply it. Bonemeal and bloodmeal can be added to the amended soil at planting time. After large cuttings during the growing season, or if basils begin to look tired with repeated harvesting, feed with dry fish fertilizer, liquid fish emulsion, or chicken manure. Basil will begin to flower quite soon after it is planted; since it is at its tastiest just before flowering, try and keep up with pinching back the heads as they develop. Pluck the most succulent flowering tip clusters, or pinch the stems back to the third node. If you use a large amount of basil in cooking, try succession plantings of 'Mrs. Burns' and 'Cinnamon' basil every two weeks to ensure a steady supply of young basil leaves. Keeping up with the flowering heads of basil is almost impossible in the southeastern growing regions of Zones 8 and 9. Mulch well with materials like smooth river stone, pecan shells, peanut or rice hulls, or chipped and shredded pine bark. 'Mrs. Burns' Famous Lemon Basil' is a good performer in these regions and reseeds prolifically. East Indian basil is also a vigorous grower in these areas.

All the above basils will grow well in containers, and some partial shade especially aids the water-thirsty potted basils. They can be fed with dry fish fertilizer or full-strength liquid fish emulsion once a month, or the fish emulsion can be applied at one-quarter strength with each watering. Decrease fertilizing when basil is on the wane, toward the end of the growing season. In colder regions, container-grown East Indian basil may be brought indoors for the winter, or set out in the garden for the summer and then repotted to winter over indoors, ideally under artificial light. Container-grown 'African Blue', 'Mrs. Burns', and 'Cinnamon' basil may be cut back and brought indoors to a sunny, south-facing windowsill so you can harvest their leaves until the plants are spent. In addition, a few sprigs of these basils placed in a glass of water will keep for an extended period and occasionally will root, which serendipitously extends their harvest even further.

CULINARY USES OF BASIL

When the garden air is perfumed with spicy scents from the abundance of these unique basils is the time to overindulge in all the different ways to prepare them, beginning with the delicious standards. 'Mrs. Burns' Famous Lemon Basil' gives a unique twist to French *pistou*, the Provençal sauce that is a combination of basil, garlic, and olive oil, with or without cheese, to spoon into vegetable soup; or to pesto, the fresh Italian sauce for pasta that is made from the same ingredients as *pistou*, but with the addition of pine nuts or walnuts. 'Mrs. Burns' adds a refreshing citrus note to the basic—and perhaps the best—basil treatment, which is to shred the leaves and strew them over large slices of fresh tomatoes warm from the garden, sprinkle with salt and pepper, and drizzle all with extra virgin olive oil. Add fresh basil leaves to the water when poaching fish, and sprinkle them over a lentil or flageolet bean salad. Use basil's cooling lemony tang in hot and sour soup or chilled tomato soup.

Use clove-scented East Indian basil to brew a cup of hot tea, called *albahaca* in Latin America, or ice the tea for a cooling summer beverage. In Curaçao, it scents soups, and in Aruba it is used to flavor fish. Infuse honey with its julienned leaves to flavor baked apples and other fruits with a more subtle taste than real cloves. The herb makes a scented stuffing for fish, poultry, and game.

The concentrated camphor taste of 'African Blue' basil dictates using a judicious amount to suit personal tastes. It complements beef, pork, and chicken dishes, and also spicy, chile-laced sauces for fish such as catfish and mackerel. One of the best ways to use 'African Blue' basil is in an herb vinegar. The deep purple variegation in its leaves magically tints the vinegar a jewellike garnet hue, and its mellowed camphorous taste makes a pleasing basil vinegar that is quite unique in flavor (see page 55).

'Cinnamon' basil stands up well to heat in cooking, retaining its true spice flavor in syrup that can be poured over poached summer fruits and is the extra fillip in a cooling fruit sorbet or ice cream. It makes an unusual herb jelly and a subtle cinnamon marinade for chicken; it is tasty combined with opal basil and lemon zest in steamed rice. Mixed with a lesser amount of East Indian basil, it gives a nice punch to chutneys. Add a bouquet of 'Cinnamon' basil to a bottle of freshly made strawberry vinegar (see page 62). Combined with walnut or hazelnut oil, this herbal fruit vinegar is an excellent dressing for green or fruit salads. A handful of fresh leaves of 'Cinnamon' basil lends spice to Darjeeling or other black teas. Its leaves can be nestled in the sugar bowl, and the sugar will be infused with its subtle cinnamon scent.

Pluck basil as close to cooking time as possible, and preferably at the end of the day, as studies have shown its keeping power is longer when it is harvested in this way. I don't generally preserve basil by drying, as it loses so much of its flavor, but both 'Mrs. Burns' and East Indian retain a nice, if less emphatic, bouquet when dried.

WHITE-FLOWERING BORAGE
(Borago officinalis 'Alba')

Hardy Annual
Native Habitat   Southern Europe, Asia Minor, North Africa

At an herb lecture I attended that was presented by a distinguished English garden author, when the slide of the gardens of Sissinghurst appeared on the screen, he described several plants, then nonchalantly noted the white borage among the other herbs, and went on to the next slide. I made a mental note of this white form, for blue borage is one of my favorite herbs. The next day I wrote a letter addressed to "the gift shop" at Sissinghurst Castle, requesting a packet of white borage seeds. A month went by, and a package from abroad appeared in my mailbox, addressed to me in carefully scripted handwriting. In it was a personal letter from the head gardener at Sissinghurst informing me (1) that there is no "gift shop" at the garden, and (2) that she was so sorry, but all she could collect that morning from the white borage in the garden were the enclosed *nine* seeds. Emeralds couldn't have been more precious! My "Sissinghurst seeds" of white borage thrive in my garden today, and I hand-collect the progeny, which I stingily pass out to deserving gardening friends. Fortunately, the seed is becoming more available in this country (see "Sources," page 279).

Ego, Borago, gaudia semper ago (I, borage, bring always courage) is the age-old Latin verse found so often in garden literature wherein borage symbolizes courage. Linguists are divided on the derivation of its name, but this rhyme perhaps explains why borage is often pronounced "burrage" to rhyme with "courage."

Historically, one of borage's culinary uses was to include its leaves in "wine cups"; they were thought to enhance the exhilarating effect of the grape, causing the imbiber to become merrier than usual, and therefore empowered with newfound "courage" to speak and behave in otherwise uncustomary ways. In ancient Greece and Rome the herb was used as both food and medicine and was grown in little formal garden plots along with basil, chervil, cilantro, fennel, and parsley. In the medieval household it had a firm position in the repertoire of herbs: its cooked leaves, eaten as a vegetable, were known as "porray," and its fresh leaves were used in salads, along with mint, sage, garlic, fennel, and rosemary. The versatile herb was also a staple in colonial American gardens and kitchens.

A rather uncomplimentary common name, ox-tongue, aptly describes its hairy leaves. In many herbals there is reference to the use of its leaves in salads. Whether the leaves are young or old, to my palate they feel like Brillo pads, so I prefer to use borage's cucumber-scented flowers, blue or white, in salads and wines and other beverages. I don't necessarily experience any giddiness drinking wine or cold drinks with borage flowers, but their contrasting beauty when served in beverages is certainly effective. Blue borage blossoms turn pink after a time in drinks, so you can always keep track of how many lemonades you have had by counting the pink borage blossoms in your glass. Since ancient times, blue flowers have symbolized loyalty, as in "true blue," and white flowers have represented light and innocence—and borage blossoms with them both.

GROWING YOUR OWN

White borage flowers are shaped like a perfect five-pointed white star, and upon close inspection, there is just a hint of pearlized iridescence in their petals; the abundant white flowers hang in loose clusters. The gray-green bristly herb is best planted in a spot that is elevated, such as a wall garden, where the flowers will be more visible, and that better highlights the herb's ornamental qualities. It grows to 2 feet tall and 2 feet wide and has prickly, large, oblong, veined leaves and hollow stems. Once an inhabitant of your garden, always an inhabitant, for it self-sows vigorously. However, where it is unwanted, young plants are easy to uproot.

It is best to sow borage where you want it, for it does not like to be moved once settled because of its long taproot, which is easily disturbed or snapped off. Or, seed can be sown indoors in winter in individual pots, and the small seedlings can be successfully transplanted outdoors. Thin or set plants 1 to 1½ feet apart. White borage likes full sun but will accept partial shade. It grows well in average soil with added bonemeal and bloodmeal at planting time and needs regular watering. It can become rangy, so cut it back often to keep it looking its ornamental best. Bees love borage; interplanted in the vegetable garden, it makes a good bedding companion to attract bees and thus help pollinate tomatoes, squash, and strawberries.

In the design of the garden, white borage's gray-green, coarse foliage contrasts with the texture of various other herbs, such as the soft, silvery gray foliage of lamb's ears or the velvet green leaves of peppermint-scented geranium. White borage blossoms are complemented by blue anchusa, forget-me-nots, anise hyssop, calamint, and dianthus, including the fringed superb pink. Borage is a must for the edible-flower theme garden or bed, for it was one of the first and most enduring of its kind.

CULINARY USES

One delicate cucumber-flavored flower of white borage can be floated as a garnish in Pimm's Cup No. 1, the English gin-based aperitif. Or the fat, hollow stem of white borage, scraped clean of its fuzz, can replace the cucumber stick that sometimes accompanies the drink.

To remember in midwinter how cucumbers *should* taste, make a delicate cucumber vinegar by steeping borage leaves, combined with salad burnet (*Poterium sanguisorba*), another cucumber-tasting herb, in white wine vinegar. Its flowers also add a scented note to white wine spritzers, pink and plain lemonade, fruit drinks, and punches. The white star flowers are most effective frozen in ice cubes (made with distilled water so the cubes remain clear), and floated in all the above beverages. They complement a pale, pale green cucumber soup or a cold curried carrot soup. They are striking sprinkled over a green salad of many young lettuces, and make an elegant contrast atop sliced strawberries. Candied, they contrast handsomely with a chocolate pudding, mousse, or a brownie for dessert.

For a recipe that uses white borage, see page 199, Good Husbandry Summer Salad with Pear Vinaigrette.

LEAF CELERY

(*Apium graveolens* var. *secalinum*)

Biennial   Zones 7–9
Native Habitat   Europe and temperate Asia

The wild celery known as "smallage" in Roman days, poisonous in its raw form, was developed into garden celery primarily by the Italians in the seventeenth century. It took until the nineteenth century before garden celery came into general use in England and America. Leaf celery is a separate variety of celery that requires no blanching of its stems (covering the growing stalks to make them white) and makes a fine seasoning. In the horticultural classic *The Vegetable Garden*, written in the 1800s by members of the French Vilmorin seed company family, leaf celery was depicted as *céleri à couper*, or "cutting celery," which in the English version was translated as "soup celery," so complementary is the herb to soups and stews. Now, on the verge of the twenty-first century, the herb is offered only by a small number of specialty seed catalogs; it remains relatively unknown and is, as one catalog describes it, "a cook's secret."

The intensely savory leaf celery is a common item in the outdoor market stalls of European countries. "Amsterdam fine seasoning celery," "French celery," "Chinese celery," "cutting celery," and "par-cel" are other names for this pungent seasoning. Its vividly green, glossy leaves are deeply cut and resemble those of another biennial, Italian parsley—hence the no-nonsense name "par-cel." They have similar growth habits.

GROWING YOUR OWN

Leaf celery is a biennial that is grown like an annual. An easy-to-grow herb, it can be seeded directly into the ground or started indoors in the very early spring so the seedlings will be large enough for transplanting outdoors when the soil has warmed. Do not be tempted to plant the seedlings too early, as the cool weather can cause the herb to bolt. Plant in rich, moist, well-drained soil. Leaf celery likes full sun but will tolerate partial shade in hot climates. Maintain a regular watering schedule, and especially in dry weather keep the plant well watered. Feed regularly with dried fish fertilizer or liquid fish emulsion mixed at half strength. Leaf celery grows to 12 to 18 inches; the narrow stalks are best harvested at about 12 inches or less, before they become stringy and fibrous. The outside stems should be removed to increase production of new stems. Leaves can be plucked as needed for seasoning. Leaf celery has a nice long growing season from spring to hard frost. It makes an attractive ornamental edible border interplanted with colorful flowering annuals.

CULINARY USES

Whenever the culinary uses of leaf celery are listed, its importance as a flavoring in both meat and vegetable soups and stews is mentioned. Its leaves have a grassy, aromatic taste that is excellent in tomato-based soups. Wrap a stem or two of leaf celery with a bouquet garni and add to white vegetable soup made with chicken stock. Its parsleylike undertones blend with and enhance the flavor of other herbs, much like parsley. And if you like the look of Italian parsley as a garnish, leaf celery is more assertive both visually and in its flavor. Its chopped aromatic leaves can be sprinkled over vegetables, their dark green color making a fine color contrast, and the young, tender tips of the leafy stems give a mesclun salad a nice bite. A creamy yogurt dressing for salads can be made using finely chopped leaf celery leaves, a little minced garlic, and lemon juice. Revive the old-fashioned Waldorf salad of diced celery, apples, and grapes, enrobed with a mayonnaise dressing and sprinkled with pecans, by using the tender diced stems of leaf celery and eggless saffron mayonnaise. (See page 227.) Another classic, cream of celery soup, has twice the punch when made with leaf celery.

Other recipes using leaf celery are True French Sorrel Vichyssoise with 'Golden Rain' Rosemary (page 244), Duck and White Bean Tacos (page 87), Malabar-Spinach-and-Prosciutto-Stuffed Tomatoes (page 159), and Good Husbandry Spring Salad with Verjus Vinaigrette (page 128).

GARLAND CHRYSANTHEMUM

(Chrysanthemum coronarium)

Annual
Native Habitat   The Mediterranean

You might think a "mum" would be untasty and bitter because of the association with the sharp fragrance of cut bunches of the autumn-blooming chrysanthemum (*Chrysanthemum* x *morifolium*) sold in flower shops and often worn in corsages at fall football games. While these chrysanthemums are considered edible, their relative, garland chrysanthemum, has a milder flavor, and its fleshy leaves of a slightly different shape are bred for use as edible greens. Garland chrysanthemum's slightly astringent qualities lend complexity and character to a number of Oriental dishes. The flowers are the size of quarters with centers the color of egg yolks and the shape of daisies; upon closer inspection, they turn out to be yellow on yellow, for the ends of the petals are the palest shade of yellow. Garland chrysanthemum also blooms in variations of white and orange. Their fringed foliage and sunny blossoms brighten the awakening spring garden.

Indigenous to the Mediterranean area, garland chrysanthemum is naturalized in Europe, Africa, and Asia. It is widely cultivated for food in Southeast Asia, China, and Japan and is also a common staple in Oriental markets in the United States, but this decorative edible is not so common in domestic herb gardens. The two forms of garland chrysanthemum most available in seed catalogs are simply called "small-leaf variety," an exuberant plant with thick, moderately serrated dark green leaves and a spreading growth habit, and "large-leaf variety," with a slightly milder taste and smooth, slightly indented broad, oblong leaves. Both grow 1 to 3 feet tall. A third variety, the one closest to the wild garland chrysanthemum, has especially lacy leaves and a short, upright growth habit.

GROWING YOUR OWN

Sow seeds of garland chrysanthemum in early spring in well-amended soil so you can harvest its young leaves before the weather gets hot and turns them bitter. Seeds can be sown again during the fall growing season. The seeds are small, so plant them shallow and cover with fine soil or vermiculite mixed with some soil. Keep the soil moist until germination, about 7 to 10 days. Garland chrysanthemum can also be started indoors or in a cold frame or unheated greenhouse and set out when the danger of frost is past. When the seedlings are 3 inches high, thin to about 4 to 6 inches apart. Garland chrysanthemum likes full sun but can tolerate some shade. Water regularly. Harvest can begin about 6 weeks after sowing.

Garland chrysanthemum is an excellent container plant. I usually plant it in a wine crate with attractive graphics that I beg from a chef friend. I line the crate with black plastic, punch holes in the bottom for drainage, and plant the seeds in a lightweight, soilless mix. I feed it fish emulsion every other week during the growing season.

To harvest the tender stems of garland chrysanthemum for cooking, snip 2 to 3 inches of the young stems when the plant is about 1 foot tall, which also will stimulate new growth for future cuttings. It should not be allowed to flower or its stems will get tough, so plant enough seeds to allow one or two plants to reach maturity and flower freely, just for the lovely ornament they add to the herb garden, and for the edible flowers. Fortunately for the gardener, this is one herb that has virtually no pests, and the Safer's soap can have a rest. Garland chrysanthemum gets tall and rangy with heat. When this occurs, discard the plants and seed again in late summer or early fall.

CULINARY USES

In Japanese cuisine, garland chrysanthemum, or *shungiku,* is popular in one-pot dishes like sukiyaki and *shabu shabu,* made with beef sirloin, and *yosenabe,* made with fish and shellfish. It is easily adapted to hearty soups made with the same ingredients. In Korean cuisine it is known as *sukkat* and is considered to neutralize the odor of strong fish and enhance its flavor. Garland chrysanthemum also harmonizes well with chicken and is healthy and delicious in a rich chicken soup prepared with various vegetables. In China, cooks know how tasty garland chrysanthemum, or *p'eng-hao,* is in soups and also add it to stir-fries at the end of cooking, for it tends to get bitter when exposed to prolonged high heat. Garland chrysanthemum's leaves are nutritious when eaten as a vegetable; they can be steamed, blanched, or boiled with just the water remaining from washing the leaves, then seasoned with soy sauce and a little sesame seed oil. For fresh green salads made with a mesclun mélange of bitter, sweet, and tangy tastes and different textures, garland chrysanthemum is a perfect new addition, either its pretty flower petals, or its leaves. The Japanese blanch garland chrysanthemum leaves to make them shocking green before eating them as a salad, in combination with other ingredients or deliciously alone.

Garland Chrysanthemum Salad with Oriental Dressing

A Korean friend who is an excellent cook shared this recipe with me. When I asked her what her favorite cookbook was, there was a moment of surprised silence before she answered, "I don't read cookbooks, my recipes are in my head." This recipe for garland chrysanthemum can be served as either a salad or side dish and is an example of the creativity of the culinary repertoire in my friend's head.

For another recipe using garland chrysanthemum, see page 128, Good Husbandry Spring Salad with Verjus Vinaigrette.

4 cups young garland chrysanthemum leaves
  and stems
4 cups fresh bean sprouts
½ cup diced tofu (optional)

Oriental Dressing
4 tablespoons red wine vinegar
2 tablespoons soy sauce
Pinch sugar
½ teaspoon dark sesame seed oil
1 teaspoon thinly sliced scallions, green part
  only
¼ teaspoon finely chopped garlic
Sesame seeds for garnish

Wash the garland chrysanthemum leaves and stems. In a large pot of boiling salted water, blanch the leaves briefly, just until the color changes. Drain, then quickly pour cold water over the leaves. Pat them dry with paper towels and set aside. The cooked garland chrysanthemum diminishes in volume, like spinach. Blanch the bean sprouts, and pat them dry with paper towels.

To make Oriental Dressing, in a small bowl whisk together the vinegar, soy sauce, sugar, and sesame seed oil. Stir in the scallions and garlic.

Coarsely chop the garland chrysanthemum and place in a large bowl. Add the bean sprouts and tofu, if being used. Lightly toss with the dressing. Divide the mixture among four salad plates. Sprinkle each salad with toasted sesame seeds and serve immediately.

Serves 4

The Cilantro Mimics

It seems a paradox that cilantro's distinctive taste makes it both one of the country's most popular herbs and, to its detractors, so decidedly *un*popular. Two of its detractors are members of my own family, so I know that just the mention of the word can cause a contorted face, and the appearance of the herb in a dish causes consternation while the diner picks out the odiferous leaves one by one. Those of us on the other side of the fence welcome the following herbs, which impersonate the flavor of cilantro with varying degrees of its enticing, aromatic scent.

CULANTRO

(Eryngium foetidum)

Tender Perennial   Zones 8–10
Native Habitat   Southern Mexico, Central and South America, and the West Indies

From the garden at Festival Hill, Round Top, Texas

It is clear that culantro is a relative of the handsome ornamental sea holly (*Eryngium mariti-mum*), because of its thistlelike, stiff, spiny foliage and decorative, conical flower heads, which look like miniature green pineapples. Culantro is a low-growing herb that grows to about 16 inches high and has a rosette of sharply toothed oblong leaves at its base, which only look menacing, but are edibly soft when young. From its center spring flowering stalks that also have toothed leaves and sharp prickers, which are harmless on young leaves, but do really prick when older.

Growing in thickets and pastures in Central America, historically the herb has been called *chardon etoile* (star thistle), *culantro de la tierra*, and *culantro del monte*. In certain regions of Mexico it is known as *cilantron*, *cilantrillo*, and Tabascan parsley. But the detractors also have their names for it: *chardon etoile fetide* or stinking star thistle, *culantro de burro*, *culantro de coyote*, and, in English, stinkweed. Long used as a culinary herb in its native Latin America, where both its leaves and roots flavor soups and stews, culantro has also gained widespread culinary appreciation throughout tropical Africa and Asia. Its Vietnamese name, *ngò gai*, means "thorny coriander," and in Thai, *pak chee farang* means "foreign coriander" (*pak chee* means "coriander"); in Cambodian, "saw-leaf herb" perfectly describes the shape of its long, edible leaves.

GROWING YOUR OWN

Culantro is grown as an annual below Zone 8, where temperatures can plummet to zero and beyond. It is treated as a short-lived perennial in warm-climate zones. Culantro can be sown from seed indoors in early winter, and set out when the ground has warmed. Be patient, for it is very slow to germinate. One positive point about growing culantro is that it doesn't bolt as cilantro is wont to do. It will be in the garden long after cilantro has bolted, and is producing coriander, its dried seedheads. Harvest culantro's basal leaves, which can grow to over 4 inches long and 1 inch wide. The flowering stems grow to 16 inches or more. Keep them cut back so the basal leaves continue to produce. Culantro likes a moderately fertile, fast-draining, moist soil. It grows in full sun or partial shade. In my Zone 10 garden, I have found that culantro likes morning sun and afternoon shade, but fries in full sun in the ground. It adapts very well to growing in containers, where it is easy to supply it with the water it needs, and to move it to follow the shade when necessary. In containers, I feed it once a month with liquid fish emulsion. In growing areas with cold winters, bring potted culantro indoors. Slugs pay no attention to the derogatory remarks about cilantro-scented culantro; their appetite for it is voracious, and the gardener must be diligent in protecting culantro from them. A flashlight and a coffee can with a lid is the foolproof method. When it is dark, use the flashlight to detect them, drop them in the can, cover, and dispose. Alternate methods are to strew wood ash or lay copper tubing, which they don't like to crawl over, or to set out a lid filled with beer, which they do like to crawl into. The edible leaves grow flat on the ground, so poisonous snail bait is not an option.

CULINARY USES

The place to use culantro is any dish you want to impart the taste of cilantro. Combine chopped culantro leaves with cumin, Mexican oregano I or II, and New Mexico ground chile to flavor a spicy guacamole, or infuse a mixture of lime juice and honey with the leaves to pour over honeydew melon. In Mexico, the flowerheads of culantro are used regionally as a spice to flavor moles, or sauces. Unlike cilantro, culantro's leaves retain their flavor when dried. An excellent method for infusing dishes with its flavor is the Caribbean *sofrito*, a savory base for sauces, soups, and other dishes. One version consists of a sauteéd mixture of onions, garlic, bell pepper, perhaps tomatoes or ham, and always cilantro, which you can replace with culantro.

Culantro is popular in soups in both tropical America and Southeast Asia; a sprig of it can be used whole and removed at the end of cooking, as with bay leaves, or it can be chopped and remain in the soup, as in the North Vietnamese classic, Hanoi soup (*pho bac*), made with rich beef stock, slices of lean beef, and rice noodles, or the popular southern Vietnamese specialty, hot and sour fish soup. Do as the Asians do and add culantro to steamed rice; cook and garnish fish with its serrated leaves; toss chopped culantro leaves into main-course vegetable, meat, and seafood stews, called curries, or add it to fiery red or green curry pastes made with red or green chiles, onions, garlic, lemon grass, cumin, and a little vegetable oil. Add a tablespoon of culantro to hummus, the earthy spread made of ground chickpeas, olive oil, lemon juice, and usually tahini, or sesame seed paste. The easiest way of all to enjoy culantro is simply to garnish a warm tasty taco topped with shredded Monterey Jack cheese with a confetti of freshly chopped green culantro.

Asian Pesto

This exotic herbal pesto is excellent served with firm-fleshed fish such as swordfish, or atop a bed of pasta, just like the basil pesto. This recipe serves 4 if it is to accompany pasta. A tasty stuffing for tricolor wonton pillows, the sauce is also delicious on steamed vegetables or on a wedge of iceberg—yes, iceberg—lettuce.

Roasting the garlic cloves instead of using them raw gives the sauce a rich, nutty flavor.

Japanese *shichimi togarashi*, or "red pepper mix," is a blend of ground red pepper, black sesame seeds, seaweed, orange peel, and mulberries. It can be found at Oriental markets.

For another recipe using culantro, see page 100, Potato Curry.

2 cloves garlic, roasted
2 tablespoons coarsely chopped ginger
1 to 2 serrano peppers, stemmed and seeded
2 tablespoons lemon juice
2 teaspoons low-sodium soy sauce
1 cup packed fresh 'Cinnamon' basil
   (page 60)
½ cup fresh coarsely chopped Vietnamese balm
   leaves (see page 255)

¼ cup rice paddy herb leaves, loosely packed
   (see page 201)
¼ cup packed fresh culantro or cilantro leaves
   (page 80)
¼ cup chopped scallions, green part only
¾ cup peanut oil
1 tablespoon dark sesame oil
shichimi togarashi *or red chile powder to taste*
Toasted sesame seeds, for garnish

To roast garlic, roast unpeeled cloves for 15 minutes in a 350-degree oven, then squeeze out the soft inside. In a food processor fitted with the metal blade, purée the roasted garlic, chopped ginger, and peppers with the lemon juice and soy sauce until smooth. Add the basil, Vietnamese balm, rice paddy herb, culantro, and scallions. Process until smooth. Combine the two oils in a lipped measuring cup. Slowly add to the processed herbs the peanut and sesame oils in a thin stream, scraping down the sides of the bowl, until the mixture is well blended. Transfer the mixture to a small bowl and add the *shichimi togarashi* or chile powder. Lay a piece of plastic wrap on the surface of the pesto while you prepare the dish it is to accompany. Add garnish and serve immediately.

About 1⅓ cups

PAPALOQUELITE

(*Porophyllum ruderale* subsp. *macrocephalum*)

Annual
Native Habitat   Arizona and Texas through Mexico and Central America to
South America

If you like the taste of cilantro, you'll love papaloquelite, which has the same distinctively pungent essential oils as cilantro, plus a dusky taste of green peppers and cucumbers to make it more complex. It's sort of like gazpacho in a leaf, sans tomatoes. Considering that cilantro has established itself as one of the most popular herbs today—despite its detractors—papaloquelite just might have the same appeal. But as with cilantro, there are bound to be two opposing camps regarding its culinary merits, for it's difficult to be neutral regarding the taste and scent of most distinctively strong herbs, and papaloquelite is no exception. Cilantro's name is derived from the Greek word for "bedbug," *koris*, and papaloquelite is also known as *mampuritu*, a corruption of the Spanish word for "skunk."

Taste is personal, but I doubt that anyone would quarrel with the ornamental qualities of papaloquelite, which means "butterfly leaf" in the language of the Nahuatl Indians of the central highlands of Mexico. Papaloquelite grows abundantly in pastures, on hillsides, in ravines, and in other waste places, and its easily availability gives it widespread use in its native habitat. Porophyllum is a tropical and subtropical American genus of perhaps 30 species. The most popular cultivated species, *Porophyllum ruderale* subsp. *macrocephalum*, grows in a graceful, multibranching, airy manner with beautiful blue-green leaves 1 to 2½-inches long. The stems seem to reach for the sky, stopping at about 3 to 4 feet in my Zone 10 garden, but they can reach 6 feet in very hot climates. The leaves are curious. They are oval and small, and elongated translucent oil glands occur at each wavy notch in the leaf and are scattered over its surface. Its botanical name means "pored leaf." These pores can be seen with the naked eye, but it's fascinating to observe the leaf structure close up through a small 15-power photographer's loupe—as I have a habit of doing with leaves and flowers. What an interesting world one finds there! Papaloquelite has quite showy purple to brownish-green starburst flowers at the ends of its branches. Gardeners in cold growing regions with short summers will have to be content with the pretty foliage of papaloquelite, for it doesn't usually flower where the growing season is short—but it is the leaves that flavor foods.

GROWING YOUR OWN

Papaloquelite is easily grown from seed sown direct in the ground. Just make sure the weather has warmed up sufficiently before sowing. It can also be sown from seed indoors 6 weeks before the last frost date, then transplanted to the ground when the weather warms. Plant in fast-draining, sandy soil, and water regularly. It grows best in full sun but can take some shade. One plant will usually suffice for one family, but if planting more than one, prick out the seedlings to leave the remaining plants spaced about 1½ feet apart. It is a midborder plant, and its oval blue-green leaves and upright growth habit are complemented by Mexican oregano II (*Poliomentha longiflora*), which has a similar growth habit and tubular, dusty-rose flowers, or Mexican oregano I (*Lippia graveolens*) with its small clusters of white blossoms. The matte blue-green lacy foliage of rue is attractive when planted in front of papaloquelite, where it complements papaloquelite's larger leaves of the same hue. When papaloquelite has gone to seed, it looks like a dandelion-ball tree, its featherlight, gossamer seedheads ready to fly through the air with just one puff.

CULINARY USES

Attesting to its popularity in areas where it grows wild in Mexico and the American Southwest, a glass of water holding little branches of papaloquelite is a staple fixture on certain restaurant tables, along with other condiments like salsa and hot chile peppers, for the diners to pluck their own leaves to add to bean dishes or roll up in warm tortillas. It is generally used fresh, and it does not dry well. In Bolivia it is a popular ingredient in salsas containing a variety of chiles. In Mexico, it is also known as *papalo*, and seasons guacamole and tacos. It is a common herb in the Mexican states of Hidalgo, Jalisco, and Puebla, and in Mexico City. A general rule of thumb for its use would be to include a few leaves of papalo-quelite in any dish where you would use cilantro. Its complex flavor is excellent in fresh tomato salsas and is especially tasty in a smoky chipotle pepper salsa. A sprinkling of chopped leaves over jicama coleslaw prepared with lemon vinaigrette is a refreshing salad with a unique flavor. Use 1 or 2 leaves in chicken, duck, pork, or beef tacos, and scatter some finely chopped leaves over a cold red or white gazpacho.

Duck and White Bean Tacos

Tacos stuffed with shredded duck breast, white beans, and Mexican white cheese (*queso fresco*), with a sprig of cilantro-scented papaloquelite tucked inside, create a deliciously eclectic version of the Mexican favorite. Serving the tacos with Spicy Beans with Mexican Herbs (page 186) and cold beer or icy margaritas makes the meal a fiesta.

To Poach Duck

1½ pounds boneless duck breasts

½ cup thinly sliced onions

1 large clove garlic, peeled

1 carrot, peeled, stem end removed, cut into 4 to 5 pieces

1 four-inch leafy stem leaf celery (see page 72) or the light green inner heart of celery with leaves attached, coarsely chopped

Bouquet garni: 4 sprigs fresh parsley, 2 sprigs fresh thyme, and 1 dried bay leaf

5 whole black peppercorns

1 teaspoon sea salt

To Assemble Tacos

3 tablespoons canola oil

1 medium-sized red onion, chopped

2 large cloves garlic, chopped

1 large fresh jalapeño pepper and 1 fresh serrano pepper, stemmed, seeded, and finely chopped

1 cup fresh tomatoes, peeled, seeded, and diced

1 teaspoon dried Mexican oregano I (page 187) or 1½ teaspoons Mexican oregano II (page 189)

Sea salt to taste

2 fifteen-ounce cans white beans, drained

About 10 corn tortillas

1 six-ounce package Mexican queso fresco or feta or domestic mild goat cheese, crumbled

About 10 sprigs papaloquelite

Place the duck in a large saucepan. Add water to cover, and bring slowly to a boil. Immediately lower the heat, and skim from the surface any rising scum. Add the onion, garlic, carrot, leaf celery, bouquet garni, peppercorns, and salt. Simmer over very low heat (there should be just a bare ripple on the surface of the liquid), partially covered, for about 50 minutes. When the juices of the duck breasts run clear when pricked deeply with a skewer, or when a meat thermometer just registers 160 degrees, remove the duck from the heat. Remove the breasts from the stock, then skin and shred them. Set aside. There should be about 3 cups of duck meat for the tacos. Reserve ¾ cup of the stock. Refrigerate the remainder and save it for a delicious base for soup.

Heat the canola oil in a large skillet. Sauté the onion until soft, about 3 to 4 minutes. Add the duck and over medium high heat, stir-fry the shredded pieces, tossing them frequently until they begin to brown, about 10 minutes. Add the garlic, peppers, tomatoes, Mexican oregano, and salt to taste. Cook over medium heat for about 5 minutes, then add the reserved ¾ cups duck stock. Cook for about 10 minutes, until the stock has evaporated.

Heat the beans over low heat in a medium saucepan, and keep them warm.

The tortillas may be steamed together or simply heated one by one on either side in a hot iron skillet and kept warm in a covered dish. To fry the tortillas, heat ½ inch canola oil over medium heat in a cast-iron skillet. Place one tortilla in the skillet and cook it flat for a few seconds. Quickly fold it in half and hold it slightly open with tongs to make room for the filling. Turn and cook on the other side. Do not fry them too crisp, or they will break apart when they are filled. Drain on paper towels and keep them in a warm oven with the door ajar while preparing the remaining tortillas.

To assemble, place a layer of shredded duck in the warm taco shells, then add a spoonful of the beans. Sprinkle over this the crumbled cheese and slip a sprig of papaloquelite into each taco. Garnish with lettuce. Serve immediately.

Makes about 10 tacos

RAU RAM

(*Polygonum odoratum*)

Tender Perennial   Zones 9–10

Native Habitat   Southeast Asia

The sprawling plant with red-fading-to-green jointed stems and a faint paintbrush line of burgundy striping its lance-shaped leaves with a flame pattern is a culinary herb belonging to the group of annual and perennial weeds of the Polygonaceae, or buckwheat, family. Rau ram, or Vietnamese coriander, as it is known in most specialty herb catalogs, is intensely aromatic of cilantro with a delightfully odd taste note reminiscent of soap. It is widely used, generally fresh or as a garnish, in Southeast Asian cooking. In Vietnamese cuisine the popular herb is also used to flavor fish, chicken, meats, and salads. It is sometimes called Vietnamese mint, but it has no resemblance to mint either in appearance or taste, so it is best to identify it by its botanical name, *Polygonum odoratum*, or use its Vietnamese name, rau ram.

GROWING YOUR OWN

Rau ram is a tender perennial that grows to about 1 foot high, then begins its horizontal spread. It tolerates no frost, and in cold-winter zones it is treated as an annual, and can be wintered over indoors as a lovely houseplant. When it is container-grown, its jointed, round, red stems with abundant 2-inch-long pointy leaves make a handsome hanging basket. It is easily propagated from stem cuttings—either from your own plant, or from the cut herb obtained at the greengrocer or in Southeast Asian markets—and by root division. Grown in the ground, rau ram likes fertile soil, shade or filtered sun, and plenty of water. It is considered invasive, but its shallow root system makes it easy to keep its growth in check. In general it does not flower in the temperate regions of the United States, although there have been reports of its pale pink flower spikes blooming in the fall in a few of our hot-climate growing zones, or in greenhouse settings after the plant has experienced a late autumn chill.

CULINARY USES

Rau ram is a key ingredient in a Vietnamese chicken salad containing citrus fruits, carrots, cabbage, and sliced onion, dressed just with a light vinegar or *nuoc cham*, a dipping sauce made with fish sauce (*nuoc mam*), lime juice, garlic, and vinegar, sweetened with a little sugar and heated with a couple of chiles. A scattering of rau ram chopped leaves over stir-fried chicken is tantalizingly fragrant. My Vietnamese lawyer friend makes *bun thang*, a delicious chicken noodle soup of shredded chicken, ham, and lettuce, plus thin strips of egg omelette, to which is added a handful of the chopped herb just before serving. A classic Vietnamese twosome is fertile duck eggs garnished with rau ram. As with cooked cabbage, the cilantro scent of cooked rau ram will pervade the house, something the cook will have to reckon with to its detractors, so the herb is generally used fresh, added at the end of cooking. Perhaps the perfect way to experience the unique citrus-and-cilantro taste of this herb is in Henry's Rau Ram Salad of marinated white onions, soft butter lettuce, and rau ram, with a hint of mint. It is the simplest of salads—spare and elegant.

Henry's Rau Ram Salad

Henry, the best landscaping contractor this side of Vietnam, where he was born, grows his own vegetables and herbs, including rau ram. This is Henry's recipe for a simple green salad made without oil. The explosion of flavor from only two herbs, rau ram and ginger mint, is astonishing and delicious.

1½ cups water

2 teaspoons sugar

1 small Vidalia, Maui, or white onion, sliced paper thin

6 teaspoons rice vinegar

1 teaspoon low-sodium soy sauce

1 teaspoon finely chopped fresh rau ram

½ teaspoon finely chopped fresh ginger mint, (page 168) or spearmint

⅛ teaspoon chile flakes

Pinch sea salt

⅛ teaspoon finely chopped ginger root (optional)

6 cups butter lettuce, washed and dried

4 sprigs fresh rau ram, for garnish

Pour the water into a medium-sized bowl. Add the sugar and stir until dissolved. Separate the onions into rings and add them to the bowl. Allow the mixture to sit for 30 minutes.

In a small mixing bowl, combine the rice vinegar, soy sauce, rau ram, mint, chile flakes, salt, and the ginger, if being used.

In a large bowl, toss the lettuce with the dressing, coating the leaves well. Divide the lettuce among 4 plates. Drain the onions. Divide and place them atop each serving. Garnish each salad with a sprig of rau ram.

Serves 4

BROADLEAF GARDEN CRESS
(*Lepidium sativum*)

Annual

Native Habitat   Iran, Egypt, and western Asia

When you want something spicy on your plate, a savory choice is broadleaf garden cress, also known as land cress to distinguish it from watercress. The land variety is actually more convenient to plant, as gardeners don't need a stream of running water if they want to grow an herb with that peppery watercress flavor.

Garden cress is an "escaped herb," a cultivated species that originally was introduced to our shores long ago from Europe and that now grows across much of North America. Over a hundred wild and domesticated varieties grow throughout the temperate regions of the world. Garden cress is one half of the "mustard and cress" duo that the English crave with butter in their lunch or tea sandwiches. Broadleaf garden cress is an annual variety, not to be confused with curly cress, the parsley look-alike with tightly curled, frilly leaves, or the perennial upland cress, a dead ringer for watercress but with tougher leaves. Broadleaf garden cress has fine-textured, light green leaves with serrated edges, notched here and there along the way, and the taste is a cross between horseradish and mustard. It makes a pretty verdant stand in early spring when you yearn for something fresh and green from the garden while you're waiting for the growing season to get going. Broadleaf garden cress rewards you quickly, as it can be harvested within a month of planting, when the leaves reach 3 to 5 inches. It is full of vitamins A and C, and for those who believe in the lore of spring tonics, its bitter taste combined with that of other newly sprouted herbs such as arugula, violet leaves, and mâche is said to stimulate the appetite and the circulation.

GROWING YOUR OWN

Broadleaf garden cress is perfect for both the new gardener who wants an overwhelming success on the first attempt at sowing seed and the seasoned gardener who knows instant gratification is near. Nothing could be easier than growing cress. Within a month, a spring-bright patch of light green appears. Seed can be broadcast free form or planted in neat garden rows. Interplanting garden cress with other spring-blooming annuals and just-awakening perennials makes a pretty design combination. I have planted it among calamint, dittany-of-Crete, superb pink, nasturtiums, *Origanum libanoticum*, and a terra-cotta pot of chocolate mint for a pleasing show of leaf contrast and color combinations. Alternately, planting garden cress in tidy rows makes it easier to harvest. Although it is not fussy about growing conditions, the richer the soil the tastier the cress. Because it is harvested often, the herb benefits by an application of organic fertilizer such as dried fish fertilizer, liquid fish emulsion, or a balanced soluble fertilizer every two or three weeks to increase leaf production. A little plot of the aforementioned English twosome, "mustard and cress," white mustard (*Sinapsis alba*) and broadleaf cress, is easy to grow, and the seasoning blend is unique in salads and sandwiches, especially in the prissy cucumber round. Sow garden cress four days earlier than the mustard so both will be ready to harvest together when they are young, about 2 or 3 inches high. Broadleaf garden cress is a cool-weather crop that can be sown every month from early spring until hot weather comes, and again in the cool fall.

CULINARY USES

The French enjoy the mustardlike taste of broadleaf cress combined with chopped fresh tomatoes in a deliciously simple Provençal dish. No Persian table would be complete without *nan-o-panir-o-sabzi-khordan*, a plate of pita bread or crisp lavash, a wedge of fresh feta, nuts, scallions, and radishes served with an assortment of fresh green herbs such as tarragon, mint, dill, cilantro, fenugreek, lemon, anise, or 'Cinnamon' basil, and *shahy*, or broadleaf garden cress. In the Middle Eastern markets where I live, it is called "Persian watercress." The platter of greens, be it large or small, is either eaten as an appetizer or nibbled on throughout the meal. Perhaps the phrase "food fit for a king," derived from the seventh-century Persian court, pertains to this piquant combination.

Broadleaf garden cress is delicious as a replacement for the lettuce in a turkey, chicken, or roast beef sandwich. Its large leaves stand on their own as a salad ingredient mixed with other lettuces or can be garnished with peppery nasturtium flowers, also a member of the cress family. Broadleaf garden cress contains peppery mustard oil, so less salad oil is needed in a vinaigrette. Substitute lemon juice for vinegar, milder paprika or white pepper for black pepper; they better complement the tangy herb. Broadleaf garden cress can be harvested for slipping into a sandwich by snipping it with scissors when it is just 2 to 3 inches high. Finely chopped, it makes a peppery herb butter. *Just* as its foliage changes form and becomes lacy as it flowers and goes to seed, its stronger mustard taste gives herb butter an extra heady bite. For those who can't use salt, spicy cress is a satisfying alternative.

Persian Garden Cress Soup

At a bustling Middle Eastern market catering to the Iranian population in Los Angeles is broadleaf garden cress, known there as *shahy*, or Persian watercress, nestled next to the fenugreek, tarragon, flatleaf chives, cilantro, and dill. Large bunches of this spicy herb are also snapped up quickly at the weekly outdoor farmer's markets. Broadleaf garden cress is quite flavorful in the following two hot soups, one with a refreshing yogurt base, the other a delightfully simple chicken consommé.

2 cups broadleaf garden cress, tightly packed
1 white onion
2 tablespoons olive oil
4 cups chicken stock, preferably homemade
½ cup ground almonds

2 cups yogurt, preferably from goat's milk .
Sea salt and freshly ground white pepper to
*   taste*
Broadleaf garden cress leaves, spearmint, or
*   nasturtium blossoms for garnish*

Wash and dry the cress, then remove the stems. Set aside. In a food processor fitted with the metal blade, finely chop the onion. Heat the olive oil in a medium saucepan. Add the onion and cook over low heat until softened. Add the garden cress and cook for 2 to 3 minutes to

allow flavors to blend, then add chicken stock. Simmer, uncovered, over low heat for 5 minutes. Stir in almonds and continue to cook for 10 minutes. Add the yogurt and *just* heat through. Do not allow to boil. Add salt and white pepper to taste. Pour into warmed soup bowls. Garnish and serve immediately.

Serves 4–6

Emerald Consommé

This delicate soup is simplicity itself. Served in clear glass bowls, its light green, jewellike effect is a lovely way to whet the appetite for the next course.

A cooking tip: Fill an ice tray with the cooled soup and freeze. Use the frozen cubes to perk up the cooking water for vegetables or other light soups.

For another recipe using broadleaf garden cress, see page 128, Good Husbandry Spring Salad with Verjus Vinaigrette.

2 cups broadleaf garden cress, tightly packed
4 cups chicken stock, preferably homemade
Lemon juice to taste
Sea salt and freshly ground white pepper to taste

Wash and dry the garden cress. In a food processor fitted with the metal blade, purée the cress until smooth. Add 1 cup of the chicken stock. Pulse several times to combine, then pour the mixture into a medium-sized saucepan. Stir in the remaining 3 cups chicken stock and simmer over low heat, uncovered, for 10 minutes. Strain soup through a fine-mesh sieve. Return to clean saucepan. Add lemon juice, salt, and white pepper to taste. Heat soup for 3 to 4 minutes. Pour into warmed soup bowls and serve immediately.

Serves 4

CURRY LEAF

(*Murraya koenigii*)

Tender Perennial   Zones 10–11
Native Habitat   India and Ceylon

Curry leaf, with its long, palmlike fronds that catch the slightest breeze, is the perfect small herbal tree to create a feeling of the balmy tropics, whether in a conservatory or outdoors under a canopy of tall trees. It grows wild in the foothills of the Himalayas and also in southern India, where it is a favored fragrant leafy herb used to flavor food. Known as *kari patta*, it is popularly cultivated in domestic gardens there, particularly in Madras. Grown as well throughout Southeast Asia, the leaves of this graceful tree find their way into numerous regional dishes.

In its native habitat the curry leaf tree can grow to 20 feet, but grown outdoors in the warm-winter regions of the United States, and in conservatories or greenhouses where the winters are cold, it grows to only 5 feet. Its 2-inch-long, shiny green lance-shaped leaves grow in alternate order, about 20 to the stem, and are the culinary arm of the plant. Its spray of white flowers is followed by ornamental, shiny purple-black berries. Its aromatic bark, roots, and seeds are utilized in medicine. Both curry leaf and citrus are members of the Rutaceae family, and in the nursery industry citrus is grafted on to curry leaf tree rootstock.

Two things not to be confused with curry leaf: curry *plant* (*Helichrysum italicum*, formerly *Helichrysum angustifolium*), a Mediterranean herb with silvery needlelike leaves that smell like a blend of Indian spices, and commercial curry powder. Fresh curry leaf is indeed used to flavor curries, the myriad vegetable, chicken, fish, shellfish, and and meat stews or sauces ("curry" in the parlance of Indian cuisine) that are flavored with an artistic and skillful blend of spices that differs from region to region and cook to cook. The word "curry" is derived from the Tamil word *kari*, meaning sauce or stew, so in the simplest terms, curry leaf could be translated as "stew leaf" or "sauce leaf."

GROWING YOUR OWN

Curry leaf is evergreen in the warm-winter regions of Zones 10 and 11, where it can be grown in the ground or in a container. Containers to hold mature plants should be at least 1½ feet wide. In areas with hot summers and cold winters, curry leaf must be brought indoors or to a greenhouse to winter over, whether it is grown in the ground or in a container outdoors. Planted in the ground, curry leaf does well in moist, fertile soil that is rich with humus. The herb should be watered regularly, and excellent drainage is a must. Feed once a month with liquid fish emulsion or a balanced soluble fertilizer. Curry leaf grown in pots will need watering more often, especially in hot weather. It can be grown in full sun or partial shade, depending on the particular microclimate of your garden. In hot summer regions where the sun is strong, place the plant under the canopy of a tall tree that will provide it with high, dappled shade, or position it so it gets morning sun and afternoon shade.

Curry leaf is a slow grower. In my Zone 10 garden I grow it in a large terra-cotta container, where it has attained a height of 5 feet in four years. The herb can be top-pruned to promote fuller growth. It can be propagated by seed, which is contained in the shiny black patent-leather-like berries, if the mockingbirds don't get to them first.

CULINARY USES

When I give visitors trips through my herb garden, I always save curry leaf for last on the tour, for the musky scent of its leaves crushed between the hands inhibits the ability to enjoy other fragrances afterward. The rather rank smell of its fresh leaves gives way to a very pleasant, unique scent and toasty flavor when cooked.

Curry leaf has a particular affinity for vegetables, especially when combined with several spices. An excellent method used in Indian cuisine to obtain optimum flavor from spices can also be used with the herbal curry leaf to form a fragrant base for cooking vegetables, chicken, fish, and meat. Choose several spices such as turmeric, coriander seed, chile peppers, mustard seed, fennel seed, anise seed, cumin, saffron, fenugreek, etc., along with several fresh curry leaves. Heat them in a skillet with a little vegetable oil, and just as the seeds begin to pop, add onions and garlic and sauté them until soft, then add the main ingredient and proceed with the recipe. The best way for the uninitiated to sample the flavor of curry leaf is to use the same method without the spices. Heat whole or chopped leaves in vegetable oil until they become crisp and start to turn brown, then add the main ingredient and continue cooking. A delicious spicy fish stew begins with a base of sautéed onions, curry leaf, ginger, and chiles, to which sole or whitefish is added, all simmered together in coconut milk. The herb also infuses marinades with its unique curry flavor.

Curry leaf is a tasty companion to lentils, either in a salad with a lemon- and cumin-scented dressing or served as a hot dish or soup, spiced with a to-your-own-taste version of Indian *sambaar* powder, a combination of ground spices that may include cayenne, coriander, cumin, fenugreek, mustard, and turmeric. Try curry leaf's warm, bouillonlike taste in basmati rice: First sauté the leaves in vegetable oil. Add the rice and cook 5 minutes before adding water or chicken stock and steaming the grains. For an unusual breakfast or luncheon omelette, add finely chopped curry leaves and bronze fennel to the eggs. Add some curry leaf to mellow fiery fruit chutneys that will accompany roast chicken or beef and grilled vegetables, or add its minced leaves to yogurt to make a cooling dip.

Combined with walnut oil, curry leaf makes an excellent bottled herb oil, a surprisingly nutty, warm, and toasty-flavored oil that is convenient to have on hand during the winter months. Fresh curry leaves can be successfully frozen, but cooks seem to be divided on the flavor of dried curry leaves. Fresh is always best, but I find sufficient flavor left in curry leaves when they are quickly dried in the microwave oven and used within a short period of time.

Potato Curry

This rich and satisfying potato curry is infused with the warm, toasty flavor of curry leaf and sweetened with coconut milk. Accompanied by a leafy green salad and Indian whole-wheat *chapati* bread, it is an especially savory part of a vegetarian meal.

2 tablespoons walnut oil
1 tablespoon chopped fresh curry leaves
1 teaspoon ground cumin
½ teaspoon ground turmeric
¼ teaspoon nigella seeds (page 177)
⅛ teaspoon cayenne pepper
2 yellow onions, finely chopped
1 teaspoon freshly chopped ginger root

1 serrano chile pepper, stemmed, seeded, and
  coarsely chopped
1½ pounds Yellow Finn or other new potatoes,
  peeled and sliced ½ inch thick and 1 inch wide
½ cup chicken stock
½ cup coconut milk
Sea salt to taste
Chopped fresh cilantro or culantro, for garnish

Heat the walnut oil in a large skillet. Add the curry leaves, cumin, turmeric, nigella seeds, and cayenne pepper. As soon as the spices and curry leaf release their fragrance, in 1 to 2 minutes, add the onions, ginger, and chile pepper. Stir to combine, and cook over low heat until the onions are soft, about 3 to 4 minutes. Add the potatoes, coating them well with the herb and spice mixture. Cover and cook over medium heat for 5 minutes, then add the chicken stock, coconut milk, and salt to taste. Cover and simmer over low heat for 15 to 20 minutes, or until potatoes are tender. Garnish with the cilantro or culantro.

Serves 4

Curry Leaf Walnut Oil

This may be perhaps the most exotically flavored oil on the pantry shelf. When heated, the curry leaves have a warm, toasty flavor. When their essential oils are combined with the rich nutty flavor of walnut oil, the blend is excellent for sautéing chicken, fish, or beef; sprinkling over cooked vegetables; combining with hot lentils; or mixing with cumin in a vinaigrette for a spicy lentil salad.

1 loosely packed cup fresh curry leaves
Boiling water
2 teaspoons freshly squeezed lemon juice
2 cups walnut oil

Wash the curry leaves in cool water. Place them in a sieve and pour boiling water over them. Drain, then pat them thoroughly dry with paper towels. In a food processor fitted with the metal blade, combine the curry leaves, lemon juice, and ¼ cup of the walnut oil. Process until the curry leaves are finely chopped, then add the remaining walnut oil in a thin stream until the mixture is emulsified. Pour into a sterilized jar with a nonreactive lid. Cover tightly and place in the refrigerator for 1 week.

Bring the oil to room temperature and strain through a fine-mesh sieve lined with cheese-cloth. Return the strained oil to the same jar and cover tightly. It can be stored in the refrigerator for up to 2 weeks. The oil will solidify again, but will liquefy at room temperature after a few minutes, or if the jar is run under hot water.

Makes 1½ to 2 cups

SUPERB PINK

(Dianthus superbus)

Perennial or Biennial   Zones 3–8

Native Habitat   Southern Europe, Scandinavia, Russia, eastern Asia to Japan

On a hot day in the garden, an invisible fragrant cloud forms around a clump of superb pinks, and as one draws near, a luscious and heady clove scent is broadcast at least five feet in all directions, as if to invite the visitor closer. The extremely floriferous scent that wafts about the garden on warm summer breezes belongs to an old variety of exotic garden pinks with deeply fringed petals. The superb pink's intensely shaggy and ragged appearance gives the impression that the flowers are multipetaled, but in fact there are only five of them. The delicious colors of the flowers, also called fringed pinks, range from powdery rose to almost magenta with soft pastels in between, and an alabaster white for punctuation. Arising from grassy tufts, the 1-to-2-foot stems have green, lance-shaped leaves 2 to 3 inches long, which complement the shredded edges of the flowers. The colors of the hybrid 'Loveliness' are more showy, its flowers a little larger and longer blooming. The seed mixture 'Rainbow Loveliness Mixed,' available from specialty mail-order seed companies, creates a hazy rainbow of carmine red, violet, and bicolored blossoms and is a stunning choice for the front of the border. If you like underplanting your roses, as I do, superb pink makes a charming old-fashioned combination, and its flowers and foliage nicely complement perennials such as French lavender, calamint, and catmint (*Nepeta* x *faassenii*). Brought indoors as a frilly bouquet, the cut flowers are pervasively fragrant. Superb pinks are excellent to plant in specialty gardens with a particular theme: a garden of heirloom herbs; a garden of antique flowers; a fragrance garden; or a cozy cottage garden.

The superb pink has a long tradition in Japanese literature. Known as *kawara-nadeshiko*, the herb is the symbol of the ideal woman: a combination of strength and grace. It is also one of the Seven Flowers of Autumn, joining six other flowers that best express the melancholy of the fall according to an ancient Japanese book of poetry extolling the virtues of nature.

The Greeks and Romans grew species of dianthus, the "divine flower," not as ornament but as culinary and medicinal herbs. Superb pink, a member of this divine family, was introduced around 1772 and was still being offered in garden catalogs in the early nineteenth century. Fortunately, with the rekindled interest in old varieties of plants, this delicate pink has been rediscovered.

GROWING YOUR OWN

Superb pink is a short-lived perennial best treated as a biennial. It blooms from spring through summer and requires moderate watering. The *Dianthus superbus* hybrid 'Loveliness' will bloom for a much longer period than the perennial superb pink, especially if it is not allowed to set seed. Plant the seeds shallow, ⅛ to ¼ inch deep, whether in the ground or in a container, for when planted too deep, dianthus is prone to stem rot. It likes a rich soil amended with well-aged compost, and sand or gravel for good drainage, which is absolutely essential. Apply cottonseed meal to alkaline soils and bonemeal and a sprinkling of agricultural lime to acid soils. Space the plants about 1 foot apart. As they are not heavy feeders, use liquid fish emulsion or a balanced soluble fertilizer mixed at half strength until their flowering stems begin to elongate; when the plants are in full bloom feeding can cease.

Growing superb pinks in full sun ensures that you will make the most of that extraordinary scent they exude. They can be propagated from stem cuttings from established plants taken in mid- to late summer. In cold climates, the cuttings should be wintered over in a cold frame or greenhouse until spring arrives.

Superb pinks are especially effective when grown in containers. Placed strategically, their scent pervades a sunny patio, and their feathery flowers create a romantic and decorative surrounding. Plant them in fast-draining commercial potting mix with a little lime mixed in to supply the slightly more alkaline soil they appreciate. Water when the surface of the soil appears dry, but take care not to allow the soil to dry completely. Feed container-grown superb pinks with liquid fish emulsion applied at half strength just until the flower buds begin to swell. In cold-winter areas, place the pots in a protected area until spring and cover with a few evergreen boughs. Do not otherwise mulch either container-grown plants or those grown in the ground, as this increases the danger of root rot.

CULINARY USES

One of the oldest culinary uses of dianthus comes from ancient Greek and Roman kitchens, where the oddly named, strongly clove-perfumed dianthus species "sops in wine" was infused into homemade vintages to add a spicy flavor. One custom was to offer a cup of this wine to a just-married bride—why it was not offered to the groom remains unclear. In the language of flowers, the messages ranged from "pure love" and "always lovely" to "boldness" and "refusal," depending upon which color dianthus was added. In later days, nutmeg was added to the brew. I have made similar infusions using superb pinks and cottage pinks in imported vodka, with interesting results—but I don't call it "sops in vodka." A scented white wine vinegar can be made with dianthus petals to give a floral fillip to fruit salads.

The intensely floral character of superb pink, however, lends itself best to sweet dishes like ice cream, meringues, sorbets, jellies, fruit soups, syrups, cookies, and cakes; chop it and mix with sweet-cream butter for spreading on scones. It is of paramount importance to use flowers from your own garden—or a friend's—that have not been sprayed with harmful pesticides unlicensed to be used on food plants.

Unless you grow fields of superb pinks, you probably won't have enough to gather at one time for experimenting with more than one or two recipes. A good way to have them on hand when you want them is to harvest small amounts when they are in bloom and infuse a small handful in a simple syrup made with equal parts water and sugar. Freeze the syrup and use it as needed. This method is also good for the plants, as the more you cut, the more flowers you will have.

Superb Pink Sorbet with 'Cinnamon' Basil

The heady, warm clove scent of *Dianthus superbus*, an extremely fragrant dianthus, perfumes this delicate sorbet. It can be served between courses as a palate freshener or as a dessert with a sugar cookie or madeleine.

This sorbet is very floral, so a small amount satisfies the desire for "a little something sweet" at the end of the meal. If larger portions are wanted, the recipe can be doubled. Its pleasingly pale pink color is natural. Make sure to use flowers that have not been grown with harmful pesticides.

For another recipe using superb pink, see page 199, Good Husbandry Summer Salad with Pear Vinaigrette.

½ cup petals of superb pink dianthus or another
   old-fashioned fragrant pink
1¼ cups water
4 tablespoons sugar, or to taste
2 teaspoons finely minced 'Cinnamon' basil
   (page 60)

1 to ½ tablespoons lemon juice, or
   to taste
1 egg white
6 superb pink dianthus flowers for
   garnish

With a pair of sharp scissors, cut off the bitter white base of the dianthus petals. Gently wash the petals, then pat them dry and set aside. In a medium-sized saucepan, combine the water and sugar and bring to a boil. Stir until the sugar dissolves, then lower the heat and add the dianthus petals and 'Cinnamon' basil. Remove the pan from the heat, cover, and allow mixture to cool with the lid on, so the "virtuous steam" does not dissipate. Strain mixture into a flat pie pan. Add lemon juice, and combine well. (At this point you will feel like an alchemist. The infusion will be green until the addition of the lemon juice, which instantly turns the mixture pink.) Place in the freezer for ½ hour, or until ice crystals have formed.

Beat the egg white until stiff, then fold into the half-frozen mixture. Return to the freezer for about 1 hour. To serve, whip the mixture into a slush with a whisk, then spoon into small chilled parfait glasses or ¼-cup ramekins. Garnish each serving with 1 superb pink. Serve immediately.

Makes six ¼-cup servings

EPAZOTE

(Chenopodium ambrosioides)

Annual
Native Habitat   Tropical America

Epazote is an annual herb, but once planted in the garden it is permanently there, for it self-sows freely. While it is an herb *for* the herb garden, it is best not planted *in* the herb garden, for aside from its spreading habit, it also saps the growth of other herbs surrounding it. Plant it in an area where it can volunteer freely without intruding on other herbs for space, and soon there will be a plantation of handsome epazote. It will probably roam, regardless, but when you see these wanderers, pull them out of the ground so they can't start another grove.

It would be an oversight not to include epazote in a book on exotic herbs, for several reasons. Epazote is definitely an exotic "ethnic" herb, widely used in Mexican cookery. Ever since Diana Kennedy extolled its virtues in her 1972 cookbook, *The Cuisines of Mexico,* and to her delight discovered it growing wild in Central Park, gardeners and cooks have been curious about this herb, and a growing number of specialty seed companies now offer its seeds, which were once difficult to obtain. Recent cookbooks on Mexican cuisine written by noted authors on the subject include epazote as a culinary herb, as do many current herbals. But it should be noted that many authoritative herb books include a warning that it should be used with discretion, and in moderation, for epazote contains a highly toxic oil. In addition, handling its leaves may cause dermatitis.

Epazote has been widely naturalized in many parts of North America, particularly the southeastern part of the country, as well as in central and southern Europe. It is often found growing wild in fields, along roadsides, and in urban settings such as vacant lots and through cracks in city sidewalks. The Spanish name, epazote, is from the Aztec words *epatl* and *tzotl*, meaning an animal with the smell of a skunk. The herb is also known as wormseed, Mexican tea, Jerusalem oak, pigweed, and goosefoot. The name of the genus *Chenopodium* is derived from the Greek words for "goose" and "foot" and refers to the shape of its leaves, which resemble the webbed foot of a goose. Medium green, deeply incised, and up to 3½ inches long, the leaves grow on a multibranched trunklike stem that grows to 5 feet tall, and its branches spread several feet wide. In late summer, dense spikes of tiny, inconspicuous, yellow-green flowers appear in clusters in the angles of the leafy branches, followed by hundreds of tiny round green seeds in the fall. The whole plant is aromatic with a resinous, camphorlike scent, about which you will definitely have an opinion. Curiously, this plant with its pungent odor is used as a fragrance component in creams, detergents, lotions, soaps, and perfumes.

GROWING YOUR OWN

Epazote grows well in full sun, in average soil that is well drained. In hot climates, it can take some afternoon shade. Classified as an annual, in warm climates epazote can be a perennial. In my Zone 10 garden, epazote grown from seeds obtained from a friend in Mexico has returned as a perennial going into its third year. Epazote can be started from seed planted directly, or sown indoors in early spring to be planted outdoors when the weather has warmed. One plant will suffice in the garden for culinary uses. It seems to thrive with carefree maintenance, and appears pest-free: certainly bugs leave it alone, and, even better, no deer approach it.

Epazote can be container-grown, but the center branch should be pinched back often to discourage height and encourage a bushy growth habit. It can be propagated by stem cuttings, best taken in the spring in warm areas. Where it is an annual, take cuttings in mid-summer, before the leaves get too strong in taste and aroma.

A theme garden of Mexican herbs could include papaloquelite (page 84); the two Mexican oreganos, *Poliomentha longiflora* and *Lippia graveolens* (pages 187 and 189); cilantro; lamb's-quarter (page 140); manzanilla, a.k.a. chamomile; and green husk tomatoes, *Physalis ixocarpa* or the more exotic purple husk tomato cultivar 'Purple de Milpa'. And, of course, chile peppers. You'll need a spacious area for such a garden.

CULINARY USES

Epazote is an assertive herb that is an acquired taste. As with the picked-on herb cilantro, there are two camps regarding epazote. To some it is akin to cooking with a kerosene-scented herb; to others its pungent taste with mint or anise overtones is addictive.

Epazote is greatly used in central and southern Mexico and Yucatan, but rarely used in Mexico's arid north and northwest. A pinch of its dried leaves is added to black bean dishes both as a flavoring and carminative (intestinal cleanser), in chicken and corn soups, and in tamale pies containing chicken and pork. In Mexico and Guatemala its leaves season corn, mushrooms, fish, and shellfish. Southwestern chefs use epazote as an aromatic for flavoring halibut, bass, shrimp, and crab. It is used to flavor fiery salsas and in other tomato sauces that are combined and cooked with scrambled eggs and green beans. Epazote flavors fresh green mole sauce and *pipian verde*, or green pumpkin seed sauce. Used fresh, it flavors toasted or fried quesadillas, turnovers made of *masa harina* (fine cornmeal), plain or with white cheese fillings. The herb can be dried without loss of flavor. When using epazote in cooked dishes, add it during the last 15 minutes of cooking so the food does not become bitter. As its flavor and aroma strengthen over the spring, summer, and fall, so it is best to assess the intensity before adding a sprig.

For a recipe using epazote, see page 186, Spicy Beans with Mexican Herbs.

BRONZE FENNEL

(Foeniculum vulgare 'Rubrum')

Perennial   Zones 6–9

Native Habitat   The Mediterranean Basin

Bronze fennel and common fennel

Bronze fennel is an exotic design feature in the garden. A large planting of the herb makes a dramatic stand that looks like glistening, fringed black feathers burnished with copper. With bronze fennel as a tall, dark background, a beautifully integrated design can be created with a variety of plants with contrasting textured leaves and complementary flowers. The graceful herb is spectacular when its broad umbels bloom golden yellow. If there is no room in the garden for a stand of bronze fennel, just one plant still provides an exotic black-and-copper accent.

Although there are only three basic fennels, a maze of fennel names exists. Common fennel (*F. vulgare*), also called sweet fennel or wild fennel, is a semihardy perennial and the one commonly used as a flavoring herb, which you will also find growing wild in certain parts of the country, notably in California and the southern United States. Florence fennel (*Foeniculum vulgare* var. *azoricum*), also called *finocchio*, is an annual vegetable with a thickened, overlapping leaf base commonly known as a "bulb," which is routinely found among the other vegetables in supermarkets (often incorrectly labelled anise or sweet anise). Bronze fennel (*F. vulgare* 'Rubrum'), is a semihardy perennial with decorative rich, reddish bronze coloring which makes it the most splendid of the fennels.

All the fennels bring something colorful with them when planted in the garden: the brightly striped green, black, and yellow swallowtail caterpillar, which ultimately emerges as the beautiful, exotically patterned western anise swallowtail butterfly, or the eastern black swallowtail and short-tailed black swallowtail. Fennel is the preferred food of these lovely creatures, and fortunately, because the leaves grow so plentifully, there is enough for both the gardener and the benign intruders. Just consider these creatures as bringing additional fluttery color to the herb garden. None other than Sir Winston Churchill kept a caged garden of fennel just for the swallowtail caterpillars at his home in Chartwell, where he raised the swallowtail butterflies. One rule to keep the butterflies in the garden: no pesticides, not even the organic B.t., or *Bacillus thuringiensis*, which is deadly to the butterfly caterpillar.

GROWING YOUR OWN

Bronze fennel can grow to 6 feet tall and several feet wide. In areas with cold-winter climates, it can be grown as an annual. Plant in full sun in well-drained, average soil. In hot climates it prefers some afternoon shade. It takes average watering and minimal fertilizing, and when established the herb is drought-tolerant. In the southern belt, fennel tends to bolt prematurely in the heat of the summer. Cut back flowering umbels after they have bloomed to keep the plant shapely. Sow seeds in early spring or fall. Seeds from established plants readily self-sow. To help remedy the situation if it gets out of hand, remove the seed heads before they bloom. Because fennel germinates easily, it is excellent for a child's beginning garden.

The graceful habit of bronze fennel with its airy, plumelike foliage makes it an interesting herb to decorate with in the garden; it combines well with golden marguerite, tansy, angelica, anise hyssop, coneflower, clary sage, and Queen Anne's lace.

CULINARY USES

One of the most fragrant uses for bronze fennel is to make of the dried stems a bed for an entire fish held in a fish rack and grilled over an open fire. Get into the habit of saving the snippings for this aromatic manner of cooking fish when you prune fennel. Finely chopped, the herb is excellent with all kinds of fish, especially salmon, as its pink flesh looks attractive contrasted with the dark fennel. Bronze fennel is also a good companion for chicken and pork. Vegetables benefit from its anise taste, which is milder than that of its green relative. Carrots, potatoes, peas, and beets—especially the red and white candy-striped Chioggia beets, and golden beets—taste good and look pretty with chopped bronze fennel leaves sprinkled over them. A salad of sliced tomatoes and bulb fennel, sprinkled with a mixture of its own green leaves and bronze fennel's, makes an attractive presentation. A short feathery frond of bronze fennel is a striking garnish for a salad of jicama matchsticks.

Baked Golden Beets with Bronze Fennel Butter

The flavor of these golden beets is intensified when they are baked instead of boiled, and their golden orange color is beautifully accented by a scattering of finely chopped bronze fennel leaves.

Fennel-Orange Butter
2 tablespoons softened unsalted butter
2 teaspoons finely chopped bronze fennel
½ teaspoon freshly squeezed orange juice

6 golden beets, about 2 pounds
1 teaspoon orange zest
Sea salt and cayenne pepper to taste
Finely chopped bronze fennel

To make the fennel-orange butter, combine the butter and bronze fennel in a small bowl. Cream together until well blended, then add the orange juice. Allow the butter to rest for 30 minutes while the flavor infuses.

Preheat oven to 375 degrees.

Brush the beets clean of any soil, and place them on a baking sheet lined with aluminum foil. Bake for about 1 hour, or until a fork easily pierces the beets. Cool slightly, then remove the skins and tops. Slice the beets ¼ inch thick. Melt the orange fennel butter in a large saucepan and add the orange zest. Add the golden

beets, and coat them thoroughly with the butter, stirring until heated through. Add salt and pepper to taste. To serve, sprinkle with chopped bronze fennel.

Serves 4

Fraises des Bois

Native Habitat   Central and southern Europe

Fraises des bois, as wild strawberries and alpine strawberries are called in French, are one of life's edible luxuries that are not easy to indulge in unless you grow your own. And what an exquisite—but fleeting—indulgence, for the amount gathered at each harvest is generally just enough to make you wish you had more. So you have to wait for a few more to ripen. Fortunately, these spring-fruiting berries remain with us through summer.

The aromatic berries are not widely available commercially because they produce too sparsely and are too perishable to ship. In the produce section of our grocery stores, where bigger is better, the small size of the fruit placed next to grand, fat strawberries doesn't lend to their marketing themselves too well, but discerning shoppers know the small size of fraises des bois belies their expansive taste, which causes a perfumed explosion in the mouth.

Growing a plot of these delightful miniature woodland strawberries is a simple task. They can be grown close by the house so you can not only enjoy their beauty as a ground cover but get at them quickly the moment you spy some ripe ones (preferably before anyone else does). The red, glossy pointed fruits sparkle, nestled against serrated, forest-green trefoil leaves. Their genus name, *Fragaria,* is derived from the Latin word for fragrance, which you will understand when you approach the plants and inhale the heady perfume of the pendulous little berries as if they were flowers.

Fraises des bois, also called alpine strawberries, were discovered in the low Alps near Grenoble, France, some three hundred years ago, and the everbearing berries were so appreciated that they were also first cultivated in that country. Unlike standard strawberries, most strains of fraises des bois are runnerless. Historically, they have long been considered a fruit and an herb because of the medicinal tea made from the leaves of the wild plant. In the fourteenth century, King Charles V of France was so enamored of the small, aromatic fruit that he planted twelve hundred fraises des bois plants in his royal garden. A popular cultivar named after the king is offered in today's nursery trade, along with several others, including 'Alexandria', 'Baron Solemacher', and 'Ruegen'. The following are more exotic variants of the charming family of fraises des bois.

VARIEGATED FRAISES DES BOIS
(*Fragaria vesca* 'Albo-Marginata')

Tender Perennial   Zones 5–9

The carmine-red berries of fraises des bois are exceptionally beautiful when complemented by the dark green leaves, shot with creamy white, of the variegated form. Its 1½-inch-long leaves have a somewhat different shape from that of the 3-inch-long green leaves of fraises des bois: a more rounded fan shape and not as deeply serrated. Their pretty white flowers with softly rounded petals have a bright, butter-yellow center. The variegated form is a lower grower than the circa 8-inch-high standard fraises des bois and hugs the ground in matlike mounds. Like its relative, the wild strawberry (*Fragaria vesca*), this cultivar spreads by runners. It appreciates more shade than sun, which helps it hold its handsome variegation. It combines well with other variegated herbs planted nearby such as the lamiums (*Lamium album*, *L. maculatum*, *L.* 'White Nancy', and *L.* 'Silver Beacon'), or Yellow Archangel (*Lamiastrum galeobdolon* 'Variegatum').

WHITE FRAISES DES BOIS

(Fragaria vesca 'White Alpine')

Tender Perennial   Zones 4–8

White-fruited fraises des bois may look like unripe red berries, but they pack the same unexpected flavor explosion as the ripe, red berries, and form a unique little green-dotted-with-white carpet for a spot in the herb garden. In comparison to their red relatives, their fruit is somewhat larger, and appears earlier in the growing season. The secret to knowing when the white berries are ripe to eat is when the seeds are burnished brown.

'White Alpine' and 'Alba' are names of two white fraises des bois available from specialty herb catalogs. Both cultivars grow about 8 inches high and spread by runners in typical strawberry fashion. Almost-white berries known as 'Alpine Yellow' or 'Yellow Wonder', with an elusive suggestion of pineapple in their yellow-tinged, ivory white berries, are runnerless cultivars that are more compact and orderly fraises des bois, and are excellent for edgings and front-of-the-border situations. These plants grow close to the ground, easily carpeting an area with their bright green, 2½-inch-long trefoil leaves and typical yellow-centered, white-petaled fraises des bois flowers.

If unique beauty and taste aren't reasons enough to grow white-berried fraises, another reason is the fact that your precious crop diminishes only when harvested by *your* hand—because hungry birds don't bother to peck at them, preferring instead the vivid red berries.

GROWING YOUR OWN

Fraises des bois, "strawberries of the woods," or wild strawberries, enjoy the same culture they do when grown in their natural woodland habitat, i.e., a cool, moist, acid soil that is rich in humus, and well drained. Plants may be obtained from specialty herb nurseries, or with luck, from a fraises des bois–loving friend's garden. Though hard to find, 'Alpine Yellow' may also be grown from purchased seed, or seeds may be collected from your own ripe berries. Fraises des bois can also be propagated by crown division from established plants.

In areas with warm-winter climates, fraises des bois can be planted in the spring or fall. In cold-winter areas plant them in the spring. If you are sowing from seed, start them indoors in late winter for planting outdoors when the weather warms. When preparing beds for plants or transplants, dig in well-rotted manure and nitrogen-rich compost. Peat moss may be added to provide acidity. Take care to plant the crowns above the soil line, and spread the roots out horizontally. Fertilize the plants with a balanced soluble fertilizer and water frequently until they are established, then continue to fertilize on a regular basis. Mulch the plants and never allow the soil to dry out. Fraises des bois like full sun or partial shade. In areas with very hot summer climates they can be grown in high shade, or in morning sun and afternoon shade. Once established, the cultivars that spread by runners and those that set seed and self-sow will need thinning to keep the beds tidy. Fraises des bois grown from seed should be planted every second year and old plants removed.

Fraises des bois look luxurious when grown in a container, especially one overflowing with the variegated-leaved form, *F. vesca* 'Albo-Marginata.' All are especially effective planted in strawberry jars with their tiny berries spilling from the pockets, accentuating the unique design of these lovely terra-cotta or ceramic pots. Lightweight, well-drained potting soil, frequent watering, and once-a-week feeding with a balanced soluble fertilizer at half strength are a must to keep the leaves and berries flourishing in containers.

CULINARY USES

Unlike strawberries, fraises des bois have a very soft texture when ripe, bursting with sugar and full of flavor. A small handful will be enough for satisfaction, and a larger handful is even better. The berries contain vitamin C as well as natural pectin, making it the perfect fruit for a (very small) batch of confiture. The red berries of *F. vesca* 'Albo-Marginata' are elegant when precisely placed atop a vanilla cream tart that is garnished with its variegated leaves. The white-berried varieties are a visual delight garnishing chocolate custard or pots de crème. Mint, lemon balm, sweet cicely, and chervil are herbs that complement fraises des bois. A handful of either red or white berries gives an extra flavor edge to a fruit salad prepared with a dressing of lemon juice, extra virgin olive oil, and honey, and made old-fashioned with poppy seeds.

Eating fraises des bois unadorned is the best method to enjoy their rare flavor, but a sprinkle of rosewater is an appropriately delicate companion, as is sparkling wine or a dry white wine with just a pinch of sugar to add to their own sugary juices. Sweet vermouth, a fruity red wine, or a dollop of whipped cream are also good companions. Fraises des bois with a touch of balsamic vinegar and a light sprinkling of pepper, as unlikely as it may sound, is a take on the Italian custom of sprinkling the two ingredients on strawberries, and is a "tiramisu" (meaning pick-me-up) of a different kind than the popular frothy meringue and mascarpone Italian dessert.

Fraises des Bois Compote with Balsamic Vinegar

Warning! This unusual combination of ingredients is addictive, and you will want to prepare it regularly when fraises des bois are at the height of their season. The recipe can be scaled up as the size of the harvest increases.

1 cup fresh fraises des bois (rounded out with regular strawberries cut into small pieces, if necessary)

1½ tablespoons finely granulated sugar or Vietnamese balm honey (page 257) or clover honey

A large pinch of freshly ground black pepper

1 teaspoon balsamic vinegar

1 teaspoon Vietnamese balm (page 255) or spearmint (optional)

If necessary, wash the berries quickly, and hull just before preparing. In a medium-sized bowl, combine all ingredients. Refrigerate for 30 minutes to 1 hour. Place in a pretty glass bowl.
Serves 1

'MABEL GREY' SCENTED GERANIUM

(*Pelargonium citronellum* 'Mabel Grey')

Tender perennial   Zone 10

Native Habitat   South Africa

Geraniums generally are noted for their showy range of red, pink, purple, salmon, and white flowers, but the scented geraniums, with their quieter range of colors, are most noted for their leaves. But in those unassuming leaves of various shape, size, and texture are the scents of rose, peppermint, coconut, nutmeg, strawberry, peach, apricot, almond, apple, orange, lime—and lemon, which 'Mabel Grey' broadcasts with abandon. Other scented geraniums have sweet and subtle citrus notes, but this one blatantly announces you are in its presence by the explosion of lemon fragrance when the leaves are only lightly grazed; its leaves needn't be crushed and rubbed to release the scent. One of the showiest forms of the scented geraniums, many of which are rangy ramblers or compacts, 'Mabel Grey' stands up tall enough to make a fragrant, stunning showpiece.

Scented geraniums are native to South Africa. They are widely cultivated in Europe, where their essential oils, especially the rose geranium, are collected for use in the perfume industry. Scented geraniums were introduced to England in the seventeenth century and to the United States in the middle to late eighteenth century. By the Victorian era these plants with their heavenly scents, along with the many other flashy varieties of geraniums, were the rage. Cultivated in quantity by nurseries and avid enthusiasts, they filled Victorian solariums and kitchens and bay windows. Leaves of the scenteds were used as romantic notions to enclose in love letters and as sweetly scented bookmarks, perhaps to note a page in a special book of poetry, and the geraniums' various fragrances gave fruit- and flower-scented variety to potpourris.

One note on botanical nomenclature: botanically, a "scented geranium" is actually a member of the genus *Pelargonium*, which is a member of the geranium family.

GROWING YOUR OWN

'Mabel Grey' scented geranium has an assertive, upright growth habit with leaves shaped like an incised maple leaf, roughly hairy and angular, 2½ inches long and 3 inches wide. For a scented, the flower is showy but of moderate size, blooming in florets of true pink streaked with purple. It makes quite a design statement in the garden and can be a strong focal point. Like all scented geraniums, it is fragrant even when not in bloom. 'Mabel Grey' is easily grown in several ways. It performs equally well in the ground, or in outdoor containers on a porch or patio. Indoors it is a scented conversation piece for the solarium or a large window that receives sun or plenty of bright light. 'Mabel Grey' can be grown as a grand scented standard topiary and if you have the patience, it can be espaliered. In cold-winter climates it must be brought indoors until spring. It is an evergreen perennial in the mild-winter areas of Zone 10.

Plant in a sunny spot in well-draining average soil with only a light amount of organic matter added. In harsh, hot climates it requires partial shade. Where it is evergreen, it can grow to 4½ feet tall in the ground but should be kept pruned to 2½ to 3 feet to keep its woody stems from sprawling and getting rangy. Take care not to overwater. A good rule of thumb is to water "when *just* dry." Don't place container-grown 'Mabel Grey' in a saucer, because water can collect there and cause rot. If possible, water container-grown 'Mabel Grey' with distilled water, which it prefers. Don't place the container directly on the ground, because the plant will root. Feed with liquid fish emulsion or a balanced soluble fertilizer at half strength once a month, or a timed-release fertilizer can be added at planting time. In containers, feed in the same manner, but restrict feeding during the winter or when its growth has matured.

You can obtain 'Mabel Grey' scented geranium from specialty plant nurseries. When the plant is large enough, you can propagate it from stem cuttings taken in late summer or early spring. It would be the crown jewel in a theme bed of lemon-scented herbs such as lemon basil, lemon balm, lemon thyme, and lemon verbena. And that aroma . . . when you are working near it in the garden and have brushed by it several times, your skin will have the clean, fresh citrus scent of 'Mabel Grey' for hours.

CULINARY USES

Add a small leaf of 'Mabel Grey' scented geranium to a cup of Darjeeling tea, and you may never drink it "neat" again. If you like floral teas, a small leaf added to Earl Grey tea makes it even more citrusy, and it is refreshing served iced, with an afternoon snack. One leaf added to the sugar bowl will perfume every crystal grain. Use its leaves, julienned, to flavor herb butter, but remove them before spreading on little finger sandwiches or morning biscuits. Better yet, whip the scented butter into a jar of honey for a delicious spread for warm bread. Many old recipes use rose geranium to flavor cakes. Substitute only two leaves of 'Mabel Grey' for a sweet lemon flavor instead of rose. An infusion of a few of its leaves also makes a delicious lemon geranium ice cream, and 'Mabel Grey' honey is a delight slightly warmed and poured over slices of honeydew melon. The other classic place for this scented geranium is in the jelly jar—the apple jelly jar.

Strawberry Salad with 'Mabel Grey' Lemon-Scented Geranium Crème Fraîche

The highly scented lemon leaves of 'Mabel Grey' scented geraniums permeate sweet crème fraiche; serve it with summer strawberries sprinkled with a balm of strawberry liqueur.
Prepare the scented crème fraîche two days ahead.

Lemon-Scented Crème Fraîche
1 tablespoon finely minced 'Mabel Grey'
*   scented geranium leaves*
2 tablespoons sugar
1 cup crème fraîche

2 pints strawberries
1 tablespoon sugar
4 tablespoons Crème de Fraises liqueur
4 small 'Mabel Grey' scented geranium leaves
*   for garnish, or flowers, if in bloom*

To make the crème fraîche, in a small mixing bowl combine the 'Mabel Grey' scented geranium leaves, sugar, and crème fraîche. Cover with plastic wrap and place in the refrigerator for 48 hours. Remove the crème fraîche and place it in a large, fine-mesh sieve. With the back of a spoon push the crème fraîche through the sieve, discarding the scented geraniums. Cover with plastic wrap and keep in the refrigerator until ready to serve.

Wash the strawberries, stem them, and slice them thin. Toss them with the sugar and moisten them with the strawberry liqueur. Divide the strawberries among 4 small chilled bowls. Spoon the flavored crème fraîche over each serving. Garnish with a small 'Mabel Grey' scented geranium leaf or flower.

Serves 4

HERBA STELLA

(Plantago coronopus)

Annual
Native Habitat   The Mediterranean Sea basins and central Europe

"Like a star lying on the ground" is how the seventeenth-century physician and herbalist Nicholas Culpeper described herba stella ("star herb") in his manifesto, *Culpeper's Complete Herbal*. "The leaves are numerous and beautiful," he continues, "spreading every way from the head of the root; they are long, narrow, and deeply jagged at the edges." The interesting-shaped leaf of this old salad herb also resembles the horns and antlers of a buck deer, hence another of its names, buck's horn plantain, or hartshorn. It is also known as minutina and crowfoot plantain.

While herba stella can't be classified as a great discovery for its aroma and scent and multipurpose use in foods, it is deserving of attention as a salad herb. You will not find it in the produce department at the market, and it is an unlikely find even at the most upscale greengrocer. It is doubtful that herba stella will join the other ingredients in the chilled cases of salad bars, but considering the affection Americans have for fresh green salads, this unassuming herb, whose humble attributes are crunchy texture, attractive shape, and bright green color, has a rightful place in the salad garden. The eighteenth-century seedsman Benjamin Townsend stated in his 1726 publication, *The Complete Seedsman* ("showing the best and easiest method for raising every seed belonging to a kitchen and flower garden"), that *Plantago coronopus* was "in all the Seedsmen's Bills, tho' it is seldom in the Garden."

The genus name of herba stella, *Plantago,* is from the Latin word meaning "sole of the foot," from its close-to-the-ground growth habit in the wild. Like arugula, purslane, lamb's-quarter, leaf celery, dandelion, broadleaf cress, salad burnet, miner's lettuce, and mâche, herba stella originally was an edible treasure growing wild in the countryside that found its way to the cultivated garden. In today's cuisine, all of these herbs have become sophisticated ingredients for the popular impromptu garden salad mix of tender young lettuces and greens called mesclun.

GROWING YOUR OWN

Herba stella is a cool-weather crop and can be sown in both spring and fall, grown alone or along with lettuces and other herbal greens such as the ones listed above. In Italy, herba stella is interplanted with endive and radicchio, which makes a beautiful ornamental edible planting. Create your own signature mesclun in which herba stella is included. An easy mesclun for a 4-foot-wide bed consists of herba stella, arugula, broadleaf garden cress, chervil, and a choice of lettuces such as frisée, or curly endive, red and green oakleaf, and baby romaine. Broadcast the seeds over a well-prepared bed of richly amended soil. Cover the seeds by raking gently first in one direction, then at right angles, or sift fine soil or compost over them. If you like a more orderly appearance, seeds can be planted ¼ inch deep in rows 4 to 6 inches apart. Make successive plantings every 1 to 2 weeks during the growing season. The mesclun likes a moist, well-drained soil. Maintain a regular watering schedule. The plants benefit from regular applications of compost and feedings with a water-soluble fertilizer high in nitrogen. When the plants are 3 inches high, cut the amount needed 1 inch above the crown with sharp scissors. Fertilize after cutting, and soon the plants will resprout for second and third cuttings. Gathered in this "cut and come again" manner, the greens are not only succulent and tasty, but are nutritious as well, as their vitamin content is higher than when they are mature.

CULINARY USES

Herba stella can be used in the above mesclun or in other salad combinations. One of the most important points is to wash and quickly dry the tender young salad greens. Spin them dry in a salad spinner, then gently place them between damp dish towels and refrigerate in the crisper if you are not using them immediately. Because herba stella and the other baby greens it best accompanies in a mesclun are so young when picked, dress them lightly with a delicate oil and vinegar or lemon vinaigrette so they don't sag under the weight of a heavy dressing, and serve immediately after gently tossing. Herba stella is delicious wilted in just a bit of hot extra virgin olive oil and used as a topping for spinach pasta or plain pasta with a sprinkling of parmesan cheese.

A little cluster of the "antlers" of herba stella makes a curiously pretty garnish for a salad of sliced tomatoes; of endive, red radicchio, and tangerine segments; or of yellow beans or sliced beets.

Good Husbandry Spring Salad with Verjus Vinaigrette

This mesclun was inspired by a detailed list of garden herbs appropriate for a spring salad in *Five Hundred Points of Good Husbandrie*, published in 1573 by the Englishman Thomas Tusser, in which he described rural life in the sixteenth century. The vinaigrette is made with *verjus*, available at specialty food stores, an ancient condiment made from the juice of unripe grapes that is somewhat sweeter than vinegar, or the salad can be made with sweetened rice vinegar. Seasonal edible flowers "of divers colors" decorate the salad. (Make sure they are pesticide-free.)

2 cups assorted lettuces

2 cups arugula

1 cup herba stella

½ cup broadleaf garden cress (page 92)

½ cup garland chrysanthemum leaves (page 75)

¼ cup leaf celery tips (page 72)

Handful of edible flowers (calendula, borage, arugula, fraises des bois, broccoli blossoms) for garnish

Verjus Vinaigrette

2 tablespoons verjus or rice vinegar

2 teaspoons sugar (use only with rice vinegar)

½ teaspoon lemon juice (omit if using rice vinegar)

Salt and freshly ground black pepper to taste

6 tablespoons extra virgin olive oil

To make the vinaigrette, combine the verjus and lemon juice (or rice vinegar and sugar) and salt in a small bowl. Dissolve the salt, then add pepper to taste. Slowly whisk in the olive oil. Makes ½ cup.

Wash and dry the lettuces and herbs. Tear the lettuces into bite-sized pieces, and place in a large bowl. Add the herbs. Gently wash the flowers and pat them dry with paper towels. Lightly toss the lettuces and herbs with the verjus vinaigrette. Sprinkle the flowers over the salad and serve immediately.

Serves 6

HOUTTUYNIA

(Houttuynia cordata)

Perennial   Zones 6–10
Native Habitat   China and Southeast Asia

Who would suspect that houttuynia, the startlingly decorative ground cover with heart-shaped leaves that nature has so richly painted blue-green, cream, pink, yellow, and red, is, along with its plain green form, a culinary herb enjoyed in Southeast Asian cuisine? The herb is also startling tastewise, as it has a strong unique pungency that may take some getting used to by Western palates. Cilantro lovers will find more than a hint of its aroma in houttuynia. Houttuynia is known as *ghee* in Cambodia, and *giap ca,* the "fish-scale herb," in Vietnam, in reference to both its leaf shape and its affinity for fish. Houttuynia is also used in salads in those lands. In Chinese cuisine it is known as *ch'i* and is sometimes included in salads, and the herb is also eaten in Japan. Cooking gardeners may be wise to seek out a

Japanese type of houttuynia, *dokudami,* with a scent reminiscent of oranges, for the widely available Chinese type (cultivated in Vietnam) is scented, some say, of raw fish, meat, and cilantro.

Even if you don't acquire a taste for houttuynia, the herb still has a place in your garden, for it is a perfect ornamental for a shade border or a partially shaded area. *Houttuynia cordata* grows from 6 inches to 2 feet tall, forming a dense ground cover with 2-to-3-inch-long matte-finish green leaves and 4 to 8 snow-white, four-part bracts (specialized leaves) with a vivid yellow conelike center spike. 'Chameleon' (pictured) is a variegated cultivar with multicolor markings and 'Flore Pleno' is a green-leaved cultivar with numerous and showier bracts.

GROWING YOUR OWN

Seeds of houttuynia are not readily available, but you can obtain plants from mail-order nurseries specializing in culinary herbs. It can also be found as an ornamental perennial at garden centers, but if houttuynia is intended to be used culinarily, make sure it has been grown for human consumption, with no harmful pesticides; poisonous systemics are often used by growers on ornamentals. When houttuynia is established it can be propagated by root division in the fall. The herb dies down and disappears after the first frost in winter. Grow houttuynia in shade or part shade with adequate water throughout the growing season. In Zone 10 the herb can be grown in full sun near the coast. Houttuynia spreads by underground rhizomes and can become invasive. If this is a problem, grow it in a container. The herb makes an excellent potted plant, beautiful with its heart-shaped leaves abundantly spilling over the sides.

To create a quiet, subtle Oriental theme, as well as a partial culinary planting, I grow houttuynia in a semishade border with Japanese anemone, velvet plant, 'Bronze' perilla, culantro, mitsuba, Vietnamese balm, rice-paddy herb, rau ram, and galangal. To add to the collection, mild Vietnamese mint grows nearby in a terra-cotta pot, rooted from a cutting of mint bought at the local Vietnamese market.

CULINARY USES

The word "stinky" has been applied to houttuynia by botanists, gardeners, and cooks alike, but it should be remembered that the same word has also been used by detractors of cilantro.

As there are also many aficionados of cilantro who grew to like the herb, perhaps the same will happen with houttuynia. There are piles of the cut green-leaved herb in a bin next to the chives, garlic chives, bean sprouts, and mint in the produce market of the Southeast Asian market where I shop. In Vietnamese cuisine, houttuynia is sometimes an ingredient in the platter of various fresh herbs, lettuce leaves, and cucumbers placed on the table to be savored throughout the meal. A personal selection consisting of several sprigs of herbs and one or two other garnishes is wrapped in translucent sheets of rice paper as a handy holder to be lightly dunked in a dipping sauce. A few leaves of houttuynia can be used in a similar manner as the tangy ingredient in a mixed salad of young lettuces, bean sprouts, perilla, mint, cucumber, tomatoes, and scallions with a vinaigrette prepared with lemon juice in place of vinegar. For an authentic Vietnamese flavor, add a dash of *nuoc mam*, the Vietnamese sauce made from fermented anchovies that is an indispensable part of Vietnamese cuisine. In this cuisine the green form of houttuynia is used as a fresh garnish for large boiled duck eggs or, at the opposite extreme, a plate of tiny boiled quail eggs to be served as hors d'oeuvre. Fresh houttuynia leaves complement robust meats and strong-flavored fish such as monkfish, shark, and sea bass, or a mélange of seafood in an aromatic fish stew or a lusty bouillabaisse.

ARABIAN JASMINE

(*Jasminum sambac*)

Tender Perennial   Zones 9–10

Native Habitat   Tropical Asia

From the gardens at Well-Sweep Herb Farm, Port Murray, New Jersey

Arabian jasmine is the nicest thing you can do to water. Its flowers make a plain pitcher of ice water a perfumed pleasure, and as inhabitants of India, China, Southeast Asia, and Italy so well know, the exquisitely scented, almost exhausting, floriferous blossoms of this exotic herb with its aromatic essential oils make an intoxicating hot infusion. So invasive is the fragrance of jasmine flowers that it will even permeate dry ingredients stored with them such as tea leaves or sugar.

In India, Arabian jasmine is sacred to Vishnu and is used in Hindu ceremonies, its flowers woven into garlands. In Asia, a new bride and groom's wedding may be etched in fragrant memory, for it is the custom there to strew fresh jasmine flowers at nuptial ceremonies.

These jasmine blossoms are considered an aphrodisiac. In Hawaii, Arabian jasmine is known as *pikake* and is a favorite fragrant component of leis.

There are two Arabian jasmine cultivars of merit. 'Maid of Orleans' has a bushy, compact growth habit and semidouble white flowers fading to cranberry, and is especially fragrant at dusk, which qualifies it for a scented planting in an evening garden. It is the national flower of the Philippines, where it is known as *sampaguita*.

'Grand Duke of Tuscany' has intensely perfumed double flowers that look like tightly petaled miniature roses, some with a tinge of cranberry on the undersides, hence another common name, moss rose jasmine. In the seventeenth century, it was imported to Pisa from Goa and was subsequently established in the grand duke of Tuscany's garden.

'Maid of Orleans' is easier to grow than 'Grand Duke of Tuscany' and is more prolific, but the intensely fragrant, fat-with-petals flowers of slow-growing 'Grand Duke of Tuscany' are irresistible. It's not a cinch to grow, but perhaps every gardener grows one favored plant that needs coddling—because the result is worth the wait and the effort.

GROWING YOUR OWN

You can obtain plants of *Jaminum sambac* from specialty nurseries. Grow in full sun or partial shade in average soil with average watering. Feed with fish emulsion every two weeks during the growning season. When the plants are about to flower, feed with a bloom formulation soluble fertilizer high in phosphorus. 'Grand Duke of Tuscany' can grow to 6 feet, but as stated above, it is very slow growing. Outdoors, place it against a south-facing wall to coax faster growth. In growing zones other than 9 and 10, 'Maid of Orleans' must overwinter indoors with high humidity and be placed in an east or west window. Keep it pruned to 12 inches. Because of their slow growth, prune both cultivars judiciously. 'Grand Duke of Tuscany' should ideally be kept in a solarium or greenhouse during the cold months.

CULINARY USES

Use the flowers of 'Grand Duke of Tuscany' and 'Maid of Orleans' to infuse simple syrups, which in turn can be the base for ice creams, sorbets, or sherbets. A jasmine-scented simple syrup is ideal to pour over delicate melons such as honeydew or Charentais. Serve it over figs or poached pears. Pair it with another exotic, star fruit, and combine with sliced oranges and raspberries. Raisins become exotic too, when plumped in jasmine simple syrup, then cooled and poured over fresh peaches or other fruits.

Iced Jasmine Water

This recipe is the shortest one in my recipe files. Forgive its simplicity, but it is indeed exotic.

'Grand Duke of Tuscany' jasmine flowers
1 tall glass refrigerator water jar—all the better
to see the jasmine flowers

As the flowers of 'Grand Duke of Tuscany' come into bloom, place several of them in the water-filled jar. Refrigerate for at least 24 hours to allow the flowers to perfume the water. Strain the liquid, discarding the jasmine. Serve in glasses filled with ice, garnished with fresh 'Grand Duke of Tuscany' blossoms and other edible flowers such as white or blue borage, or English lavender, or rose petals, if desired.

NOTE: Make sure the flowers are collected from a plant that has not been grown with harmful pesticides.

KAFFIR LIME

(Citrus hystrix)

Perennial   Zones 10–11
Native Habitat   Uncertain. Widely naturalized in Southeast Asia

From the gardens at Well-Sweep Herb Farm,
Port Murray, New Jersey

Trees may be classified as herbal if they have the characteristics that define an herb: plants valued for their culinary, fragrant, household, medicinal, or economic use. The exotic citrus tree commonly called Kaffir lime, known in Thailand as *bai magrood*, in Vietnam as *la chanh*, and in Indonesia and Malaysia as *daun limau purut*, qualifies on several points. Its lemon-scented, curious-looking rounded leaves, which are notched in the middle, giving the appearance of two leaves in one, are used whole to flavor Southeast Asian curries and soups. Its bright-green, pendulous fruit with a knobby, wrinkled texture peculiar to the Kaffir lime has a florid scent in its thick oily rind, which is used to flavor a wide range of Southeast Asian foods, including curry pastes and soups. In some parts of Indonesia, fragments of the peel have been used for women's headdresses. The sour to bitter juice from the limes is rarely used in cooking, but is traditionally used in soaps and shampoos, and in native folklore the fragrance is said to ward off evil spirits. Its leaves, fruit, juice, and bark are used medicinally, which rounds out all the qualifications for being an herbal tree.

GROWING YOUR OWN

Kaffir lime, a low tree or shrub, is grown as a perennial tree in Zones 10 and 11, but in other regions it can be container-grown and enjoyed outside in the summer and brought indoors to a solarium for the winter. Placing the container on rollers will facilitate this in-and-out task. For the best drainage, plant the lime in a large clay pot, in a commercial fast-draining soil. Maintain a regular watering, fertilizing, and lookout-for-pests schedule. Watering needs to be decreased when brought indoors. A good rule of thumb is to allow the soil to dry out between waterings until the top half inch feels dry. Fertilize once a month with a houseplant fertilizer such as 20-20-20 or timed-release fertilizer pellets. Indoors it prefers temperatures from 50 to 60 degrees and lots of bright light, but no direct sun, which will burn its leaves. Like all citrus, it is a heavy feeder during its growth period, and iron chelate should be added to the soil at that time; when the leaves have soft growth it should also be foliar fed with a micronutrient formula containing chelated iron, zinc, and manganese.

In Zones 10 and 11, Kaffir lime can be planted in containers or in the ground, where it should be planted in well-drained native soil; it should be amended—not more than 50 percent—with well-rotted manure, compost, and bloodmeal and bonemeal. Mulch the top of the soil around the plant with compost. Beginning in the spring feed it with an all-purpose high-nitrogen fertilizer every 4 to 6 weeks, or use timed-release fertilizer pellets. Continue feeding until the fall, tapering off in late summer to discourage more growth and to help new growth harden before frost. Feed container-grown Kaffir lime once or twice a month with high-nitrogen fertilizer mixed at half the recommended strength. The leaves can be foliar fed with a micronutrient formula when they are soft and young. In the spring when the rains are over, begin watering deeply when the soil has dried several inches deep. When the lime is in bloom, water regularly, allowing the top 3 to 6 inches of soil to become almost dry before watering again. Kaffir lime is cold-sensitive, so plant in full sun, preferably in front of a south-facing wall or protected spot—a microclimate that simulates a tropical climate. This especially applies to areas where frost occurs. In a container, it is a conversation-piece ornamental edible with its rough and bumpy fruit. The leaves may be picked year-round for cooking, but the fruit ripens at nonspecific times during the year, depending on the severity of the previous winter. It can also be picked when green.

CULINARY USES

The exquisite citrus aroma of Kaffir lime leaves is used to flavor curries, soups, and slow-cooked foods. Added to a dish at the beginning of cooking, the leaves slowly release their flavor, in the manner of bay leaves. Excellent for flavoring meat, they are also complementary companions to fish and shellfish. Kaffir lime leaves, lemon grass, and hot-and-sour shrimp soup make an uncommon, citrus-fragrant first course. Used whole, the leaves provide a subtle taste of citrus, and finely shredded leaves impart a sharper citrus tang, which is tasty in stir-fried beef dishes, for example.

The fresh leaves of Kaffir lime can be kept in plastic wrap in the refrigerator for up to a week. They cannot be successfully dried, but can be frozen and used straight from the freezer.

With all herbs, fresh is best, and this is true also of the extremely fragrant, oily rind of Kaffir lime. Nevertheless it can be "harvested" with a vegetable peeler and dried for flavoring dishes when there is no fruit on the tree. In Indonesia the rind is candied and used in confitures. In Thai dishes it imparts a sharp, sour note to curry pastes that are used in hot-and-sour soups and vegetable, meat, and fish dishes, sometime diluted with coconut milk, tamarind liquid, lime juice, or stock. When using dried kaffir lime rind, reconstitute it by soaking in warm water before using. To make the simplest of dishes taste exotic, include freshly grated Kaffir lime rind in a spicy curry paste and add the paste to stir-fried chicken and green beans.

Poached Kaffir Lime-Leaf Chicken Soup

This citrus-fragrant soup is an ideal first course to whet the appetite for the next. Thai fish sauce, *nam pla*, or Vietnamese fish sauce, *nuoc mam*, can be added for an authentic, exotic Southeast Asian flavor. 'Cinnamon' basil added just before serving imparts another fragrant note.

6 cups homemade chicken stock

2 stalks lemon grass, ½ inch thick

1 pound boned, skinless chicken breast, cut
   into bite-sized pieces

1-inch piece fresh ginger, thinly sliced

2 scallions, sliced crosswise, including 2 inches
   of the green part

¼ cup chopped cilantro leaves, stems, and
   roots, if available

1 serrano pepper, stemmed, seeded, and sliced
   into lengthwise quarters

6 Kaffir lime leaves

1 tablespoon fresh 'Cinnamon' basil leaves,
   julienned

1 to 2 tablespoons fish sauce (optional)

In a large saucepan heat the chicken stock and bring to a gentle boil. While it is heating, cut about 4 inches of the white base of the lemon grass, then slice each stalk in half. Pound the pieces with a kitchen mallet or wooden pestle to release their fragrance. Add the chicken breasts to the chicken stock, then add the lemon grass, ginger, scallions, cilantro, and serrano pepper. Break each Kaffir lime leaf in several places, then add to the saucepan. Reduce the heat to low, and simmer the mixture for 15 minutes. Add the 'Cinnamon' basil, then remove from the pan from the heat. Stir in the fish sauce, if being used, and serve immediately.

Serves 4

MAGENTA LAMB'S-QUARTER
(Chenopodium giganteum)

Annual
Native Habitat   Northern India

Magenta lamb's-quarter starts out of the gate blooming true magenta pink amid a swirl of green. Its signature color covers some of its small leaves entirely, dusts others at their base, and coats the underside of a score of its other leaves a deep cerise. Throughout the growing season, the center clusters of its new leaves begin their growth in this manner, looking somewhat like pink Easter eggs in a green-leaved basket. As the season progresses, the color may fade somewhat, but the clusters still retain a pink shading scattered over the plant to punctuate the color of its light green leaves.

Magenta lamb's-quarter is a species more lyrical both in looks and name than its common lamb's-quarter relative, *Chenopodium album,* known as goosefoot, pigweed, muckweed, and fat hen, and is used for food in the same manner. In specialty herb catalogs, it is also known as magentaspreen lamb's-quarter. If you grow this magenta beauty in your garden yet have a certain déjà vu sense that it resembles a plant you have seen somewhere before, you have—in its green form—in empty lots, along roadsides, and in pastures, cultivated fields, and waste places. The annals of culinary history know common lamb's-quarter as a nutritious herbal "weed." Its abundant production of seeds can be dried and ground into a nutritious flour. Napoleon is said to have dined on black bread made from its seeds when food was scarce and he was hungry. Lamb's-quarter was introduced to the United States from Europe, ultimately becoming yet another escaped herb. The genus *Chenopodium* contains many annual and perennial species, including a number of annual pest species introduced from foreign soils. If one consults a colored map of the United States showing where these lamb's-quarter species grow, the only part that is uncolored is the Great Lakes. However, its genus also contains some respected species such as the Andean "supergrain of the future," quinoa, known as "the mother grain," whose origins are ancient and which today is found among cereal and grain boxes in well-stocked markets; and the equally ancient Good King Henry (*C. bonus-henricus*), the beloved medieval potherb.

On magenta lamb's-quarter's leaves, the version of the mealy white powder characteristically formed on common lamb's-quarter looks like a dusting of magenta talcum powder with a matte finish. Both plants have the same characteristic goosefoot shape with doubly serrated leaves, about 2 inches long when young and 5½ inches long when mature. Its alternate-branched leaf stems are streaked with deep rose. *Chenopodium album* means white goosefoot, and magenta lamb's-quarter is a giant species with a magenta foot. This vigorous herb can grow from 4 to 6 feet, depending upon the length of the growing season.

GROWING YOUR OWN

Seeds of magenta lamb's-quarter are available from several specialty herb catalogs. They may be planted indoors for transplanting to the garden after the danger of frost is past, or they may be direct-sown when the weather has warmed. Space transplants, or thin seedlings, to about 1½ feet apart. Grow in moderate, well-drained soil in full sun. Water regularly. Cut back the tips of its many branches to keep the plant looking lush and full. Allow the plant to set seed at the end of the season if you would like to harvest them to dry for cooking. I would suggest planting magenta lamb's-quarter in an area where it can grow freely and is satisfactory to the gardener if it reseeds. It definitely qualifies as a back-of-the border herb. I plant two or three in a large area where they lend a strong sentrylike statement to the garden. Because of its upright growth, it looks best underplanted with herbs with soft foliage such as costmary, Roman chamomile, 'Blue Wonder' catnip (*Nepeta cataria* 'Blue Wonder'), or catmint (*Nepeta* x *faassenii*).

CULINARY USES

This pretty, edible ornamental is packed with nutrition—it contains iron, calcium, and protein but eating it is not like "taking medicine" just because it's good for you. It's easy to like "a mess of magenta lamb's-quarter." Its cooked taste reminds me of the grape-leaf wrapping of Greek dolmathes, a mixture of rice, pine nuts, dill, and lemon juice, made with or without ground lamb or beef. When some of magenta lamb's-quarter's midsummer leaves spread to 5½ inches long and as wide, they could certainly be used in the same manner. Its cooked leaves have a grassy, spinach, or swiss chard taste, and as they are all members of the same family, magenta lamb's-quarter can be substituted with good results in any dish calling for one of those leafy greens. The fresh, soft seeds are a unique introduction to a mesclun, or plain green salad. A cold summer cream soup made with shallots and magenta lamb's-quarter, garnished with its pink leaves, is stunning. The soup won't be pink, for magenta lamb's-quarter's leaves turn to green when cooked. Equally lovely in a salad of greens are those rose-pink leaf clusters, tossed with a light vinaigrette.

Steamed Magenta Lamb's-quarter with Bronze Fennel

For another recipe using magenta lamb's-quarter, see page 199, Good Husbandry Summer Salad with Pear Vinaigrette.

4 cups loosely packed magenta lamb's-quarter
    leaves
1 tablespoon olive oil
1 small white onion or 6 to 8 Egyptian onions,
    chopped (page 39)
1 medium clove garlic, finely chopped
½ cup rice

½ cup crushed fresh tomatoes
½ cup chicken stock
1 tablespoon plus 1 teaspoon finely chopped
    bronze fennel (page 110)
1 tablespoon butter
Sea salt and freshly ground black pepper to
    taste

Wash the magenta lamb's-quarter leaves thoroughly. Place them in a medium-sized saucepan. Cover and cook in only the water clinging to leaves over low heat for 5 minutes. Drain, then coarsely chop the leaves. In a medium-sized skillet, heat the olive oil, then add the onion and garlic. Sauté until soft, then add the chopped lamb's-quarter, rice, tomatoes, chicken stock, and 1 tablespoon of the bronze fennel, combining well. Bring the mixture to a boil, then lower heat, cover, and cook for 20 minutes. Add the butter and the remaining teaspoon of bronze fennel. Season to taste with the salt and pepper. Serve immediately.

Serves 2

WHITE LAVENDER

(Lavandula angustifolia 'Alba')

Perennial
Zones 6–8

Courtesy of White Flower Farm; photo by Michael H. Dodge.

DWARF WHITE LAVENDER

(Lavandula angustifolia 'Nana Alba')

Perennial
Zones 5–8

PINK LAVENDER

(Lavandula angustifolia 'Jean Davis')

Perennial
Zones 5–8
Native Habitat   The western half of the Mediterranean Sea basins

Courtesy of White Flower Farm; photo by Michael H. Dodge.

The color purple is associated with fragrant lavender, but its flowers come in other colors: lilac-blue, violet-blue, royal purple, mauve, yellow, pink, and white. The herbalist John Parkinson wrote in *Paradisi in Sole Paradisus Terrestris* in 1629:

> *There is a kind hereof that beareth white flowers and somewhat broader leaves, but is very rare and seene but in a few places with us.*

Spikes of large pure white flowers with broad silvery-gray foliage belong to white lavender, which has the characteristic clean sweet scent associated with all fragrant lavenders. The charming dwarf white lavender is a miniature with floral-scented snow-white dainty flowers and silvery-white leaves. So fragrant are its leaves that just by brushing against them lightly you will release their clean, cool scent. In the garden, white and dwarf white lavenders perfectly complement each other in a billowy white haze.

White lavender is not a modern cultivar, but an exceedingly old English lavender that has been treasured in gardens for 350 years. Queen Henrietta Maria, the English queen whose recipes for lavender, among others, were revealed in the seventeenth-century book *The Queen's Closet Opened*, had a great knowledge and love of gardens, and in particular of white lavender, which she grew in huge borders along with rue and rosemary. Dwarf white lavender is an English lavender cultivar, though it is not a recent introduction, for this white gem has been available for almost 60 years.

The compact cultivar 'Jean Davis' English lavender with its romantic pale pink flowers is the perfect complement to the classic lavender-blue blossoms of English lavender, and a lovely color companion to flatter the white-flowering lavenders. The whorls of pink blossoms on its flowering spikes are well separated, and its leaves are green instead of the more typical gray-green. Its baby pink color looks superb in a garden of other soft pastel flowering perennials. This sedate lavender with its old world charm can be successfully paired with the modern English lavender cultivar 'Lady' with its rich purple flower spikes.

It is interesting to note that 'Jean Davis' lavender is identical in form, color, and essential oils to two other pink-flowering lavenders, 'Loddon Pink' and 'Rosea,' according to Dr. Arthur O. Tucker, herb authority and research professor at Delaware State University. It is unknown whether these lavenders were ever three distinct cultivars, but the pink lavenders available in the nursery trade and grown under these names are essentially identical.

Cheerful cottage gardens of the nineteenth century were treasure troves of hardy and unusual field flowers, gallica and damask roses, fruit trees, vegetables, gaily colored flowers, herbs, and fragrant English lavender. When the proverbial washday came around, the washing was spread out on the aromatic lavender hedge so that sheets, clothing, and petticoats and other undergarments could soak up its refreshingly clean smell. Lavender was a part of the housewife's medicine cabinet for headaches and other "slight maladies," and its leaves and flowers were used in sachets not only to perfume drawers and linen cabinets but also to keep the moths away. Lavender water was sometimes mixed with rosewater for a delightful cosmetic to refresh the skin. Entire hedges of lavender were planted not only for the wash but for the delight of the bees so that an intoxicating lavender honey could be collected from the hive. Lavender, with its softly penetrating scent, fits in perfectly with this exuberant, unstudied paradise.

GROWING YOUR OWN

White lavender grows to about 3 feet in open rounded mounds. Dwarf white lavender grows from 8 to 12 inches and from 6 to 18 inches wide. 'Jean Davis' lavender grows to about 1½ feet high. Plant all three lavenders in full sun and fast-draining, alkaline soil, in an area with protection from winter winds. Add sand and compost at planting time, and in acid soil add about 1 cup of dolomitic lime per plant. Keep the plants watered until they put out new growth. After that they need little watering. Water established plants every week or two, but less often in cool growing climates. Once established these lavenders are drought-tolerant. In areas where the soil is not naturally fast draining, plant with the crowns above the soil line to provide faster drainage.

Ideally a mounded planting should be prepared in the fall previous to spring planting, which allows for settling problems to be solved. A topdressing of 2 inches of sterile white builder's sand is beneficial, as its reflectivity increases the light available to the lavenders, which helps to deter fungus. Provide good air circulation to minimize fungus disease, which attacks English lavender in humid climates. Space the plants 3 feet apart from one another or other perennials. Lavenders don't tolerate wet feet, and their roots will rot in wet soil.

Cut back flowering stalks of white lavender on a regular basis to encourage new growth, and prune several inches off tips in early spring. In cold-winter areas, do not prune after midsummer so new shoots will not be killed by frost. In mild-winter growing regions, the lavenders can be cut back hard in early spring to renew untidy plants with a "black hole" in the center. Dwarf white lavender and 'Jean Davis' lavender are naturally compact, and only their spent flowering spikes need pruning to keep the plants shapely.

In cold-winter areas, mulch the lavenders with evergreen branches after the ground has frozen to protect them from heaving out of the ground because of constant freezing and thawing. Obtain all three lavenders as plants from specialty nurseries, as seed is not readily available. They may be propagated by stem cuttings and layering.

To harvest—the best part of growing fragrant lavenders—snip the flowering spikes just above the foliage, just as the flowers begin to open. Dry the spikes in a warm, dry place out of direct sunlight. The flower buds should be dry within 2 weeks. Strip the buds from the spikes, and store in an airtight container in a cool, dark place.

White lavender is beautiful in the garden when massed in threes, if space allows, and is elegant in a tapestry hedge mixed with the pale pink blossoms of 'Jean Davis' lavender, the fringed green leaves of *Lavandula dentata*, and the gray-leaved *Lavandula dentata* var. candicans, silver-leaved curry plant (*Helichrysum italicum*), blue-green rue, the densely felted whitish leaves of English lavender 'Sawyers', and the prolific hybrid lavandins such as 'Grosso', 'Dutch', and 'Provence'. If room doesn't allow for a large planting of white lavender, one plant looks just as lovely, as a backdrop for roses or planted next to a single plant of rue (a dynamite combination), rosemary and its cultivars, white and blue borage, and the lower-growing, pale-colored nasturtiums, costmary, and rose and white campion.

Dwarf white lavender makes a tidy edging and is beautiful contrasted with the dark purple flowers of lavender 'Hidcote' and the mauve blossoms of lavender 'Munstead' or clove pinks and sweet williams, thymes, purple sage, and the often brilliant colors of the micro-mini roses. 'Jean Davis' lavender is also a perfect foil for the compact lavenders 'Hidcote' and 'Munstead'. With its sweetly scented flowers, this powder-puff-pink lavender makes a charming feature in a theme garden bed of fragrant herbs and flowers.

Alas, gardeners in the South have a hard time growing *L. angustifolia*; the tender *L. dentata* and *L. stoechas* fare better in their humid climate. Lavenders there should be grown in pots to provide them with better drainage, but generally even the tender lavenders are grown as annuals. Fortunately, *L. stoechas* 'Alba' is white, so those in Zones 8 and 9 can still try a white lavender.

CULINARY USES

In Elizabethan England, lavender was a favored flavoring in a conserve used with meats, game, fruit salads, and desserts. It can be recreated in today's cuisine in the form of lavender jelly used in the same way, but with a cinnamon stick added for extra flavor. The jelly is wonderful spread over cream cheese and crackers. Another favored use for lavender in the old days was as a tisane, an infusion of its flowers to make an herbal tea, which can also be brought into this century as a fragrant and calming cup, flavored with honey if desired. Its leaves can also be infused into honey, which is delicious with morning biscuits, and into both plain and fruit vinegars, for deglazing skillets used for sautéed chicken or meat dishes. Embed a tiny tip of a lavender leaf in a pot of applesauce for a surprising flavor. Its flowers and leaves also provide the fragrance in a simple syrup to pour over fruit salads and desserts; in their simplest use, the white lavender blossoms can be lightly strewn over a dessert as a pretty garnish.

Herbes de Provence Made in the U.S.A.

This fragrant dried herb blend, so essential to the cooking of Provence, can also be made with the same herbs from your own garden. Although it doesn't have the taste identical to the imported French mixture, it has a fresh-from-your-own-garden signature, and the addition of white lavender buds makes it unique. Make sure the marjoram is the true sweet marjoram (*Origanum majorana*).

1 tablespoon dried knotted sweet marjoram
1 tablespoon dried summer savory
1 tablespoon dried 'Orange Balsam' thyme
   (page 248) or dried French thyme
1 teaspoon dried rosemary
1 teaspoon Greek oregano

2 teaspoons dried orange peel
1 teaspoon dried white English lavender buds
1 teaspoon fennel seeds
1 dried bay leaf, grated to a powder with a
   mortar and pestle, or finely ground in a
   spice grinder.

In a medium-sized mixing bowl, combine the sweet marjoram, summer savory, thyme, rosemary, and oregano. Lightly crush the herbs with the tips of your fingers, then add the remaining ingredients. Stir to combine. Store in an airtight jar, in a cool, dark place, so the colors remain vividly bright.

Makes about ⅓ cup

Lavender Crème Fraîche Chocolates

Sadie Kendall is the owner of Kendall Farms in Atascadero, California and purveyor of a premium crème fraîche product to the food and restaurant industry. She developed this chocolate and lavender lover's recipe for her book, *The Crème Fraîche Cookbook* (Ridgeview Publishing). These exotic bonbons cause quite a sensation when served for dessert with a cup of strong espresso. The couverture chocolate used provides a thinner, glossier coating than baking chocolate, and is available at specialty food stores.

1 cup crème fraîche
2 tablespoons finely chopped fresh leaves of
*   lavender 'Jean Davis' or other English*
*   lavender, or 1 teaspoon dried leaves*

2 tablespoons superfine sugar
4 ounces bittersweet or milk chocolate,
*   couverture chocolate, or semi-sweet or*
*   milk chocolate baking squares*

Combine the crème fraîche and lavender in a medium bowl. Stir well. Cover the bowl and refrigerate for 24 hours to allow the lavender to scent the crème fraîche.

Strain the mixture through a fine sieve, discarding the lavender leaves. Stir in the sugar and combine well.

Line a colander with damp cheesecloth. Pour the lavender-infused crème fraîche into the colander. Gather up the cheesecloth and fold it over the mixture. Place a weighted saucer on top to hasten draining (such as a 6-ounce can). Drain at room temperature for approximately 3 hours, or until the mixture is dry in texture. Refrigerate the drained mixture until cold.

Melt the chocolate in the top of a double boiler set over very hot water, but do not allow the water to touch the bottom of the insert. When the chocolate is melted, 88 to 91 degrees F. for dark chocolate and 84 to 87 degrees F. for milk chocolate, transfer to a small deep ceramic bowl, or custard cup.

Remove the chilled crème fraîche mixture from the refrigerator. Scoop up about a teaspoon of the mixture at a time, and form 8 spheres, about 1 inch in diameter, gently shaping them between the palms of your hands. Place the spheres on a cold plate. Dip each sphere into the melted chocolate so that it is completely enrobed. Lift out the spheres with a spoon, and return them to the plate. Set aside in a cool, dry place until the chocolate has firmed, then store in an airtight container in the refrigerator until ready to serve. (If possible store the candies for several days before serving, as the flavors mellow).

Makes 8 candies. (Recipe may be doubled.)

LEMON GRASS
(Cymbopogon citratus)

Tender Perennial   Zone 10
Native Habitat   Southern India and Ceylon

Confirming the popularity of the citrus-scented subtropical herb lemon grass, it has recently had its debut—as a convenience food—on grocery shelves. No longer need you peel, trim, slice, grind, or pound the herb yourself because it is available as a ready-made paste. But that misses the point, because to harvest this beautiful fountain of sweet grass from your own herb garden and to personally perform the above culinary activities in your own kitchen is a fragrant pleasure.

Known as *xa* in Vietnam, *ta krai* in Thailand, and *sereh* in Indonesia, lemon grass is a versatile staple ingredient in Southeast Asian cookery. In South and Central America, where it is known as *limoncillo,* it is used principally to make a beverage. This billowy, lime-green perennial is a large, clump-forming herb that grows 2 to 3 feet tall and as wide. Its pointed, translucent, arching leaf blades, 2 to 3 feet long and 1½ inches wide, rise gracefully above its bulbous stems. Flowering is rare in cultivation in temperate gardens. The lemon-fragrant essential oil, the tantalizing ingredient that subtly flavors foods with its elusive balm scent, lies in the thick, fibrous stalks that form tough, concentric sheaths.

GROWING YOUR OWN

Lemon grass, a frost-tender perennial, requires protection in all zones but the most tropical growing areas of Zone 10. In cold climates, lemon grass can be grown as a container plant and brought indoors for the winter, or dug up in the fall, divided, and potted. It can also be cut back to 2 or 3 inches, and overwintered in a greenhouse. Probably the easiest approach in cold climates is to treat lemon grass as an annual, obtaining new potted plants every spring. Grow lemon grass in richly amended, moist, well-draining soil. It likes full sun but will accept partial shade. Although the herb is sturdy and drought-tolerant when established, it does need frequent watering, and a thick mulch is helpful in keeping the soil moist. It should not be allowed to dry out completely. Feed with fish fertilizer or liquid fish emulsion regularly throughout the growing season, or add timed-release fertilizer at planting time, or scratch it into the soil later. The lemon grass I planted in my kitchen garden outgrew and dwarfed every nearby herb, so I planted it in a 20-inch-diameter pot, where it thrives. In its container I feed it regularly with fish emulsion mixed at half strength. Planted in the ground, lemon grass is dynamic planted with other lower-growing ornamental grasses. The morning and afternoon sun shining through its leaves creates a lovely focal point in the garden. Because of its sharp leaves, it is not an herb to plant in areas where it will be brushed against, pleasantly scented though it may be.

CULINARY USES

When harvesting lemon grass for cooking, choose outside stems that are about ½ inch thick. Cut each one at its base, discarding the leafy upper section. Depending on the recipe, the fat-scallion-like stems are cut into 2- or 3-inch lengths, or thinly sliced crosswise, or chopped, or pounded into a paste with other herbs. Most often, lemon grass stems are removed from the dish before serving, as they are fibrous and tough. Fortunately for gardeners who live in cold climates, where lemon grass is treated as an annual, the stems can be stored for future use.

Wrapped individually in aluminum foil, they can be frozen indefinitely or stored in the refrigerator for up to two weeks.

The subtlety that fresh lemon grass adds to a Southeast Asian or other dish is incomparable. It lends beverages a delicate "eau de Cologne" rather than "perfume" scent of citrus, and it is quite soothing in iced or hot teas, alone or mixed with other herbs. A lemon grass lemonade is citrusy, yet not as tart as lemonade. One of the basic ways to enjoy lemon grass is in soups, especially those with a rich chicken-stock base. Mixed with coconut milk it is "liquid manna." Added to soups with a fish-stock base, it is equally sublime. Sliced lemon grass gives up its aromatic flavor to poached or steamed shellfish, and the flavor is improved by the addition of perhaps one complementary star anise. Finely minced, lemon grass lends a unique taste to a stuffing for fish or roast chicken and is exotic when added to a peanut sauce to spoon over a wedge of crunchy lettuce, or for a dip, or tossed with fine egg noodles. Lemon grass can be pounded into a paste to enhance a marinade for beef, pork, or fish made with other Oriental and Southeast Asian ingredients such as sesame oil, culantro or cilantro, Thai basil, ginger, and hot chiles. A simple sugar syrup infused with lemon grass and poured over fresh fruit makes a floral salad or dessert, and a sorbet made with lemon grass has the ideal understated note on which to end a meal.

Lemon Grass and Vietnamese Balm Cooler

This cooling summer drink tastes like a delicate lemonade but with more complex citrus notes, mingled with the beguiling scent of Vietnamese balm.

For another recipe using lemon grass, see page 204, Fragrant Fish Soup.

Lemon Grass–Vietnamese Balm Infusion
3 to 4 stalks lemon grass
1 cup water
1 cup sugar
½ cup lightly packed Vietnamese balm (page 255) or lemon balm

5 cups water
3 to 4 tablespoons freshly squeezed lemon juice, to taste

To make the lemon grass–Vietnamese balm infusion, trim the leafy tops of the lemon grass and discard. Remove the tough, outer leaves from the base of the stalk, and cut away any hard root section. With a sharp knife, cut the trimmed stalks diagonally into ¼-inch slices. Combine water and sugar in a medium-sized saucepan. Bring the mixture to a boil, stirring to dissolve the sugar. Add the lemon grass, and turn heat to low. Cover, and simmer for 15 minutes. Remove cover and bring the mixture to a boil. Add the Vietnamese balm, and boil for 1 minute. Cover pan and remove from heat. Allow mixture to cool with the lid on. Pour the syrup through a fine-mesh sieve placed over a bowl, pressing down on the lemon grass and Vietnamese balm with the back of a spoon to extract as much of the flavorful oils as possible, then discard the herbs. There should be ¾ to 1 cup herb infusion.

Pour the syrup into a glass pitcher, and add the water and lemon juice. Stir well, then pour into ice-filled glasses. Garnish each glass with a sprig of Vietnamese balm.

Makes six 8-ounce servings

MALABAR SPINACH

(Basella alba)

Annual

Native Habitat   Tropical Asia, probably India and China

Malabar spinach, the herb eaten as a vegetable, has many names that confirm—in case there is any question—that it is a replacement for true spinach: Ceylon spinach, climbing spinach, Indian spinach, country spinach, Surinam spinach, and vine spinach. In addition, it is descriptively called slippery vegetable, soft juice leaf, wood ear vegetable, red vine, and red wine vegetable (because of the burgundy-red stems of *Basella rubra*). The most exotic name is Malabar nightshade. Personally, Malabar spinach reminds me of goats—the four lovable Nubian goats my family and I cared for over several years on our little farm in rural northern New Jersey, who were named after our favorite vegetables and herbs that we grew in our garden: Batata, Cauliflower, Coriander, and handsome Malabar.

Malabar spinach, widely cultivated in tropical Asia, West Africa, and the Carribean, is the model of an ornamental edible. Its vining habit makes it the ideal plant to scamper up a vertical trellis or conical "tepee," where it soon becomes a lush, thick-leaved focal point for either the herb or vegetable garden. And it will be there as a replacement for spinach in the hot summer weather when even the slow-bolting spinach varieties begin to bolt. In warm climates, the plant can be perennial for several years. As nutritious as it is ornamental, Malabar spinach is rich in vitamins A and C and is a good source of calcium and iron. There are two types to choose from. The red form, *Basella alba* 'Rubra', with its burnished purplish-red stems, thick green or purple-green 4- to-5-inch leaves, and pale pink flowers is hands down the prettiest, both in the garden and on the plate. *B. alba* is the green-on-green form, with larger, dark green oval leaves. Both grow from 2 to 6 feet or higher in long-hot-summer climates.

In China, the violet-red dye yielded by the fleshy succulent berries of Malabar spinach historically was used by government officials to stamp documents as well as in rouge to cosmetically color female cheeks. The same dye colors jellies, pastries, and sweets in China.

GROWING YOUR OWN

Where the growing season is short, start Malabar spinach indoors in individual pots 8 to 10 weeks before the date of the last frost and transplant outdoors when the night temperature has warmed to 58 degrees or above. Seed may also be direct-sown when the soil has warmed; plant it 1 inch deep at the foot of a 3-to-6-foot trellis, crossed and tied bean poles, or at the base of a fence, and thin the seedlings 6 to 12 inches apart. Seed can also be sown in a 5-to-10-gallon container set with a short trellis. Malabar spinach is an ideal specimen for a heated greenhouse, where it will grow as a perennial for several years. As it is a tropical plant it grows poorly in cold weather and will accept no frost. In the ground it likes a well-amended, moisture-retentive, rich soil with plenty of manure. Grow the herb in full sun, but in hot weather climates provide afternoon shade. It appreciates regular feedings of nitrogen-rich fertilizer throughout the growing season. Gathering may begin 12 weeks after planting; cut 3 to 5 inches from the tip of the branches, which encourages succulent new growth and produces a lush and beautiful twining vine. It is easily propagated from stem cuttings. Malabar spinach is an economical herb, for if its seeds are collected, they are viable for 5 years.

CULINARY USES

Malabar spinach is a succesful replacement in any recipe that calls for spinach, including all the classics: spinach soup, soufflés, quiche, omelettes, frittatas, and au naturel with a little butter, nutmeg, salt, and pepper. It retains its beautiful emerald green color when cooked and tastes like a succulent form of chard, but with more substance. Unfortunately, the beautiful garnet red of B. *rubra* dissipates in cooking, but no mesclun is prettier than one with a scattering of its wine-colored stems contrasted against its rich green leaves shiny with a simple vinaigrette. Because of the thickness of the leaves of Malabar spinach, it doesn't cook down as much as spinach or chard, so less is needed for a healthy portion. To retain all its vitamins, it is best to steam Malabar spinach or use it in soups and stews or stir-fry it with meat or chicken. Like okra, it has a mucilaginous quality when cooked at length, so unless you want to produce a dish with a natural thickener, take care not to overcook the herb.

Malabar-Spinach-and-Prosciutto-Stuffed Tomatoes

These savory stuffed tomatoes are delicious when tomato season is in full swing. They can be served as an accompaniment for an outdoor barbecue or as the first course for a summer dinner indoors.

If using fresh sweet marjoram, make sure it is the true sweet marjoram (*Origanum majorana*).

If the prosciutto is too salty, pour hot water over it to cover and allow to sit for 20 to 30 minutes, then drain.

4 large tomatoes

2 tablespoons olive oil

½ cup red onion, finely chopped

1 clove garlic, finely chopped

2 three-inch sprigs leaf celery, finely chopped (page 72)

1 tablespoon chopped fresh parsley

2 teaspoons chopped fresh sweet marjoram, or 1 teaspoon dried

1 teaspoon chopped fresh thyme, or ¼ teaspoon dried

8 cups chopped Malabar spinach

½ cup bread crumbs

¼ teaspoon freshly grated nutmeg

4 tablespoons chopped imported prosciutto

1 tablespoon lemon juice

Freshly ground black pepper, to taste

2 eggs, lightly beaten

4 tablespoons Parmesan cheese

1 tablespoon butter, cut into small pieces

Preheat the oven to 350 degrees.

Slice the tops off the tomatoes and scoop out the interiors. Cut a small horizontal slice from the bottom of the tomatoes so they will sit flat, taking care not to create a hole for the stuffing to leak through. Drain the tomatoes upside down on paper towels. Reserve.

In a large skillet, heat the olive oil and sauté the onion, garlic, and leaf celery until soft, about 3 minutes. Add the parsley, sweet marjoram, and thyme. Stir over medium heat for 1 minute, then add the Malabar spinach. Turn the heat to low. Cover and cook for about

5 minutes. Remove the cover and gently turn the Malabar spinach with 2 spatulas to combine the mixture. Cover and cook for another 5 minutes, or until the Malabar spinach is
completely wilted. Break apart the leaves, if necessary, with a wooden spoon. Stir in the
bread crumbs and nutmeg and combine well. Stir in the prosciutto, lemon juice, and black
pepper. Add the eggs and cook for 3 to 4 minutes, stirring constantly.

Stuff the reserved tomatoes with the mixture. Sprinkle 1 tablespoon of the Parmesan
cheese over each tomato, then dot with the butter pieces. Place the tomatoes on a baking
sheet and bake for 10 to 15 minutes. Serve immediately.

Serves 4

MEXICAN TARRAGON

(Tagetes lucida)

Tender Perennial   Zones 8–10
Native Habitat   Mexico and Guatemala

Yerbanis, anisillo, Santa Maria, and *pericon* are mellifluous Spanish names for Mexican tarragon, a highly fragrant herb reminiscent of star anise mixed with French tarragon. Its equally poetic English common names are Mexican marigold mint, cloud plant, sweet mace, and sweet-scented marigold. A member of the marigold genus, the herb is a bushy, erect perennial growing to approximately 2½ feet high, with finely serrated, 3-inch-long, lance-shaped leaves and clusters of butter-yellow flowers the size of small golden coins. In its native habitat it grows on dry, rocky slopes, in meadows, and in oak woods. It was known as a substitute for French tarragon in European gardens of the nineteenth century. It is marketed in quantity in Mexican markets as a culinary herb, but its soothing fragrance also perfumes babies' bathwater and it is used in baptisms and other ceremonies. Its dried leaves and flowers are also mixed with tobacco or used alone and smoked in pipes and cigarettes.

Mexican tarragon has a rich history of culinary, medicinal, and magical uses. The anise-scented herb was supposedly used to flavor the humble Mexican gruel, *atole*, as well as the haute-cuisine chocolate beverage of ancient Aztec royalty, *cacahuhuel*. In its native Mexican habitat, its leaves are infused to make a medicinal tea to soothe minor ills. The Huichol Indians who live in the Mexican Sierra Madre north of Guadalajara use the freshly picked golden flowers to make ceremonial crosses and colorful household decorations, and they dry and burn Mexican tarragon's leaves as a fragrant, anise-scented incense.

GROWING YOUR OWN

Mexican tarragon is a tender perennial that is cultivated as an annual in the colder climates of the United States. In the Northeast it flowers rather sparsely several weeks before the first frost. In warmer climates, the plant is almost evergreen, dying back for only a few months, and blooms from late fall to early winter. In the mid-South it usually flowers in October, just before the frost nips it. The beauty of growing Mexican tarragon in the southern states is that it can take the place of French tarragon, which is difficult to maintain in that humid region.

Mexican tarragon thrives in average, well-drained soil in full sun with regular watering. Start seeds indoors 6 weeks before the last frost date, or set out young nursery plants in spring, spaced 1 foot apart. If you grow Mexican tarragon as a perennial in warm climates, cut the herb back to the ground after it flowers. Soon thereafter it will begin its cycle again. To prolong its life, divide the thick clumps of Mexican tarragon in the early spring just as the plant shows new growth. Keep divisions moist until they are established. Stem cuttings can also be propagated in the spring. In cold climates, where the herb cannot overwinter, stem cuttings can be taken in late summer or the entire plant can be potted up before frost and brought inside until spring arrives.

Mexican tarragon is complemented by a low-growing border of herbs such as winter savory, broadleaf English thyme, golden variegated thyme, and golden sage, which highlight its rich green foliage and vivid yellow flowers.

CULINARY USES

Mexican tarragon makes a nice anise-scented herb tea to serve with a typical tea platter of small sandwiches, scones, and pastries. Southwestern chefs prize Mexican tarragon because of its affinity with corn, chayote and other squashes, robust meats, quail, and *pavo*, or turkey, the domesticated staple fowl of ancient Mexican culinary history. The tarragon- and lemon-flavored herb is well paired with catfish, and its leaves can be pounded with pecans to make a sprightly pesto. Chopped, it can be combined with goat's or sheep's milk cheese to prepare an anise-perfumed spread for crackers or squares of toasted bread. Add it to a hot or cold tomato soup, and toss a few of its leaves in the water when cooking corn. One Texan hostess, an afficionado of southwestern cuisine, replaces sweet woodruff with *yerbanis* for an unusual Mexican May wine, the festive punch served at her annual Cinco de Mayo party celebration.

Mexican tarragon can be substituted for any dish where French tarragon is called for, but it should be used with a lighter hand, as its anise flavor is much more pronounced. A fragrant herb vinegar is made by steeping the fresh leaves in white wine vinegar, and the essence of this robust herb can be captured by preserving it in olive oil. Dry the leaves of Mexican tarragon to have on hand during the winter months when neither French nor Mexican tarragon is available from the garden, and save an extra handful to lend a spicy note to a fragrant potpourri.

Jicama Matchstick Salad with Mexican Tarragon Vinaigrette

Jicama, also known as Mexican yam bean, is a rather nondescript tuber in a plain brown skin wrapper until it is peeled and sliced into crunchy matchsticks for a cool, ivory white salad anointed with a tart lime and Mexican tarragon vinaigrette. With the addition of green and sweet red pepper, the salad contains the red, white, and green colors of the Mexican flag.

When handling chiles, I wear thin rubber gloves to keep from getting the hot capsaicin contained in the seeds and ribs on my hands. It's no fun to go around with a burned tongue or tearing eyes, as you invariably forget and lick your fingers or rub your eyes—*ouch*.

2 tablespoons lime juice
½ teaspoon ground cumin
Salt and freshly ground white pepper to taste
¼ teaspoon ground chile powder, preferably New Mexican
⅓ cup peanut oil
2 tablespoons finely chopped fresh Mexican tarragon

1 pound jicama
½ cup diced red bell pepper
½ cup diced green bell pepper
1 fresh jalapeño chile pepper, finely chopped (optional)
Fresh Mexican tarragon sprigs (and flowers if in bloom), for garnish

In a small mixing bowl, whisk together the lime juice, cumin, salt, white pepper, and ground chile. Slowly whisk in the oil until the dressing is emulsified, then add the Mexican tarragon. Set aside.

Cut the jicama into lengthwise chunks, and with a paring knife peel off the skin, cutting away the fibrous underlayer. Slice the peeled jicama lengthwise into thin matchsticks about ⅛ inch thick and ¼ inch wide. Place in a large mixing bowl and add the red and green peppers and the jalapeño. Pour the vinaigrette over the mixture, combining well. Refrigerate for 1 hour before serving, if desired.

Serves 4

MINER'S LETTUCE

(Claytonia perfoliata)

Annual
Native Habitat   North America from British Columbia to Mexico

Miner's lettuce is one of those plants that is truly almost too ornamental to eat. Its succulent, shiny green leaves, threaded along thin stems, look like dainty, miniature, heart-shaped lily pads cupping its white-flowering stalk, which grows right through the center like a floppy tassel. It is a unique herb with a refreshing taste when eaten as a salad or as a healthy steamed vegetable, which the California Gold Rush miners knew firsthand. Although they might not have considered how pretty it looks in a mesclun mélange, as a vitamin C–rich salad and vegetable herb it helped keep them healthy during their forays to search for gold, hence the common name. While a contemporary cook probably won't want to go to the tedious effort of digging up miner's lettuce's roots and boiling them to enjoy their water chestnut flavor, the root remains available for the taking, just in case. Savvy gardening cooks aren't the only ones who appreciate miner's lettuce; the mourning dove coos over the herb's black seeds, and songbirds also know it is a plentiful source of food for them.

Miner's lettuce is a member of the purslane family, and in Europe, where purslane is a culinary "weed of the wild" enjoyed in the warm months, winter purslane is the name earned there for naturalized miner's lettuce. In Cuba, where it was also introduced and naturalized, miner's lettuce is called Cuban spinach and is eaten as a vegetable. From winter to spring in the American West, it grows wild both in damp, shaded glades and on the dry, sandy lower slopes of the mountain ranges from the Rocky Mountains to the Pacific Ocean. In cool months it can be seen growing wild by the side of the road and, rather more grandly, luxuriating in its own shiny verdant meadow in San Francisco's serenely green Golden Gate Park, where you can look—but not pick.

GROWING YOUR OWN

Miner's lettuce is an easily grown herb that can be cultivated and enjoyed in the cool months of the growing season. It is ready to harvest in about 6 weeks. In regions with mild winters it can be sown in the fall and harvested right through late spring, but it tolerates only light frosts. In mild-winter areas leave a few plants to go to seed, to see whether miner's lettuce will naturalize in a cool, moist spot in the herb garden. In areas with freezing cold winters, sow seed directly in the early spring in part sun and harvest until hot weather begins. Seed can also be sown indoors in the late winter for transplanting outdoors come spring. Sow again in early fall in a cold frame or unheated greenhouse for an all-winter-long harvest.

Grow miner's lettuce in well-draining soil enriched with organic compost. Sow seeds about ½ inch apart, then thin seedlings to about 6 inches apart or more. The plants grow to about 1 foot. Miner's lettuce benefits from the cut-and-come-again method of harvesting. It can be treated as a "seedling crop," where the seeds are broadcast thickly and snipped when the young leaves are only 2 or 3 inches high. In this manner, they are especially fresh and tasty, and the vitamin content is twice that of the fully grown leaves. Seedling crops can be grown indoors or out, depending on the season. Or you can allow miner's lettuce to grow and cut the leaves as needed from the mature plant. You can also cut the mature plant back to an inch above the ground, and it will sprout again. Miner's lettuce can also be grown in containers in fast-draining potting soil, with regular feedings of fish emulsion mixed at half strength.

CULINARY USES

Miner's lettuce looks most exotic in a grand salad composed of greens of many shapes and textures along with brightly colored edible flowers, and most often it outshines them all. One or two leaves placed alongside a beautiful plate of food also make a dramatic garnish. On the other hand, a pot of its leaves cooked in a light chicken stock makes a homey and nutritious vegetable, to which a pinch of chopped rosemary could be added. Its mild flavor is complemented by a sharp cheese in a fluffy breakfast omelet, or chop the fresh leaves with chives in an egg salad sandwich.

Because it tastes mildly of spinach, it would make an interesting ingredient in a classic soufflé. For an up-to-date version of a wilted green salad, use miner's lettuce and substitute for the old-fashioned bacon grease a warmed good-quality olive oil; you could add a sprinkling of lean chopped bacon with no guilt. The herb has an affinity for potatoes, and the two result in a delicious soup made with a rich beef-, chicken-, or vegetable-stock base, add a dollop of crème fraîche just before serving. Cooked chopped miner's lettuce with a sprinkling of dill or a dusting of nutmeg could serve as an elegant bed for grilled salmon.

For a recipe using miner's lettuce, see page 262, Sweet Violet Salad.

GINGER MINT

(*Mentha* x *gracilis* 'Variegata')

Perennial   Zones 5–9
Native Habitat   Europe and Asia

from left to right: Ginger mint, curly mint, and Hillary's lemon mint in the back

I find all variegated plants intriguing because of their serendipitous "nature-gone-haywire" coloration and design, and those that taste and smell fragrant as a bonus are all the better. Ginger mint is such a plant. It has another, actually more suitable, name, golden apple mint, for the yellow striping in the herb's mottled leaves is the color of a Golden Delicious apple. Besides being tasty in all sorts of foods, ginger mint flatters a dish as a bright and handsome garnish. Its cheerfully colored variegation is also an excellent design tool to brighten up a dark spot in the garden, and you can play up its duotone leaves by setting them against the complementary greens and textures of other herbs.

Among the bewildering maze of mints, ginger mint is one of the most economically important of the so-called "pure" mints, valued for its lavenderlike essential oil with fruity notes. To some its aroma is similar to basil mixed with mint, and its green form is so described in the 1640 herbal, *Theatrum Botanicum*, by John Parkinson. The 1633 edition of John Gerard's *The Herball or Generall Historie of Plantes* contains a detailed line drawing of the herb, then known as M. *cardiaca*, or heart mint. Other names of the green-leaved form of this mint, which is widely used in Asian cuisine, include red mint and Scotch mint. The handsome variegated form with its lavender flowers, headlights-on leaves, and red-tinged stems is simply more decorative.

GROWING YOUR OWN

The first decision with all mints is where to grow them, as they are invasive, and soon gobble up space needed by less tenacious herbs unable to defend themselves against mint's vigorous growth habit. Ginger mint can be successfully grown in pots, or can be contained when planted in the ground (discussed below). Obtain ginger mint in plant form from specialty herb nurseries; when the plant is established, it can be easily propagated by root division, layering, or cuttings.

Ginger mint's milky-yellow and light green leaves make it an excellent decorative potted plant for the patio, especially if it is near an outside dining area, where the leaves can easily be snipped for refreshing iced teas and lemonades. Choose a 10-to-12-inch pot and plant the herb in lightweight potting soil. Do not allow the soil to dry out. Depending upon the climate and season, mint in pots needs to be watered regularly every few days, and in dry climates, perhaps every day. Feed container-grown ginger mint with a liquid fertilizer every other week during the growing season. Prune regularly to keep it looking shapely. Like most mints, it prefers to grow in full sun and partial shade. While many yellow-variegated leaves color best in full sun, I have found the variegation in ginger mint's leaves dissipates if it gets too much sun during the hot summer months, and the beauty of potting up the herb is the ability to move it to follow the shade.

Ginger mint beautifully complements other mints. I grow mine in a cluster of pots containing light green lemon balm; shiny, dark green Morroccan mint, also with reddish stems; the picoteed leaves of curly mint; and a "Vietnamese market mint," propagated by rooting a cutting from a bunch purchased at a Southeast Asian market. In cold winter areas, store pots in a cold frame or unheated garage until spring, then divide and repot. You'll eventually have enough for a plantation of pots and a host of garden gifts for friends.

Planted in the ground, ginger mint prefers a moist, rich, fertile soil amended with well-rotted manure or compost. Prune regularly to encourage lush growth, and cut back after flowering. In cold-winter areas, cut it to the ground in winter. Every few years, the beds must be divided, amended again, and replanted. The trick to planting ginger mint in the ground so it doesn't get out of hand is to provide a barricade to its roots. This is easily accomplished by surrounding the mint with a 5-gallon plastic nursery pot with the bottom cut out that is sunk in the ground; then fill it with soil and plant the ginger mint in the center. This method is not necessary if there is a bare area in the garden where a planting can run rampant. What a pretty sight unfettered ginger mint would be.

CULINARY USES

Among the multitude of uses for ginger mint in cooking are those that result in domestic kitchen products such as an infusion of its leaves in honey, sugar, butter, and rice wine vinegar. It makes a restorative steaming hot cup of ginger mint tea, and a fresh sprig also brightens other herb teas for a fragrant combination. When making lemonade, before adding the water muddle ginger mint and the zest of a lemon, ideally a florid Meyer lemon, and sugar to taste for a particularly soothing, cool summer beverage. A snippet of ginger mint is equally nice in a cup of breakfast or bedtime hot chocolate. For an hors d'oeuvre, add chopped ginger mint to a mashed-sweet-pea "guacamole," a unique version of the savory avocado dip made with fresh green peas, or combine it with chopped parsley and sprinkle over a first-course hot or cold fresh green pea soup. A sliced fennel salad dressed with a light vinaigrette and strewn with chopped ginger mint leaves is a delightful combination, as is a cucumber and tomato sandwich with a lemony mayonnaise infused with ginger mint. The pairing of mint with carrots and potatoes remains tried and true, and works particularly well with ginger mint. It is a good partner with basil, which has minty overtones, and in Southeast Asian dishes the twosome is good with steamed clams flavored with ginger, garlic, and fiery chiles, or used to subtly flavor a pot of steamed rice. Chicken is excellent marinated in a mixture of ginger mint, onions, and yogurt. A culinary trick for common mint is to steep the leaves in a little crème de menthe and use it to give extra minty flavor to a pot of fresh peas, a trick that also works with ginger mint. An exotic and floral dessert is balls of honeydew melon macerated in rosewater and ginger mint. Ginger mint's essence marries well and gives up its subtle fragrance with other fruits macerated in complementary liqueurs such as Grand Marnier with oranges, framboise with raspberries, or strawberry liqueur with strawberries or fraises des bois.

Hot Ginger Mint Tea with Candied Ginger

Like all mint teas, this ginger mint tea is soothing and refreshing. The candied ginger gives it a spicy kick.

For another recipe using ginger mint, see page 91, Henry's Rau Ram Salad.

2 tablespoons fresh ginger mint leaves
2 cups boiling water
2 pieces candied ginger

Rinse the ginger mint leaves with cold water, then gently bruise them with a wooden spoon or pestle. Rinse a 2-cup teapot with boiling water. Place in it the mint leaves, then pour in the boiling water. Cover the teapot so the "virtuous steam" doesn't escape. Steep for 3 to 5 minutes. Strain the tea into 2 warmed cups rinsed with boiling water. Place 1 piece of candied ginger in each teacup.

Serves 2

MITSUBA

(Cryptotaenia canadensis)

Perennial   Zones 4–9
Native Habitat   Africa, Asia, Europe, and eastern North America from Manitoba
south to Georgia and Texas

Although the pretty fleur-de-lys-like herb known as mitsuba, white chervil, or wild
honewort grows prolifically in its shaded woodland habitat in eastern North America, it is
in Japan that the culinary merits of this herb are most widely recognized. Because the herb
also grows wild in Japan, mitsuba (meaning "three leaves") has found its way into many traditional Japanese dishes as an important native herb, and it is widely cultivated there. Every
part of the plant—leaves, leaf stalks, and roots—is used in Japanese cookery. So popular is
the herb in Japan that there are *two* strains grown just for the stems, one to grow green, and
one to blanch white. The stems are then stacked log style in that artful Japanese manner and
appear in salads or vinegared dishes. In France, mitsuba's spring leaves are used like the

French favorite, chervil, in green herbal soups. In our own hemisphere, wild honewort was used as a flavoring herb and vegetable by North American Indians.

You will find mitsuba listed by other names: Japanese parsley, Japanese wild chervil, and Japanese honewort and trefoil, the latter describing the form of the leaves of this graceful, ornamental culinary herb with long slender stalks. Its young, double-serrated leaves are light green, turning to dark green as they grow larger. Its white, star-shaped flowers are so tiny that they are are ornamentally insignificant. Mitsuba looks attractive in a serene shade border with other herbs of like culture such as violets, fraises des bois, bee balm, lemon balm, chervil, and sweet cicely. In cooler garden climates, grown in full sun, mitsuba reaches only 2 feet, making it a unique edging for a vegetable garden. The taste of mitsuba is a combination of Italian flatleaf parsley and slightly bitter celery leaves, but its character changes somewhat when lightly parboiled and becomes more mellow.

GROWING YOUR OWN

Mitsuba grows 2 to 3 feet tall, and while it is classified as a perennial, it is often grown as an annual. It likes a rich, moist soil and does best in part shade. I have tried growing mitsuba between two taller herbs so their foliage shades the plant, with some success, but it is much happier in full shade in my hot Zone 10 growing climate. Sow mitsuba in the spring or early fall. In cold climates seeds can be sown indoors for transplanting in late spring. In temperate, frost-free areas, mitsuba can be planted outdoors from fall through late spring; avoid planting only in the hot summer months. Thin seedlings to about 6 to 9 inches apart. Successive sowings can be made every 6 weeks to ensure a continual supply of the young leaves. Plant the seeds about ¼ inch deep, and keep the soil evenly moist until germination. You might like to blanch the long stems to make them more tender, as is done in Japan, by mounding up soil to block the light, but unless you are a production grower this may be more trouble than it's worth. The same effect can be achieved by sowing mitsuba densely and not thinning the seedlings, so that the crowded stems become naturally blanched. Harvest mitsuba grown in this manner when the stems are 5 or 6 inches high. The easiest way to grow mitsuba is to make successive plantings and harvest the young stems and leaves when they are 8 to 10 inches high, or as you need them. Feed regularly with liquid fish emulsion mixed at half strength. The older leaves become tough, and can be used for longer-cooking dishes, if desired.

CULINARY USES

Mitsuba is used in such Japanese standards as sushi, tempura, sukiyaki, *chawan-mushi* and other egg dishes, and *sunomono,* or vinegared foods. It is included in cooked seasoned greens, *ohitashi,* which are served in moderate amounts, and in one-pot dishes. A garnish of mitsuba nicely accompanies a salad of chilled, bite-sized tofu squares with a vinaigrette of rice wine vinegar, safflower oil, and soy sauce. It is used in soups and cold noodle dishes with fish or shellfish.

All of these uses are easily adapted to Western cookery. Mitsuba can be substituted in any recipe where parsley would normally be used. A simple pleasure is to sprinkle minced mitsuba leaves over rice. Young seedling thinnings are especially tasty in green salads. Minced mitsuba and 'Bronze' perilla, daikon sprouts, and a small amount of melted butter makes a nice herbal sauce for vegetables. Combine minced mitsuba with thyme or marjoram, finely chopped chives, and fromage blanc for a tasty mixture to spread on toast rounds. Its stems can be candied like angelica for decorating pastries. Some years ago I purchased a plastic gadget at Takashimaya, a Japanese department store in Manhattan, that made *square* hard-cooked eggs. I artfully embedded a leaf of mitsuba atop the uniquely shaped eggs and served them on a bed of lettuce accompanied by a dab of homemade mayonnaise shot through with minced mitsuba; the eggs may be odd, but they certainly turn heads as a tasty first course. If you don't have access to the square egg maker, mitsuba is just as flavorful minced in a filling for everyday hard-cooked eggs.

Many years ago my Japanese friend Yuki showed me how to blanch three-leaved stems of mitsuba in boiling water just long enough to make them turn bright green and limp, tying a knot mid-stem, then artfully laying one knotted stem over each steaming hot bowl of *miso shiru,* or miso soup. I still serve this soup in inexpensive lacquered and lidded Japanese soup bowls. When the lid is lifted, the subtle aroma that arises from the mitsuba mingling with the fragrant soup and coupled with the beauty of these simple bowls is an elegant way to begin a meal.

Orange Crescents and Cucumber Rounds with Mitsuba Dressing

This is a cooling and refreshing first-course salad. The subtle, grassy taste of mitsuba blends nicely with the mild flavor of rice wine vinegar, and the color of its bright green stems punctuates the golden oranges and pale cucumbers with a sense of Oriental aesthetics. Serve with lacquered soy crackers.

4 small oranges

1 hothouse cucumber

Mitsuba Dressing

16 young mitsuba stems 4 to 5 inches long with
    leaves attached

2 tablespoons seasoned rice vinegar

2 teaspoons light soy sauce

2 tablespoons freshly squeezed orange juice

¼ teaspoon dark sesame seed oil

Pinch cayenne pepper

Pinch sea salt (optional)

Toasted sesame seeds, for garnish

Peel the oranges and separate the segments, removing the membrane. Slice the cucumber into thin slices. Set both aside.

To make the dressing, wash the mitsuba. Remove the leaves from 12 of the stems and pat dry with paper towels. Julienne the leaves and set aside. Parboil the deleafed stems plus the 4 stems with leaves attached for 2 minutes. Strain through a sieve. Refresh with cold water and pat them dry with paper towels. Set aside the 4 mitsuba stems with attached leaves. Finely chop the deleafed mitsuba stems.

In a small bowl, whisk together the rice vinegar, soy sauce, orange juice, sesame seed oil, cayenne pepper, and salt, if being used. Stir in the chopped mitsuba stems.

Arrange the orange segments in the center of four salad plates. Place a ring of cucumbers around the oranges. Drizzle 1 tablespoon of the mitsuba dressing over each salad. On this scatter the finely chopped mitsuba leaves, then a sprinkling of sesame seeds. Place a mitsuba stem on each salad plate, tying a knot in the stems if desired.

Serves 4

NIGELLA

(Nigella sativa)

Annual
Native Habitat   The Mediterranean Sea basins and western Asia

Matte-black nigella seeds, shaken like grains of pepper from their own dried parchment-colored, nut-shaped cases, have a unique taste all their own. Nigella's other common names suggest culinary associations with other herbs and spices: black cumin, black caraway, nutmeg flower, fennel flower, and Roman coriander. It is known as *charnuska* in Russia, *kalonji* in India, and *habbat baraka* in the Arab world. Its lovely French name is *cheveu de Vénus*, because of the delicate structure of its leaves, and *toute épice* or *mille épices*.

Nigella's beautiful young blossoms are as exotic as they come. Moonlight-white five-petaled flowers painted with the palest of blue shadows are cradled in a spray of needlelike, fringed foliage. In the center, a small, segmented oval green casement arises from a ring of dark purple, encircled with another ring of delicate filaments. The whole effect gives the impression that the flower is surrounded by exploding miniature green sparklers. Nigella also blooms in varying shades of mauve and purple-blue. When the flowers are spent, the oval green pods, which hold the three-cornered seeds, begin to inflate. When dry, these pretty fruit pods turn into parchment-colored seed shakers (which are sought after as elements for dried flower arrangements in the florist trade). After shaking enough of the seeds from the pods for use in the kitchen, you can save the attractive empty cases for your own dried floral arrangements. This herb elicits true wonder at the complex intricacies of growth and the beauty of nature.

Nigella is one of those ancient herbs that has endured through the ages and has been cultivated for both culinary and medicinal uses. It is mentioned in the Bible, and was probably used in biblical times to give variety with its unique peppery taste to the staple fare of bread. The herb also has its place of honor as one of the 75 plants decreed to be grown in every royal garden by the ninth-century emperor Charlemagne. Historically, nigella's essential oils have been used in wine and in scented infusions. Nigella offered its attributes to an appealing sixteenth-century recipe for a restorative floral water, a sensuously fragrant brew that mingled it with marjoram, cinnamon, ginger, clove, basil, borage, calamint, rose, sage, rosemary, and thyme. In the Egypt of the past, the seeds were supposedly eaten by women to help them attain a stouter figure, considered an attribute of beauty.

Nigella is native to western Asia, the Middle East, and the sunny countries bordering the Mediterranean. In the eighteenth century, *Nigella sativa* crossed the Atlantic with the newcomers to America. In the nineteenth century, the curious gardener Thomas Jefferson planted this culinary nigella in his gardens at Monticello. Another nigella species, the poetically named love-in-a-mist (*N. damascena*) is more widely available than *N. sativa*, but its seeds do not have the same pungency and culinary qualities. Many Indian, Middle Eastern, and Mediterranean cookbooks contain references to the use of the aromatic seeds of this exotic herb, despite its use through the centuries, it remains deserving of wider discovery and adaptation.

GROWING YOUR OWN

Nigella is an annual that grows to 2½ feet tall with flowers 1½ inches in diameter. Once it is planted in your garden, you will never be without it, for it readily self-sows. Seeds can be direct-sown in the early spring or in the autumn, which will result in an extra early start the next spring. Gardeners who live in areas with long winters and short summers should sow the seeds indoors and carefully set out the seedlings in the spring without disturbing the roots. Thin seedlings to 3 to 4 inches. Nigella likes full sun in a richly amended, well-drained soil. A little fertilizer such as a side-dressing of well-rotted manure when plants are just beginning to put on growth will help them off to a good start. The references in works of garden history regarding nigella's ability to deter insects when interplanted with "potherbs"—vegetables— is reason enough to try companion-planting nigella in the vegetable plot. In the herb garden or flower border, sky-blue forget-me-nots look lovely with the blue tones of nigella flowers, as do the purple puffball blossoms of garden chives (*Allium schoenoprasum*), and the deep, rich blue of cornflowers. To harvest nigella: Just as the balloonlike containers turn parchment-colored and the black seeds are visible through slits in the top, gently break open the pods and shake out their contents. You must be vigilant, and collect the seeds before they drop to the ground—but leave a few stems with a balloon pod or two full of seeds to ensure next year's growth. Nigella is an economical plant, for the seeds are viable for three years.

CULINARY USES

In Indian cuisine nigella's seeds are used with lentil dishes, vegetables, curries, pickles, breads, and fish. Along with cumin, fennel, mustard, and fenugreek, they are a prominent component of the unground spice blend *punch phoran*, used for chutneys and vegetables and especially nice with eggplant. This blend, or a variation thereof, is easy to make in small amounts and can also be used for sprinkling over chicken or lamb. A sprinkling of nigella is an excellent addition when making preserved lemons to season salads, vegetables, and chicken. In Middle Eastern and Eastern European cooking, nigella seeds are used to flavor cakes and cookies and to flavor and top breads and breakfast rolls; they even flavor wine. They are irresistible as part of a savory mélange with one or several herb seeds—sesame, poppy, rye, ajowan, fennel, cumin, and caraway—for flavoring a loaf of freshly baked home-made bread. Although the seeds are widely used in the baking industry, they still should be used with restraint because of possible irritant effects of the oils. In Eastern Europe, the seeds, known as *czerniska*, are used to flavor lamb and rice dishes and to infuse sauerkraut, an interesting change from juniper berries. To spruce up canned sauerkraut, strain the liquid and heat the sauerkraut in equal amounts of chicken stock and white wine with a sprinkling of nigella seeds and two or three peppercorns. Armenian string cheese is lifted out of the ordinary by the addition of the savory perfume of nigella seeds.

Nigella has a subtle, slightly peppery, slightly nutty taste, and when softened has an unexpected taste of carrots. Sprinkle whole nigella seeds in scrambled eggs or an omelette for an intriguing breakfast treat. Include them in a lemony yogurt dressing with finely chopped spearmint to enrobe a dish of sliced cucumbers. The same dressing would be equally complementary spooned over slices of fresh oranges or tangerines and sliced bananas for a refreshing fruit salad. Use nigella in an Indian *raita*, the cooling yogurt-based counterpoint to pungent dishes, and spoon it over cumin-spiced zucchini spears garnished with fresh cilantro. Vegetable pickles and fruit chutneys both benefit from nigella's beguiling and pervasive flavor. Crushed with the back of a rolling pin or ground in a pepper mill, the seeds can be sprinkled over all manner of vegetables. Blended with the Middle Eastern *labneh* or your own homemade yogurt cheese, fromage blanc, or goat cheese and spread on flat or French bread, it becomes an herbal addiction.

Chèvre Preserved in Spice-Scented Oil

A lot of flavor is packed into these little black seeds, and a surprisingly small amount will permeate tangy balls of goat cheese with their unique taste. The cheese is preserved in extra virgin olive oil infused with other spices. Several little balls are delicious atop a salad of greens or with fruit, or they can be spread on crisp sesame crackers accompanied by a few black olives for an hors d'oeuvre sure to stimulate the appetite.

For another recipe using nigella, see page 100, Potato Curry.

⅛ teaspoon plus ½ teaspoon nigella seeds

⅛ teaspoon cumin seeds

⅛ teaspoon fenugreek seeds

⅛ teaspoon fennel seeds

⅛ teaspoon mustard seeds

⅛ teaspoon coriander seeds

1 dried red chile

1⅔ cups extra virgin olive oil

12 ounces imported French chèvre or
    domestic fresh goat cheese

Place ⅛ teaspoon of nigella seeds, the other seeds, and the red chile in a sterilized, wide-mouthed, 4-cup jar with a nonreactive lid. Add the olive oil and set aside.

In a medium-sized bowl, lightly crumble the goat cheese. Sprinkle the remaining ½ teaspoon nigella seeds over the cheese and combine well. Gently form the cheese mixture into balls about 1 inch in diameter. Carefully place them into the spiced olive oil, which should cover the cheese by 1 inch. Add more olive oil if necessary. Seal the jar and store in the refrigerator for 2 to 3 days to allow the flavors to meld. Remove the amount of cheese balls to be served, and place them on paper towels to drain. Store the jar of cheese in the refrigerator and use within 2 weeks.

Makes 12 to 14 balls

The Oregano Mimics

There are many herbs that smell like oregano because of the presence of carvacrol, and to a lesser extent, thymol, the essential oils responsible for this flavor. Consequently, major confusion exists regarding the identification of the "real oregano," so herb researchers have begun to call oregano a *flavor* instead of focusing on a single genus or species, which makes it less confusing for everyone: botanists, horticulturists, plantsmen and plantswomen, nursery owners, seed companies—and gardeners.

The three oregano mimics that follow may be used in recipes that call for commercially sold oregano. Because of their varying degrees of strength, begin by using small amounts, then increase or decrease according to personal taste.

CUBAN OREGANO

(Plectranthus amboinicus)

Tender Perennial   Zone 10
Native Habitat   Tropical Africa, Asia, and India

From the herb garden at the National Arboretum, Washington, D.C.

Cuban oregano is exotic in numerous ways, though it has the familiar taste and scent of oregano. The essential oils that give this herb its characteristic oregano scent are carvacrol combined with camphor. The plant has light green, succulent, scalloped leaves, and there is a striking variegated green and white form with ivory-white-banded, picoteed leaves. Cuban oregano is so decorative that it looks as if it could only be an ornamental. But when its velvet leaves are touched ever so lightly, you are overwhelmed by a resounding culinary oregano scent mixed with some other undefinable, exotic note, and you can almost taste the fragrance. Cuban oregano *is* ornamental—an edible ornamental.

Plectanthrus amboinicus was introduced to the Americas from Spain. It is cultivated in home gardens in the West Indies and throughout the tropics from Africa, India, Malaysia, and the Philippines to the Virgin Islands, Cuba, and Mexico. From the Bahamas to Yucátan it is sold in native markets, but not in great abundance, probably because it is grown in home gardens. In Spanish it is known as *oregano de Cartagena,* and *oregano de Espana;* its other several names in the Caribbean are Spanish thyme, Indian borage, Puerto Rican oregano, "French thyme," oregano, and Mexican or Indian mint. In India it is known as *suganda,* and country borage, and in Vietnam as *can day la.* Obviously, it is necessary to purchase Cuban oregano by its botanical name from reliable and knowledgeable specialty herb nurseries to be assured of acquiring the true Cuban oregano. It is often sold under its former name *Coleus amboinicus.*

GROWING YOUR OWN

Cuban oregano grows in a soft, spreading mound 2 to 3 feet tall and 2 to 3 feet wide. It has oval, succulent leaves velvet to the touch, with wavy edges. In cold-winter zones it is treated as an annual and makes a fragrant potted plant or unusual hanging-basket herb. It can be brought indoors and placed in a sunny window, or overwintered in the greenhouse. Fresh cuttings can be taken in late summer, as they root easily in either soil or water and grow quickly. It is a warm weather lover and cannot tolerate temperatures below 50 degrees. Grow Cuban oregano in full sun and a sandy, quick-draining soil. In containers, add timed-release fertilizer at planting time, then feed monthly during the growing season with fish emulsion or a balanced soluble fertilizer mixed at half strength. Keep the leaves pinched back often to maintain a full and lush appearance. In very hot climates it can be grown in partial shade.

CULINARY USES

In India, the leaves of Cuban oregano, or *suganda,* are dipped in batter and fried. In Vietnam the pungent herb is used to scent meat dishes and stews. Throughout the tropics it is often used to mask the flavor of strong-tasting fish, goat, and mutton. In Aruba it is used to season meat, fish, and soups, and in Cuba it is especially popular in black bean soup. In Java it is a substitute for another strong herb, sage, and in Trinidad, Cuban oregano enhances a savory herbal green sauce of onions, scallions, garlic, curry leaves, and thyme. A similar green sauce, the Puerto Rican *recaito,* redolent with cilantro, is also made more complex with the addition of fresh Cuban oregano leaves. It is perhaps the cooling ingredient for a traditional, spicy *rougail*, a chile-hot Creole condiment, popular in the Carribean, to serve with cold meats, rice, and seafood, made with various spices and tropical fruits such as mango and tamarind, or with a vegetable such as eggplant as its base. Cuban oregano is a surprising ingredient in Jamaican-prepared salt cod. Add it to give pungent flavor to the meat or vegetable fillings for empanadas, or Jamaican meat patties, the tasty little fried turnovers of which you can never eat just one.

A good way to experience the taste of Cuban oregano is to sprinkle a small amount of the chopped fresh leaves in bean dishes or bean soups. When used in salad, the intense oregano flavor can be mellowed out by first lightly toasting the leaves before sprinkling them over the greens. Add a leaf of two to the spiced boiling water when cooking shellfish. Chop a few of the fresh leaves in with the onion, garlic, and other herbs for the basic Spanish dish, *arroz con pollo*, or chicken with rice.

Spicy Beans with Mexican Herbs

A mound of fluffy white rice, warm tortillas, and a bowl of black and white beans and red peppers, fragrant with Cuban oregano and epazote, accompanied by a large, tossed *ensalada* of crunchy romaine lettuce, makes a hearty, healthy, and comforting meal.

2 tablespoons peanut oil

1 large red onion, chopped

1 clove garlic, chopped

2 red bell peppers, diced

1 to 2 jalapeño peppers, stemmed, seeded, and chopped fine

1 twenty-eight-ounce can crushed tomatoes

2 teaspoons ground cumin

1 small sprig fresh epazote (page 107)

Sea salt to taste

1 fifteen-ounce can black beans, drained

1 fifteen-ounce can white beans, drained

1 tablespoon chopped Cuban oregano

Shredded Monterey Jack or cheddar cheese for sprinkling

In a medium-sized saucepan, heat the peanut oil. Add the red onion, garlic, red bell pepper, and jalapeños. Sauté over medium heat until soft, about 10 minutes. Stir in the tomatoes, cumin, epazote, and salt to taste. Simmer the sauce, covered, for 10 minutes. Add the beans and Cuban oregano and cook over low heat for about 10 minutes. Remove the epazote sprig. Divide the beans among 4 warmed bowls. Sprinkle with the cheese. Serve immediately.

Serves 4

MEXICAN OREGANO I

(Lippia graveolens)

Tender Perennial   Zones 8–10
Native Habitat   Tropical Africa and Latin America

The most popular Mexican oregano for flavoring foods in Mexico, *Lippia graveolens*, is commonly known as *té de pais*, meaning country tea. Growing on rocky clay roadsides, hills, and cliffs from southern Texas and Baja California to Nicaragua, it is one of about two hundred *Lippia* species native to Latin America and Africa. A member of the verbena family, it has oregano's characteristic flavor, a penetrating, creosotelike taste that leaves a tingling, hot sensation on the tongue. This handsome herb grows as an upright shrub with pretty, rough-textured, rich-green ellipical leaves, which bear a strong resemblance to another member of the verbena family, the nonculinary ornamental lantana, which has a rank scent. In summer, minute clusters of cream-colored flowers occur at the leaf bases of L. *graveolens*, to punctuate the green of this herbal shrub.

GROWING YOUR OWN

L. *graveolens* likes full sun and moderately fertile, well-drained, sandy soil. It accepts arid conditions and can grow to 6 feet in hot climates, but it is easy to keep it pruned lower. I prune it to 3½ to 4 feet, about the same height as *Poliomentha longiflora*, another Mexican oregano that is its neighbor in my Zone 10 garden (see next entry). L. *graveolens* is not winter-hardy in cold climates, but gardeners can grow it in a pot so it can overwinter in a sunny greenhouse or indoor window with a southern exposure. Take care to keep the potting soil quite dry, and do not overwater. L. *graveolens* tolerates only light frost even where hardy, and it sometimes dies back during the winter months, but it generally revives in the spring. Seeds of L. *graveolens* are not readily available, so purchase the plant from specialty herb nurseries, and when it is mature it can be propagated from cuttings taken in late summer. A woody shrub, it is best pinched back to encourage branching. Plant lower-growing herbs in front of it to camouflage its long, woody stems, choosing plants that also like soil on the dry side. It looks attractive planted with Greek oregano or other origanums and other interesting lippias such as the lemon-fragrant anise verbena (L. *alba*), the sprawling Aztec sweet herb (L. *dulcis*), or another member of the verbena family, moujean tea (*Nashia inaguensis*), a handsome herb with small, dark green, shiny leaves.

CULINARY USES

The leaves of L. *graveolens* have a dusky lemon-and-camphor flavor, which lends an authentic spicy oregano taste to traditional Mexican dishes such as *guisados*—thick, rich stews—*sopas* such as tortilla soup, and *pozole rojo*, hominy and red chiles simmered with pork. It enhances familiar foods like fresh corn kernels sautéed with diced red and green peppers; black, white, and pinto beans; an herb butter to melt over pattypan squash; and a vinaigrette for a cold beef salad. L. *graveolens* can be dried successfully, and its camphor notes mellow somewhat. An interesting note: carvacrol and thymol, the two chemicals that create the flavor of oregano in plants, are said to contain properties that inhibit bacterial growth, thereby helping to preserve foods.

MEXICAN OREGANO II

(Poliomentha longiflora)

Tender Perennial   Zones 8–10
Native Habitat   Southwestern United States and Mexico

Of the two herbs that are called Mexican oregano, *Poliomentha longiflora,* with its soft, mauve-pink, deep-throated flowers and shiny, lance-shaped, light green leaves, is the more striking. A highly ornamental edible shrub with woody branches, it is also known as rosemary mint, but it tastes like neither rosemary nor mint, although the herb is a member of the mint family, Lamiaceae. Its glossy leaves contain a high amount of carvacrol, resulting in a very spicy, hot oregano flavor. It can grow to 4 feet high and as wide in hot climates like the Southwest. In my garden in midsummer, when it is drenched in pink blossoms, the hummingbirds, sipping its nectar, speedily flit upward to each succeeding flower like a vertical sewing machine making evenly spaced stitches. It's terrific to see your garden so alive, and it is rewarding to know that the plants there are pleasing others besides you!

GROWING YOUR OWN

Poliomentha longiflora grows best in full sun but accepts some afternoon shade. It likes a fast-draining, sandy soil and can tolerate dry conditions. It is hardy only to Zone 8, but gardeners living in cold regions can successfully grow it in a pot and bring it indoors for the winter. Its shiny, glistening leaves and long, tubular dusty-rose flowers make it a stunning container plant for the summer patio. Obtain the plant from specialty herb nurseries, as seed is not readily available. It can be propagated by stem cuttings taken in late summer, overwintered indoors, and planted outdoors the following spring. I keep it pruned to 3½ feet tall in my Zone 10 garden, where it is planted in the ground and dies back somewhat in winter but is generally evergreen. As it has woody stems, I like to underplant it; rigani (*Origanum onites*), sweet marjoram (*Origanum majorana*), and winter savory (*Satureja hortensis*) are good cover-up choices. Adding an "underplanting" of several terra-cotta pots containing the very ornamental Cuban oregano hides the base of *Poliomentha longiflora* in a decorative manner and makes a nice oregano-themed collection.

CULINARY USES

The leaves of *Poliomentha longiflora* are hotter than those of *Lippia graveolens* and somewhat less hot than Greek oregano, one of the origanums (*Origanum vulgare* var. *hirtum*) with a superb culinary flavor. When preparing robust Mexican food, *P. longiflora* lends an appropriately assertive taste to the dishes, although it is equally tasty on Italian (and American) pizza. Commercially, its oils are used in condiments and relishes. To release its unique flavor, the leaves can be toasted in a cast-iron skillet just until their essential oils become fragrant. It can be successfully dried, which makes it just a beat hotter. *P. longiflora* imparts a spicy note to a fresh tomato salsa made hot with chile peppers and sweet with diced avocado; complexity to an herb and spice marinade to rub on grilled chicken; extra flavor to the refried beans that accompany a plate of chiles rellenos; depth to a pot of rich chicken soup; and character to a ceviche made with scallops, mackerel, or other fish fillets. That simple kitchen staple, Chicken Oregano, takes on new meaning when made with this extra spicy Mexican herb.

Roasted Pumpkin Seed Dip with Mexican Oregano I or II

In Mexico, pumpkin seeds are called *pepitas*. Sprinkled with ground New Mexican chile, this unusual spicy dip is an excellent appetizer served with "chips" of sliced jicama and frosty cold Mexican beer or frothy margaritas.

For another recipe using Mexican oregano I or II see page 87, Duck and White Bean Tacos.

2 cups green pumpkin seeds

1 cup finely chopped red onion

1 large clove garlic, finely chopped

1 teaspoon finely chopped fresh Mexican Oregano I or ½ teaspoon finely chopped fresh Mexican Oregano II

2 teaspoons finely chopped culantro (page 80) or cilantro

1 to 2 jalapeño peppers, stemmed, seeded, and finely chopped (optional)

3 to 4 tablespoons lemon juice

½ to ¾ cup chicken stock

Sea salt to taste

In a medium-sized cast-iron skillet, heat the pumpkin seeds over medium heat until they begin to pop and turn golden brown, about 10 minutes. Stir them so they do not burn. Allow to cool. Put the seeds in a food processor fitted with the metal blade and process into a fine meal. Pour the ground seeds into a large bowl and add the onion, garlic, Mexican Oregano, culantro or cilantro, and the jalapeño peppers, stirring well. Add the lemon juice gradually, to taste, then add the chicken stock, thinning the mixture to the desired consistency. Add salt to taste.

Makes 2 cups

PERILLA

(Perilla frutescens)

Annual
Native Habitat   Himalayas to eastern Asia

The ruffled green or purple herb with a startling spicy taste that looks like a frilly basil is actually perilla, an indispensable herb in Oriental cuisine.

Perilla's native habitat is from the Himalayas of India through Myanmar, China, and Korea, to Japan. In ancient China, perilla was eaten as a vegetable, and the oil from the seeds of its purple variety was used—as it is today—both medicinally and in cookery. The Chinese, who call perilla *bai su zi*, introduced it to the Japanese, who adopted it as their own, and today *shiso*, as it is called in Japanese, is widely cultivated in Japan. In the United States, wherever the Japanese have settled, they have planted perilla in cultivated plots; now it also grows wild throughout the eastern part of the country. The flatleaved green variety, *ao-shiso*

(*P. frutescens*), is spicier than the purple cultivar, *aka-shiso* (*P. frutescens* 'Atropurpurea'), and they have a more ornamental frilly-leaved relative, *P. frutescens* 'Crispa', with both green and purple forms. Perilla is also known as beefsteak plant either because of its use as a Japanese garnish or wrapping for beef or because of the similarity in color of the purple form's leaves to red meat—though to my eye it looks more like burgundy wine. In Japan, purple perilla is used to color *umeboshi*, sour pickled plums (actually, small apricots), a deep magenta. It is also used to stain the pale pink strips of ginger that traditionally accompany sushi. The classic uses of the green form of perilla in Japanese cuisine are in sushi rolls, deep fried in tempura batter, and as a fresh garnish.

Tia to is a perilla cultivar with a coat of two colors. On top its leaves are matte green fused with purple, and on the bottom a shade of garnet. This perilla is generally found in cut bunches at Southeast Asian markets. It is especially prized in Vietnamese cookery, where it is used almost exclusively as a salad or garnishing herb. A perilla cultivar with the same markings that is available in plant form from specialty herb catalogs is called 'Bronze' perilla. It has two-tone green and burgundy coloring in its leaves, and in another color variation, plants have a touch of bronze in the center of their new leaves with an iridescent bronze cast on the underside. It is distinguished from the purple and green perillas as the preferred culinary perilla, with a warm, spicy scent. It combines the cinnamon, mint, and lemon notes of green perilla and has a richer flavor.

It should be noted that studies have shown that chemicals in perilla are potent lung toxins, and prolonged skin contact with the plant can cause dermatitis.

GROWING YOUR OWN

Perilla is a self-seeding annual that grows to about 3 feet tall with uniformly veined, broad, pointy leaves 3 to 4 inches long, with serrated edges and square stems, which is characteristic of the mint family. It flourishes in well-drained, moist soil. Pinch back the leaves to encourage bushy growth. To produce the tastiest leaves, amend the soil with rich compost or well-rotted manure. Be aware that snails and slugs also love its leaves. Perilla can be grown in full sun or part shade, but in hot growing regions, partial shade is best. Its wide, picoteed, green, purple, or garnet-and-green duotone leaves make strikingly ornamental plants in the garden. They are visually effective planted near opal basil, Thai, and 'Cinnamon' basil with their purple cast, and pink-flowering hyssop. If you allow the plants to flower, you can use the elongated stems with their dried seedheads to create a decorative contrast in dried flower arrangements. Obtain 'Bronze' perilla as plants from specialty herb catalogs, as seeds are not available commercially. Sow the seeds of the other perillas in the ground either in early spring or in the fall for germination the following spring. Tamp them lightly, as they need light to germinate. Perilla self-sows freely, but volunteers are easy to pull out to keep the population manageable. In my own garden, when the plant is spent I simply lay the dried branches with their seedheads in the area I want them to grow, and I am rewarded the following growing season with more perilla. In order to contain the population of prolific self-sowing perilla, simply cultivate judiciously in the surrounding soil in early spring to uproot or inhibit extra seedlings. Unfussy perilla is easily grown in a container, and I often see the green, purple, and two-tone varieties in pots along with other ethnic herbs on the back doorsteps of Southeast Asian restaurants.

CULINARY USES

Perilla's taste is all its own, but mint, lemon, clove, cinnamon, and basil are flavors associated with the herb. The whole leaves of green perilla enliven soups and can be fried in tempura batter, one of perilla's classic uses. The flowering stems are particularly effective prepared this way. A small handful of fresh seeds makes an unique addition to a soy dipping sauce, and they can also be salted to include with a little dish of pickled vegetables as spicy bites to whet the appetite as a prelude to the meal.

Green perilla goes well with tofu and is a savory addition to vegetables and rice. In cooked dishes, add the herb at the last minute so its essential oils are not diminished. It is tasty in dishes of rice noodles and grilled pork or beef, and its whole leaves can be used as a wrapper for these two meats and for fish. Wrap a 'Bronze' perilla leaf around small shrimp, bite-sized blanched vegetables, or white daikon radishes. The essence of green or bronze perilla can be captured in vinegars to sprinkle on foods when the fresh herbs are not available, as they lose their flavor when dried. An added leaf or two of purple perilla will color the vinegar a deep rose. Purple perilla imparts a spicy flavor and pink color to creative pickling notions—pearl onions, shallots, Egyptian onions, cucumbers, white radishes, turnips, and Chinese artichokes (*Stachys affinis*). Serve these pretty pickles as an hors d'oeuvre platter with soy-lacquered crackers spread with cheddar cheese blended with finely chopped green or 'Bronze' perilla: a savory snack accompanied by little cups of sake.

Avocado Salad with Curried Tofu and 'Bronze' Perilla

This pungent salad is worth the extra effort to obtain some unusual ingredients: *Ume* plum vinegar, made from *umeboshi*, Japanese pickled plums, can be found in Oriental markets or health food stores. Homemade 'Bronze' perilla–flavored vinegar (see page 27) is an excellent replacement. *Shichimi togarashi* is a spicy mix of red pepper, sesame seeds, seaweed, orange peel, and mulberries. It is available in Oriental markets.

1 tablespoon ume *plum vinegar or unseasoned rice vinegar*

Pinch sea salt

Pinch shichimi togarashi *or cayenne pepper*

1 teaspoon curry powder

2 tablespoons safflower oil

1 tablespoon dark sesame oil

1 tablespoon finely chopped 'Bronze' perilla (page 193)

10½ ounces extra firm silken tofu

4 large avocados

1 tablespoon freshly squeezed lemon juice

8 leaves red and green butter lettuce

Toasted white sesame seeds, for garnish

In a small bowl, whisk together the vinegar, salt, *shichimi togarashi* or cayenne pepper, and curry powder. Slowly whisk in the oils until an emulsion is formed, then add the 'Bronze' perilla. Set aside.

Cut the tofu into cubes and place in a food processor fitted with the metal blade. With the machine on, pour the vinegar mixture through the feed tube and purée until smooth. Scrape mixture into a bowl and set aside.

Cut each avocado in half lengthwise. Remove the pits, and peel. Cut each half lengthwise into even slices. Lightly sprinkle the slices with lemon juice to prevent darkening. Line 4 salad plates with the lettuce leaves. Arrange equal portions of the sliced avocados atop the lettuce on each plate. Spoon about 2 tablespoons of the tofu dressing over the avocados, then sprinkle with the toasted sesame seeds.

Serves 4

PURSLANE

(Portulaca oleracea var. sativa and Portulaca oleracea var. aurea)

Annual

Native Habitat   India, the Middle East, Europe

Purslane, a mat-forming plant that hugs the ground and is routinely rooted out of gardens as a weedy troublemaker, is not only a tasty herb, but a beneficial one. It is reportedly the richest source in the plant kingdom of the omega-3 fatty acids, important because they bolster the immune system, and have been found to be effective in maintaining a healthy heart. Purslane's succulent rounded leaves and stems have a sorrel flavor that lends a tart note and a pleasant crunchy bite to foods.

Purslane is not a new herb, but a rediscovered one. In the seventeenth century, Louis XIV delighted in dining on salads of golden purslane, a variety his gardeners cultivated for him. In *The Forme of Cury*, the earliest English cookery manuscript, published around 1390 by the cook or cooks of King Richard II, a savory fresh "salat" included "purslarye" mixed with sage, garlic, fennel, parsley, and rosemary, among other herbs and vegetables. *Pourpier* in French, *verdolagas* in Spanish, *glistritha* in Greek, *Burgelkraut* in German, *porcellana* in Italian, *semizotu* in Turkish, *bahlee* in Arabic, and *pussley* in our early American herb vernacular, purslane has a long culinary history in many countries, and is deserving of greater attention in ours than it has received.

The wild form, *Portulaca oleracea*, originally a native of India, has grown in Europe for centuries. Mentioned by various names in ancient herbals, purslane was held in high esteem by the Assyrians, Greeks, and Arabs, who believed it had the power to chase away magic spells cast upon a person or his—or her—cattle, and if sprinkled around the bed, to chase away evil spirits and erotic dreams. . . .

Purslane was brought to the New World by the colonists (introduced to Massachusetts in 1672). Along with basil, dill, mint, and sage, it was prized in their kitchen gardens as a flavoring herb and a condiment when pickled in vinegar. Culinary purslane is a relative of the popular ornamental garden annual, portulaca, or rose moss (*Portulaca grandiflora*), which has fleshy, needlelike leaves and brilliant red, rose, white, and yellow flowers.

Common purslane, naturalized widely in the United States and southern Canada, is indeed a wild, edible weed that I like to refer to as an "escaped herb" because of its long culinary history. It is invasive because it retains moisture in its fleshy leaves and stores energy in its stems, enabling seeds to mature even after purslane has been uprooted. The allusion to its mat-forming growth habit is referred to in French as *pied de poulet*, or "chicken's foot," and it's probably best to root wild purslane out of your garden, for there are two other varieties with superior taste. Both green purslane (*P. oleracea* var. *sativa*) and golden purslane *P. oleracea* var. *aurea* are readily available in seed catalogs, and these varieties are better behaved in the herb garden than their wild relative. Green purslane has an upright growth habit, is enticing in both form and flavor, and tastes subtly tart with lemon overtones. It grows to about 1 foot tall and 1½ feet wide with clusters of leaves ½ inch long. Golden purslane has larger, light golden-green leaves 1½ inch long, with thicker stems and a more upright growth habit to 1½ feet. Its acerbic flavor is more lemony than green purslane's, and is reminiscent of spinach. Both these varieties, like the wild purslane, are rich in omega-3 fatty acids and are an exceptionally rich source of natural vitamins E and C and calcium and iron.

GROWING YOUR OWN

Purslane is easily grown in average soil in full sun with regular watering. Sow seed in place in the warm spring soil, or seed indoors 6 weeks before the last frost. It also grows well in cold frames during the spring or fall. Sow successive plantings every 3 or 4 weeks to assure a continual supply throughout the growing season. Sow seeds thickly, then prick out the seedlings, leaving the remaining plants 6 to 9 inches apart. The goal is to have tender, succulent leaves to harvest, so keep plants well watered and cut them back often to force new growth. If purslane is allowed to get leggy, snip the plants low on the stem so more leaves will form. As the tiny yellow flowers with little fruit capsules appear, cut them off so the herb does not become tough or go to seed.

Both green and golden purslane can be used as front-of-the-border plants and can be grown in containers, either alone or with other herbs such as basil, golden bay, or golden sage. Purslane planted with other culinary salad herbs such as chives, samphire, arugula, and true French sorrel, or a variety of lettuces with different shapes and colors, creates a pretty container of decorative edibles.

CULINARY USES

Purslane was known as a "cooling herb," according to Nicholas Culpeper, the seventeenth-century English herbalist, which is indeed true, for its fresh leaves and stems impart a citrus note and a pleasant, crunchy snap to mesclun or other salads. The herb can also be cooked as a "potherb," the old-fashioned term for cooked leafy vegetables. Purslane's specific name, *oleracea*, roughly translates as "vegetable herb used in cooking." Exotic ethnic recipes call for purslane cooked with beets, in beef or lamb stews, and as an unusual filling for pastry turnovers. It has a prominent role, along with mint and parsley, in *fattoush*, the savory Middle Eastern bread salad containing chopped cucumber, tomatoes, and onions. It is one of the exotic ingredients used to flavor the Scandinavian spirit, Akvavit. Cooked, versatile purslane tastes delicious in omelettes, soups, and stews of robust meats. In long-cooking dishes its mucilaginous quality becomes evident, and acts as a thickener. Purslane has a special affinity for pork, and in Mexico—where the wild variety is known as *verdolagas*—it is used to make an excellent pork stew with tomatoes, tomatillos, and fresh chiles; the dish is even tastier when made with the cultivated forms. Purslane's culinary attributes give foundation to the story that it was Gandhi's favorite vegetable.

Good Husbandry Summer Salad with Pear Vinaigrette

This bountiful bowl of greens follows the spring version of a good husbandry salad and contains the fruits of the gardener's labor from the summer garden. The addition of purslane with its sprightly tart taste is countered by a sweet pear vinaigrette made with raspberry vinegar. Seasonal edible flowers (make sure they are pesticide-free) decorate the herb greens to make a festive mélange.

For another recipe using purslane, see page 42, Petits Pois with Purslane and Egyptian Onions.

2½ cups lettuce leaves
1 cup fresh green or golden purslane leaves,
  or a combination of the two
½ cup red radicchio leaves
½ cup silene leaves (page 241)
½ cup true French sorrel leaves (page 244)
⅓ cup small magenta lamb's-quarter leaves
  (page 140)

⅓ cup samphire sprigs (page 237)
¼ cup African valerian (page 253)
6 to 8 Belgian endive leaves
Large handful seasonal edible flowers (white
  or blue borage, antique pink pansies, rose
  geranium, superb pink dianthus)

Pear Vinaigrette
2 tablespoons raspberry vinegar
1 tablespoon canned pear nectar

Pinch sea salt and freshly ground white pepper
  to taste
⅓ cup extra virgin olive oil

Wash and dry the lettuces and herbs. Tear the lettuces into bite-sized pieces and place in a large bowl. Add the herbs and Belgian endive leaves. Gently wash the flowers and pat them dry with paper towels. Place them on a fresh paper towel and reserve them in the refrigerator while the dressing is being prepared.

To make the pear vinaigrette, in a small mixing bowl whisk together the raspberry vinegar, pear nectar, sea salt, and white pepper. Slowly whisk in the olive oil until emulsified. Makes ½ cup.

In a large bowl, toss the lettuces, herbs, and Belgian endive with the vinaigrette. Divide among 6 salad plates, then sprinkle the reserved flowers over each salad. Serve immediately.
Serves 6

RICE PADDY HERB

(*Limnophila aromatica*)

Tender Perennial   Zone 10
Native Habitat   Southern Asia, India, and Australia

A delightfully scented herb with a complex aroma was introduced to the American culinary scene by the Vietnamese communities that settled in the United States. Rice paddy herb is a semiaquatic trailing herb with long, succulent stems. Its name is self-explanatory, as it grows right along the rows of rice plants in the watery rice paddies of Vietnam, and it is also known by the less attractive name, "swamp plant." Its small serrated leaves emit an exotic, florid fragrance with hints of citrus, cinnamon, and curry and defy taste comparisons to other culinary herbs. The leaves grow in whorls of three at intervals along the lax stems, with pretty, ½-inch-long, pale lavender-blue flowers with cream-colored throats blooming at the ends. The herb grows to about 1 foot high. Known as *ngo om* in Vietnam, the whole herb is eaten both fresh and cooked, and is indispensable in Vietnamese sweet-and-sour dishes.

GROWING YOUR OWN

Rice paddy herb, being a semiaquatic plant, prefers mud and shallow standing water, but if this ideal environment cannot be provided, it can nevertheless be grown in fertile soil in full sun or partial shade, in the ground or containers in a protected, damp location. In my Zone 10 garden it grows successfully in moist soil in a semishaded area, but it is equally content in a terra-cotta pot placed just 5 feet away in the identical environment. Mulching helps keep the soil moist. Fertilize regularly with liquid fish emulsion or a balanced, soluble fertilizer. In cold-winter areas the plant can be grown in containers and brought indoors for the winter, or in a greenhouse. Mist the plant often during its stay indoors to increase humidity or provide a saucer filled with pebbles, keeping it wet to provide local humidity. Rice paddy herb can be propagated by stem cuttings. Stems from cut bunches of the fresh herb available in Southeast Asian markets are easily rooted in water. A well-traveled gardening friend shared with me a method that the Vietnamese use to grow rice paddy herb in containers. The hole in the bottom of the pot is plugged with a cork, and holes are drilled in the upper sides of the container, making a nice "swampy" environment for the herb below, yet providing drainage from the top of the pot. He also informed me of another unlikely source for *Limnophila aromatica*—aquarium supply stores.

Planted in the ground, rice paddy herb is attractive grown with other low-growing, rosette-forming plants. In my Zone 10 garden, I grow it next to rampion (*Campanula rapunculus*), culantro, and Labrador violets, which have complementary blue flowers and dark purple shaded leaves, in a narrow, moist border with morning sun and afternoon shade.

CULINARY USES

Rice paddy herb is the traditional companion for Vietnamese curries (stews), especially chicken curry, and soups, such as sweet-and-sour soup. A sprig or two lends an elusive exotic note to a homemade vegetable soup. As in the American South, frog's legs are a delicacy in Vietnam, the difference being that they are paired with rice paddy herb instead of parsley or thyme.

When cooking strong fish or shellfish, rice paddy herb is used to absorb the pungent odors besides lending its flavor to the dish. The herb lends a unique character to vegetable stews or a mélange of roasted summer vegetables. The citrusy character of rice paddy herb blends well with lemon grass to perfume poultry dishes. Boned and sautéed chicken breasts benefit from the herb's unique combination of flavors; strew a confetti of its finely chopped leaves over them just before serving. Chicken legs are removed from the ordinary when dusted with curry powder, sautéed golden, and sprinkled with chopped rice paddy herb.

Fragrant Fish Soup

This exotic soup has the elusive flavor of three herbs popular in Vietnamese cuisine: rice paddy herb, Vietnamese balm, and lemon grass. A surprising element is fresh chunks of pineapple, a refreshing counterpoint to the lusty fish stock. If you live near a Southeast Asian market you can obtain there a spongelike vegetable resembling green bamboo and known as "white carrot" or "greenbriar" (*rau rap mong*); it can be peeled and sliced diagonally to lend interesting texture and an authentic ingredient to this rich, herby soup.

The fresh chiles provide a degree of heat to the soup, so be forewarned that consuming a whole slice is incendiary unless you are a true pepper aficionado!

Bottled *nuoc mam*, the fermented fish sauce of Southeast Asian cuisine that is made from anchovies, can be found in the ethnic foods section of supermarkets, at specialty food shops, and at Oriental markets.

For another recipe using rice paddy herb, see page 83, Asian Pesto.

1 pound red snapper fillets

2 large garlic cloves, chopped

Freshly ground black pepper to taste

4 teaspoons excellent-quality nuoc mam
    (Vietnamese fish sauce)

1 cup boiling water

4 ounces lump tamarind

2 stalks lemon grass, ½ inch thick (page 149)

2 tablespoons vegetable oil

*2 large 'Échalote de Jersey' (page 35) or other
    shallots, thinly sliced*

*1 large tomato, seeded and cut into 1-inch
    squares*

1½ cups fresh pineapple, cut into 1-inch pieces

6 cups water

*2 fresh serrano or Thai chiles, stemmed, and
    sliced diagonally*

¼ cup thinly sliced scallions, green part only

1 cup bean sprouts

2 tablespoons chopped rice paddy herb leaves

*2 tablespoons chopped Vietnamese balm
    (page 255) or spearmint*

Red chile powder (optional)

Lemon wedges, for garnish

Cut the red snapper fillets into strips about 2 inches long and 1 inch wide. Place them in a medium-sized mixing bowl and add the garlic, pepper, and 2 teaspoons of the *nuoc mam*.

Combine well. Place in the refrigerator for 30 minutes to allow the mixture to marinate.

In a small bowl pour boiling water over the tamarind and allow to soften for 20 to 25 minutes. With the back of a wooden spoon, force the tamarind through a *fine* sieve. (There should be 1 heaping tablespoon.) Set aside and reserve.

Cut about 4 inches of each white base of the lemon grass, then slice each stalk in half. Pound the pieces with a kitchen mallet or wooden pestle to release their fragrance. In a large saucepan, heat the vegetable oil and add the lemon grass and shallots. Sauté for 3 or 4 minutes, just until the shallots are soft. Add the tomato and cook for several minutes, until just soft, then stir in the pineapple. Cook for 1 minute, then add the water and bring to a boil over high heat. Stir in the tamarind and remaining 2 teaspoons *nuoc mam*. Reduce the heat and simmer for 5 minutes. Raise heat slightly, and add the serrano or Thai chiles, scallions, and the marinated red snapper. Cook for 3 or 4 minutes, until the red snapper is just cooked through. With a slotted spoon, discard the pieces of lemon grass. Add the bean sprouts, rice paddy herb, and the Vietnamese balm. Combine well, then remove from heat. Allow the soup to sit for several minutes while the flavors blend, then pour into warmed bowls. Sprinkle the chile powder, if being used, over the soup. Garnish with the lemon wedges. Serve immediately. Makes 2 quarts.

Serves 4 to 5

ROMAN MINT

(*Micromeria* species)

Tender Perennial   Zones 5–10
Native Habitat   The Canary Islands, the Mediterranean basin region, the
Caucasus to the Himalayas, and southwest China

It is always a delight to discover a new herb to cook with, and many are mentioned in pass-
ing in cookbooks featuring a particular region of the world. Just such a reference was made
by the food authority Giuliano Bugialli in his 1984 book, *Foods of Italy*, to nepitella, also
known as *mentuccia*, a wonderfully savory herb that grows wild in the Italian countryside. He
pronounced it indispensable when preparing mushrooms, as well as potatoes and young June
peas. Curious, I conducted some herbal sleuthing and discovered that the herb was calamint
(*Calamintha nepeta*), native to southern Europe and the Mediterranean basin. An Italian
friend directed me to the classic Italian cookbook *La Scienza in Cucina e L'arte di Mangiar
Bene* (*Science in Cooking and the Art of Eating Well*) by Pellegrino Artusi, and there I found a

simple recipe for nepitella and mushrooms. My friend, an Italian chef, confirmed the delight of seasoning foods with nepitella but had never seen it in this country, so he just substituted apple mint where he wanted its flavor. By summer's end, I had six plants of "nepitella" growing in my garden. Obtained from four specialty herb catalogs and nurseries, there were three calamints plus a closely related *Micromeria* species known as Roman mint, as well as another *Micromeria* species called emperor's mint, and each had only a slightly different flavor. One summer day, Giuliano Bugialli himself paid a serendipitous visit to my garden, escorted by a mutual friend who was as curious about the herb as I was. I asked Bugialli to conduct a test: Which one, if any, was nepitella? He tried them all, and Roman mint won, hands down. To my taste buds, the difference in flavor was so slight as to be almost undetectable. As gardener and cook you can be the judge, as all of the above minty herbs are available from specialty herb nurseries.

In the rural Italian countryside, sprigs of nepitella are often included with the purchase of wild mushrooms, so complementary are the two considered to be. References to the fragrant *erba da funghi*, or mushroom grass, as nepitella is known in Italy, usually pertain to calamint, the taste of which is so subtly similar to that of Roman mint. Two other culinary calamints of note that are available from specialty herb catalogs are called 'Pompeii' and 'Niebita'. The late writer and Italian food authority Angelo Pelligrini considered that nepitella is to mushrooms what dill is to pickles.

GROWING YOUR OWN

Both roman mint and calamint have the same cultural requirements. In its third growing season, the Roman mint in my Zone 10 garden, initially planted from a plant in a 3-inch pot, had grown to 5 feet wide and 1½ feet tall; the calamint was only somewhat smaller, though not as wide. Roman mint's inch-long, rounded, rich gray-green opposite leaves are evenly spaced on long branches, and when the plant is in bloom, summer through fall, it has an icing of the palest lavender-blue tubular blossoms. Calamint has similar round leaves, which are slightly toothed, and its flowers are whitish lilac. The herbs can be planted in average garden soil with good drainage; add sand or gravel to achieve this, if necessary. They are not fussy and like only moderate watering. They will grow in full sun, but prefer afternoon shade, especially in hot climates. Initially, obtain plants of of these herbs from specialty nurseries, and when they are established, they can be propagated by root division or cuttings. Cut back after the first flowering and apply a side-dressing of well-rotted manure to promote a lush second growth. In cold-winter areas, protect them with a mulch of pine boughs after the ground has frozen.

Brushing by a graceful mound of Roman mint or calamint is a fragrant experience, and their low-bush form makes a handsome edging or attractive, soft border planting. Cascading over a stone wall, Roman mint planted alongside prostrate rosemary produces quite a visual show. Both mints can spend several seasons in a container before repotting, and the branches drape gracefully over the edges. Perhaps the delightful minty fragrance of both herbs is the reason they are so notably disease-free.

CULINARY USES

Both Roman mint and calamint are reminiscent of sweet spearmint with a little spice added, like mild oregano or winter savory. Because of this complexity of taste, use these mints sparingly. Calamint is mentioned in many herb books as an herb tea, but it contains an active ingredient, pulegone, that is known to cause abortion. Calamint and Roman mint are so similar in taste that neither should be used by pregnant women.

Mushrooms seem to be the best partner for the herbs, but vegetables such as zucchini and artichokes benefit equally from their minty flavor, as do the aforementioned peas and potatoes. Cooked with braised rabbit and other game such as quail and duck, a few sprigs impart a delightful savory flavor to the dishes. In France, a wild mint called *la nepita* sounds suspiciously like the Italian nepitella; it flavors fine omelettes stuffed with fresh, soft sheep's milk cheese. The minty notes of sweet basil are a complement to Roman mint's own.

Polenta Canapés with Mushrooms and Roman Mint Sauce

This recipe was adapted from one created by my friend, the angelic Italian chef Celestino Drago. The polenta canapés can be served singly with the mushroom topping and a dab of the sauce, or as a zesty first course "sandwich," by stacking 2 canapés on top of one another with the mushroom filling in between, and garnished with radicchio leaves.

Polenta

6½ cups water

Pinch sea salt

2 tablespoons butter

1½ cups imported polenta

Mushrooms

2 tablespoons butter or extra virgin olive oil

¾ pound cremini mushrooms, washed, stemmed, and thinly sliced

Sea salt and cayenne pepper to taste

Roman Mint Sauce

1 can (15.5 ounces) garbanzo beans

½ cup liquid from the can of garbanzo beans

2 tablespoons extra virgin olive oil

1 clove garlic, finely chopped

1 tablespoon freshly squeezed lemon juice

1 tablespoon Roman mint leaves, finely chopped (spearmint can be substituted, although it won't have the exact flavor of Roman mint)

Sea salt and cayenne pepper to taste

Roman mint sprigs, tomato concassé, and radicchio leaves, for garnish

To make the polenta, oil a 1½-quart rectangular loaf pan (11½ × 4½ × 2½ inches). In a 4-quart saucepan, bring the water to a boil, then add the salt and butter. When the water returns to the boil, slowly add the polenta in a thin, steady stream, stirring with a whisk. Reduce the heat to low, and with a long-handled wooden spoon, cook, stirring continuously, until the polenta has thickened and pulled away from the side of the pot, about 30 minutes. Pour the hot polenta into the loaf pan, and smooth with a rubber spatula. Set aside and allow to cool.

To prepare the mushrooms, melt the butter in a large sauté pan. Add the mushrooms. Cover and cook over medium heat until they release their liquid, about 5 minutes. Remove the cover and sauté for 3 to 4 minutes, until the liquid has evaporated and the mushrooms are lightly browned. Add salt and pepper to taste. Set aside in the covered sauté pan.

Preheat the oven to 300 degrees.

For the Roman mint sauce, drain the garbanzo beans, pouring a ½ cup of the liquid from the can into a small saucepan. Cover and warm the liquid over low heat. In a medium-sized saucepan, heat 1 tablespoon of the olive oil and add the garlic. Cook just until the garlic releases its fragrance. Add the garbanzo beans. Cover and cook over low heat for 5 minutes. In a food processor fitted with the metal blade, purée the warm garbanzo beans and garlic. Pouring the warmed garbanzo bean liquid into the food processor through the feed tube, process the garbanzo bean mixture until smooth. Add the lemon juice, Roman mint, salt, and cayenne pepper. Pour in the remaining 1 tablespoon olive oil and process for a few seconds. Return the mixture to the saucepan and cover. Place the saucepan in another larger pan filled with water over low heat to form a water bath.

Unmold the polenta loaf. With a sharp knife, cut the polenta lengthwise into slices ⅓ inch thick. With a 2¼-inch-diameter cookie cutter, stamp 4 rounds from each slice of the polenta and place them on a baking sheet lined with parchment paper. Place the chopped mushrooms on 6 of the polenta rounds. Heat all the rounds in the oven for 10 to 15 minutes, until they are thoroughly warm.

To assemble the sandwiches, spoon the warm Roman mint sauce over the mushroom-topped polenta rounds, then crown each one with the other half of the polenta. Place the canapés on radicchio leaves, and garnish each serving with tomato concassé and fresh sprigs of Roman mint. Place the remaining mint sauce in a warm bowl to serve at table.

Makes about 6 double-faced canapé sandwiches

ROSELLE

(Hibiscus sabdariffa)

Tropical Annual   Zones 8–11
Native Habitat   Tropical Asia and Africa

Many people unfamiliar with the name "roselle" have undoubtedly enjoyed its tart flavor and vivid, ruby-red color in the popular herb tea known as Red Zinger. Widely cultivated and naturalized throughout the tropics, roselle is known as jamaica, Jamaica sorrel, Indian sorrel, and Guinea sorrel. If you browse through books on Caribbean cookery, you are apt to come across a drink simply called "sorrel," prepared not with true French or garden sorrel, but with roselle. It is called *rosa de Jamaica* in Spanish, and *vinagreira* in Portuguese. Africans make a tart, currant-colored tea with roselle that they call not Red Zinger, but *karkadé*. In Japan, roselle's fleshy heads are sometimes a refreshing substitute for *umeboshi*, the extremely tart pickled plums so popular in that cuisine. In the United States, roselle is also called

"Florida cranberry," which gives a hint as to one of its uses: a tart condiment to accompany turkey and other poultry, game, and meat.

Roselle is a handsome shrub that can grow to 5 feet tall. It has large, flat, lobed leaves that look like wide green hands, and small, ivory-yellow flowers. Its fleshy red flower parts are the main reason to grow roselle for culinary use. They are as beautiful in the herb garden on their carmine-streaked stems, nestled against the plant's dark green leaves, as is the rich garnet color they release into food and drink. In botanical parlance, it is actually the calyx that is collected for use—the plump outer covering of the ripened fruit.

GROWING YOUR OWN

Roselle requires a long growing season, for it does not bloom until the hours of daylight are reduced in the fall to less than 11 hours. To provide the longest possible growing season, sow seed indoors in early winter for planting out when the weather has warmed the soil, or sow directly into the ground in the spring. Roselle can also be propagated by cuttings. It likes average soil, moderate water, full sun, and hot summers. Feed it once a month with liquid fish emulsion or a balanced soluble fertilizer at half strength during the growing season. Those living in regions with short growing seasons should not despair, for the packaged dried herb labeled "jamaica," is readily available in markets stocking Latin American products; in stores selling herbal teas it is sometimes labeled "hibiscus flowers."

CULINARY USES

The simplest preparation for roselle is an infusion of its dried calyxes strained into a tall frosted glass, and sweetened to taste, for a lovely iced roselle tea. This pretty, rose-colored beverage will undoubtedly inspire you to consider other ways to use the refreshingly tart herb. In the Caribbean, the infusion is known as "red sorrel," a drink, that is particularly popular during the Christmas holidays during the rounds of gift-giving visits, probably much like our traditional holiday eggnog. The popular drink is also enjoyed fortified with herbs and spices; with other stronger fortifications such as rum, it is perfect as a cooler on a steamy, hot afternoon. In the tropics, fresh roselle is combined with sugar to make a thick jam that resembles cranberry sauce in taste and texture, an interesting idea for a departure from the ever-traditional Thanksgiving relish. A liquid infusion of roselle's lemon-acid calyxes mixed with white wine and olive oil makes an excellent marinade for poultry and game, quail in particular. Roselle makes a tangy-sweet jelly, and a syrup to pour over sweetened ricotta cheese–filled crepes. Indian and Southeast Asian curries benefit from its mouth-puckering flavor. In the culinary lore of the West Indies, its seeds have been used as a substitute for coffee. Besides making a tasty brew, the drink—whether myth or reality—was considered an aphrodisiac.

Roselle Rum Fizz

The ruby red color of this refreshing summer drink is as lush as its taste. The rich flavor of ginger gives it a feel of the tropics, and it is so festive, it would be perfectly permissible to garnish it with a little colored paper umbrella or other frivolity.

1 cup dried roselle calyxes
2 tablespoons freshly grated ginger
4½ cups water
1 cup brown sugar

1 cup Mount Gay Barbados rum
1 cup ginger ale
Fresh sprigs of pineapple sage (see page 233),
* for garnish*

Place roselle and ginger in a stainless steel bowl. Boil 3½ cups of the water and pour it over the roselle mixture. Cover the bowl and allow mixture to steep for 4 hours. In a small saucepan, bring the remaining 1 cup water and the brown sugar to a boil, stirring until the sugar is dissolved. Remove the pan from the heat and allow the sugar syrup to cool. Strain roselle mixture through a fine-mesh sieve into a pitcher. Add the cooled sugar syrup in increments, according to the desired sweetness. Add the rum and ginger ale. Fill 6 glasses with ice cubes, then pour in the mixture. Garnish with the pineapple sage, and serve immediately.
Serves 6

Rosemary

An herb garden without rosemary is unthinkable. The familiar resinous herb from the dry hills and scrub of the Mediterranean region is the linchpin of design in our ornamental gardens and the aromatic and flavorful focal point in our culinary herb gardens. Long cultivated in European and North American herb gardens, rosemary is also popular in unexpected places. It is widely grown in home gardens in Central and South America, where it has both culinary and other applications. In Curaçao, its dried leaves are used for preparing a decoction used to shampoo hair, with the hope of avoiding baldness. In Cuba, a paste of rosemary stems crushed with ginger is placed between a folded cloth and tied around one's head to cure insomnia. In folklore, rosemary's flowers scattered over the bed supposedly protected the dreamer from nightmares; and carrying powdered rosemary, with its aroma of heliotrope and pine, in the pocket made one "merry, glad, gracious and well-beloved of all men." How true.

This enduring herb is the symbol of fidelity and of remembrance, so said Mr. Shakespeare. In days past, rosemary sprigs were part of a bride's bouquet, placed there to ensure the fidelity of the groom—and thus her happiness. Rosemary's piney scent flavors many commercial foods: baked goods, meat and meat products, condiments, relishes, snack foods, gravies, and alcoholic and nonalcoholic beverages. Although the formula is kept secret, Chartreuse, the light-green liqueur made by the Carthusian monks since 1607, is thought to contain rosemary. Rosemary's fragrant notes are used in cosmetics as well, and constitute a subtle element of the venerable eau de Cologne.

Rosemary, the herb with a wealth of human history in its genes, known since the time of Dioscorides, is generally thought of as an "an upright herb with shiny, dark green, needlelike camphorous leaves and blue flowers," and this does aptly describe *Rosmarinus officinalis*. Variety is the spice of life though, and there are many other rosemary varieties with differences in leaf, flower, size, color, and manner of growth. Garden writers have extolled rosemary as "an exotic plant that has been cherished and cultivated for its quiet beauty in the garden." The following are two uncommon rosemaries to cherish for the same reason.

'GOLDEN RAIN' ROSEMARY

(*Rosmarinus officinalis* 'Joyce DeBaggio' syn. *R. officinalis* 'Golden Rain')

Tender Perennial   Zones 8–10
Native Habitat The Mediterranean region

A lucky discovery for all gardeners occurred when a stem sporting golden-margined leaves with a thin green strip down the center showed up on an otherwise standard green rosemary, as plantsman Thomas DeBaggio observed in his nursery. 'Golden Rain' rosemary was born, giving gardeners a shining, golden-green shrub to use as an accent in the herb garden or to complement other plants in the landscape, and another mottled leaf to study for those who are fascinated by the serendipitous designs of variegated-leaved plants.

'Golden Rain' grows to 5 feet tall; it has all the culinary attributes of common rosemary, but a better branching habit. In the landscape, 'Golden Rain' combines handsomely with pineapple and other sages, oregano, golden marguerite, feverfew, Mexican tarragon, fernleaf tansy, fringed lavender (*Lavandula dentata*), and the artemisias. A planting of 'Golden Rain' with other variegated herbs and perennials makes a stunning theme bed, and a challenging one to design. Such a brilliant, sunny bed could include golden sage, golden sweet bay, golden marjoram, and golden lemon thyme, with bronze fennel, yellow coreopsis, costmary, and Roman chamomile as accents.

For a recipe using 'Golden Rain' rosemary, see page 247, True French Sorrel Vichyssoise.

'MAJORCA PINK' ROSEMARY

(Rosmarinus officinalis 'Majorca Pink')

Tender Perennial Zones 8–10

Native Habitat The Mediterranean region

The amethyst-pink flower of 'Majorca Pink' rosemary from the Balearic Islands in the Spanish Mediterranean is one of the richest in color to be found among the pink-flowering rosemaries. Similar in its growth habit to common rosemary, but with an arching columnar habit, its blossoms are tiny gems nestled next to its shorter resinous leaves. It grows to about 4 feet high and several feet wide. It looks especially effective planted next to white-flowering rosemary (*R. officinalis* 'Albus') and blue-flowering rosemary such as *R. officinalis* 'Severn Sea', both of which accentuate the color of its vivid pink blossoms. Lavenders, santolina, the artemisias such as Roman wormwood and 'Silver King' and 'Silver Queen', sages, oreganos, and both blue- and white-flowering borage are good companions that like similar, dry growing conditions.

GROWING YOUR OWN

Plant 'Golden Rain' and 'Majorca Pink' rosemary in full sun, in light, well-drained average soil with a pH range from 5 to 8. They can be planted in the spring when the weather has warmed in all regions, and in the spring or fall in Zone 10. In warmer climates, they will accept some high shade. Apply a general all-purpose fertilizer in early spring. A little bone-meal added at planting time will stimulate root growth. Once established they like only moderate watering; excessive water causes rank, woody growth, and root rot. Pinch back 2 or 3 inches of the tips of the stems during the growing season to promote bushy plants, but cut back hard only in early spring to give the new growth time to mature.

Obtain plants of both rosemarys from specialty herb nurseries, and when mature they can be propagated by layering or stem cuttings. Cuttings are best taken from vigorous spring growth. Both rosemarys are evergreen in Zone 10. In cold-winter climates, they can be grown outdoors in containers in the summer and brought indoors before a hard frost. Rosemary is best overwintered in a greenhouse, but when grown indoors, set the plants in a cool spot with good air circulation; mist the leaves regularly, and water the roots minimally. In humid southeastern gardens where rosemary is prone to root rot, mulch 'Golden Rain' and 'Majorca Pink' with 2 or 3 inches of pecan shells, rice hulls, or pea gravel to help protect them from soil-borne diseases. They can be grown in large containers or in raised beds and mulched with the same materials to keep the roots cool. Actinovate TM, a concentrate of beneficial soil microorganisms, helps ward off wilt problems when applied to the soil before planting.

CULINARY USES

In trendy restaurants, the presence of sprigs of rosemary infusing little puddles of extra virgin olive oil in which to dip crusty bread in place of butter attests to the herb's continuing popularity. Like oregano, parsley, and thyme, rosemary has myriad culinary uses. Starting with the hors d'oeuvre, whole salted pecans can be toasted with finely chopped rosemary and a dash of paprika, and eggplant caponata can be dusted with minced rosemary before being spread on toast rounds. For an entrée, chicken breasts can be sautéed with prosciutto and rosemary; the classic combination of rosemary with lamb can take a new turn when lamb is coated with storebought plum jam infused with rosemary sprigs—or try pouring the same mixture over poached fruit for dessert. For vegetables, a pinch of fresh rosemary enlivens chopped spinach, and sliced potatoes roasted with rosemary are succulent and hearty. Biscuits made with finely chopped rosemary and sharp cheddar cheese added to the dough are a savory accompaniment to a meal. Rosemary combines well with fish, shellfish, chicken, game, pork, and beef. Did we miss anything? Both 'Golden Rain' and 'Majorca Pink' make an excellent contribution to cranberry vinegar—a marriage of assertive tastes good in salad dressings for crunchy radicchio, escarole, and frisée lettuces; in braised red cabbage; and in a tangy marinade.

Place a whole sprig of rosemary in the soup pot instead of chopping it, then remove, in the manner of bay leaves, when it has done its job. With rosemary, remember the adage "A little goes a long way." The essential oils contained in its leathery leaves produce a warm, resinous taste, which if used with a light hand can make a dish sing with flavor.

Rosemary retains its flavor when dried, and it is always handy to have on the herb shelf— it may be raining or snowing outside, preventing you from plucking. Always crush or crumble the leaves of dried rosemary, as it is unpleasant to find "needles" in your food.

Swordfish with 'Majorca Pink' Rosemary

Rosemary 'Majorca Pink' infuses swordfish with a pine-scented aroma after brief marinating, and then the fish can be broiled, grilled, or sautéed. Strew the pink flowers lightly over the dish for a lovely garnish.

1 cup olive oil
2 tablespoons lemon juice
Big pinch sea salt
Cayenne pepper to taste
¼ cup fresh 'Majorca Pink' rosemary leaves
  and soft stems

4 swordfish steaks, 1 inch thick
  (about 5 ounces each)
4 teaspoons finely chopped 'Majorca Pink'
  rosemary, plus a handful of its flowers
  if in bloom, for garnish
Lemon wedges

In a large, deep platter, combine the olive oil, lemon juice, salt, and cayenne pepper. Stir to combine. Add the rosemary and bruise with a wooden pestle, then combine mixture again. Rinse the swordfish and pat it dry. Turn each steak over in the marinade to coat well. Cover and refrigerate for 1 hour, turning the swordfish once after 30 minutes.

Place the swordfish on a broiler pan. Broil about 6 inches from the heat, then turn the fish after 5 minutes. Continue to broil until its flesh is opaque when cut in the thickest part, about 5 minutes more. Remove to 4 warmed plates. Sprinkle 1 teaspoon of the chopped rosemary over each serving. Garnish with flowers and lemon wedges. Serve immediately.

Serves 4

Cranberry Vinegar with 'Golden Rain' Rosemary

The tart, assertive taste of cranberry meets its match with the pine-scented, assertive taste of 'Golden Rain' rosemary in this berry-red herb vinegar.

2 cups fresh or frozen cranberries
3 cups white wine vinegar
Sugar to taste
2 cups 'Golden Rain' rosemary leaves and
   soft stems

Place the cranberries and the vinegar in a medium-sized saucepan. Bring to a boil, and simmer until the cranberries pop. Add sugar to taste. Set aside to cool.

Strain the mixture through a fine sieve, discarding the cranberries. Pour the cranberry vinegar into a sterilized wide-mouthed jar with a nonreactive lid. Rinse the rosemary, and pat dry with paper towels. Add it to the jar, making sure all the leaves are submerged. Cover tightly and place in a cool, dark place for 1 week. Taste the vinegar, and if a stronger infusion is desired, allow to stand for 1 more week. When the rosemary has infused the vinegar to suit your taste, strain the vinegar through a fine sieve, discarding the rosemary. Pour the vinegar into a sterilized glass bottle and seal with a cork or nonreactive lid. Fresh rosemary sprigs may be added for decor. Store and use within 3 months.

Makes about 3 cups

SAFFRON

(Crocus sativus)

Perennial   Zones 6–9
Native Habitat   Thought to be the eastern Mediterranean

The familiar vivid violet saffron crocus that gardeners associate with autumn is probably the culinary garden's most exotic herb. Only a few of its thin scarlet stigmas will color and flavor an entire pot of rice, and just a little more colors and flavors two larger signature saffron dishes, risotto and paella. Calendula, safflower, and turmeric will color rice like saffron, but nothing *but* saffron will impart that alluring, oddly metallic, slightly addicting saffron taste. Technically, saffron is called "true saffron," and for good reason, for it is often adulterated with safflower and calendula (causing these innocent herbs to be known as "false saffron" and "poor man's saffron," respectively) and other "untrue" ingredients. The facts astound regarding just how many man- and woman-hours it takes to plant and pick and cure a pound of saffron (200), and how many stigmas of the "saffron rose" are in a pound (about 75,000); it would be more astonishing if it took any less work, for if you have ever picked the stigmas from your own saffron crocus, you appreciate firsthand the effort to pluck more than 10. But even if you collect just enough to color only one pot of golden rice, your reward is that *you* grew the saffron that flavored the dish, and that you have a representative of the true saffron industry in your garden.

This unassuming, pretty purple flower that heralds autumn with springlike blossoms and vermilion filaments occupies an impressive position in both ancient and modern history; Homer wrote of the "saffron-robed morn," and the author of the biblical Song of Solomon describes "an orchard of pomegranates with all choicest fruits . . . and saffron, calamus and cinnamon, with all trees of frankincense and myrrh and aloes, with all chief spices." Today saffron is associated with the culinary arts, but historically it has been linked with medicine, religion, perfumery, and cosmetics and—in one of its most exotic applications—used as a brilliant natural golden dye. According to Irish folklore, women dyed their bed linens with saffron as it was considered that lying between golden sheets would strengthen their limbs. Its wealth of attributes both aesthetic and utilitarian appear to qualify saffron as both herb and spice.

GROWING YOUR OWN

Saffron crocuses grow from flattened corms that can be obtained when bulbs and other corms begin to appear in nurseries in the fall, but to assure good quality and the best selection, order them from a specialty bulb nursery in early summer, and they will be delivered at the proper time according to your growing zone. A white form of saffron crocus not easily obtained from garden center shelves is available through specialty bulb or herb nurseries, and it makes a lovely autumn planting when combined with the vivid purple crocus. In late summer, plant the corms in rich, loamy soil that is well drained, one of saffron crocus's most important needs, for it will rot in soil with poor drainage. In warm-winter growing climates, plant saffron crocus by mid-September. Grow them in full sun or dappled shade. Plant the corms several inches apart, and 3 times their size in depth. When growth begins, feed them with a balanced soluble fertilizer and water during their growing season when the soil becomes dry. Slender, grasslike foliage with a white midrib follows the flowers. Do not cut the leaves back, for that is where the energy for next year's growth is stored. Simply allow them to die back naturally. Provide a mulch in cold-winter growing zones where there are hard freezes.

Propagate saffron crocus by dividing the corms every few years during the summer when dormant. Mark the area so you will know where the corms are when they are dormant. Plant them in a bed of plants that don't need much summer water; also, choose an area where the plant companions will not obscure the late fall view of the pretty, ground-hugging saffron crocus. Some ideal spots are in between stepping stones, in a rock garden, at the front of a small border, under trees, or in containers, where a mass planting of saffron is especially effective. To harvest your saffron "crop," collect the three red stigmas from each blossom with a pair of tweezers as early in the morning as possible. Place the stigmas on a sheet of paper and dry in a cool dark place. Store in an airtight vial, *not* the refrigerator. *Crocus sativus* is the only crocus that produces edible stigmas; no other part of the plant is edible. Do not confuse saffron crocus with the larger, and poisonous, autumn crocus, or meadow saffron (*Colchicum autumnale*), which blooms at the same time.

CULINARY USES

Saffron threads need to be "activated" to release their unique taste and aroma. Good liquid vehicles for doing this are warm water; lemon, lime, or orange juice; white wine or other alcohol (red wine is too heavy to use with saffron); stock; vinegar; and rose or orange water. Generally, a 20-minute soaking is sufficient to release the dye and flavor. When recipes call for ground saffron, toast the threads over low heat for about 2 minutes in a heavy, light-colored skillet and grind them with mortar and pestle. Use only glass mortars and pestles or plastic utensils when working with dried saffron, as wooden ones "eat up" some of the precious saffron. Half a teaspoon of threads will crush down to ⅛ teaspoon powdered saffron. When combining saffron in sauces, butters, and dressings, do not use a whisk, as the valuable threads will stick to the wire. Instead, use a fork or spoon.

Handmade pasta made with a healthy pinch of saffron is a most glamorous dish in which to "paint" with saffron, and the gilded strands glisten on the plate. Saffron butter is excellent melted over vegetables, and elegant poured over salmon. Scalloped potatoes have an affinity for saffron; as they bake they are imbued with a beautiful yellow hue. Saffron vichyssoise is as visually stunning as it is delicious, and a plain vegetable soup takes on unique taste notes when saffron is cooked with the stock. Saffron is a classic in mussel soup and bouillabaisse, and in breads and rice. Powdered saffron, cardamom, cinnamon, rosewater, and toasted slivered almonds make rice pudding a dessert treat as exotic as they come.

Saffron Faux Mayo

This is not a true mayonnaise because it is made with just egg whites for today's health-conscious cook. To make the yolkless sauce a little regal, saffron is added, which imparts its unique slightly bitter flavor and tints the mayonnaise with a subtle hue of the herb's signature vermilion color.

1 large egg white

2 tablespoons lemon juice

⅛ teaspoon crushed saffron strands

2 tablespoons water

3 teaspoons Dijon mustard

1 cup canola oil

Sea salt and cayenne pepper to taste

In a small jar, shake together the egg white, lemon juice, and saffron. Cover tightly. Refrigerate the mixture for 1 hour while the saffron "bleeds." Place the mixture in a blender or a food processor fitted with the metal blade. Add the water and Dijon mustard. Blend the ingredients for several seconds, then, adding the oil in a thin stream, process until the mixture has thickened. Add salt and cayenne pepper, and process again for several seconds. Spoon the mayonnaise into a sterilized jar and cover tightly. Store in the refrigerator for up to 2 weeks.

Makes 1 generous cup

Sage

The generic name for sage, *Salvia*, is derived from the Latin word *salvere*, meaning "safe," also translated as "in good health." Down through the ages since medieval times, garden sage (*Salvia officinalis*), probably the most well known herb in the salvia group, has been used as a popular household remedy for numerous minor ills. Over 750 species of sage are widely distributed throughout the world. They are beloved for their ornamental beauty in the garden and are valued for their medicinal properties and use in perfumery and cosmetics, both the commercial and homemade fresh-from-the-garden varieties. But perhaps most of all they are appreciated for the distinctive flavor they impart to foods. Each of the two following sages lends its own unique perfume to a wide variety of culinary dishes.

CLEVELAND SAGE

(Salvia clevelandii)

Tender Perennial   Zones 8–10

Native Habitat   Coastal and inland foothills of San Diego County, California

"Aromatic shrub" barely describes the overwhelming pungency of Cleveland sage. This is one herb that doesn't need the "pinch and sniff" offering when you tour your garden with visitors. Just walking in its vicinity lets you know you are definitely in its fragrant territory. And its looks are as sensational as its scent is pervasive. One of the more showy native sages, Cleveland has rounded thistlelike flower clusters with vivid lavender blue tubular petals exploding at intervals along its stems. It grows to about 4 feet high and 4 to 5 feet wide. Its strongly veined, elliptical 1-to-2-inch-long leaves look like pebbly gray-green suede. My impression of its strong sage aroma on a very hot day is reminiscent of the Thanksgiving dressing my mother always made with too much dried sage. But it's an unfair overall culinary assessment, for Cleveland sage is a good savory herb to use in cooking. Just a few leaves can permeate a whole game hen or roasting chicken. Hummingbirds don't put it in chicken, but they can't seem to get enough of the rich blue sage blossoms, for they furiously flutter around them constantly when the plants are in bloom from May to August. At the end of the season, the lingering dried flower clusters, sans petals, left behind on the stalks serve two purposes: they form a tall, natural garden ornament in the late-summer-to-fall garden, and the long stems with bark-brown pom-poms can be used in dried-flower arrangements. Cleveland sage is named after the botanist and taxonomist Daniel Cleveland, who was a collector of the plant in San Diego County.

GROWING YOUR OWN

In mild-winter climates, Cleveland sage is best planted in late fall to take advantage of the ensuing seasonal rains and cooler weather, perfect conditions for it to begin to set down a deep root system, which ultimately allows it to survive with little or no water. Obtain plants from specialty or native plant nurseries. Amend the soil with organic compost so the ratio is one third amendment and two thirds soil. Add a tablespoon of a slow-release fertilizer to the planting hole. A 3-to-6-inch mulch of shredded wood or leaf litter will help hold in moisture and lower soil temperatures. Water the newly planted sage during its first season once a week or every 10 days with a good soaking until the rainy season begins. The following summer, a good soaking every three weeks should be sufficient. In its second summer it should be thoroughly established with minimal need for water.

Cleveland sage flourishes in full sun in well-drained soil, which approximates the fast-draining gritty slopes of the chaparral plant community that is its native habitat. It has a rangy growth pattern, so underplant it with other herbs or ornamentals. Just make sure they can also survive without much water. In my dry garden area, its gray-green leaves and flaxen blue flowers look great with the greenish-yellow flowerheads of yellow lavender (*Lavandula viridis*) at its feet, and salvia 'Plum Wine' planted next to it provides eye-catching pinpoints of vivid red color pushing up through Cleveland sage's spreading canopy, all the better to show off its lavender-blue flowers. Equally rugged complementary companions are *Jasminum odoratissimum*, with its small, butter yellow flowers and dark green shiny leaves; the brilliant yellow flower balls and fat, green-felted leaves of Jerusalem sage (which is not a true sage, but *Phlomis fruticosa*); blazing orange-flowered lion's tail (*Leonotis leonurus*); and the green and silver of santolina. The flowering stems of purple or yellow butterfly bush towering behind

Cleveland sage create quite a fanciful garden show with the attendant fluttering butterflies and swooping hummingbirds cavorting around on a summer day.

While Cleveland sage is most effective planted in the ground in a large gardening area to contain its spread, there are several more compact named selections suitable for growing in less space. *Salvia clevelandii* 'Winifred Gilman' and *S. clevelandii* 'Allen Chickering' grow to about 3 feet. These two sages produce lusher foliage, as they will accept more summer water, but they will be shorter-lived.

Cleveland sage and its progeny can be grown in containers, allowing gardeners below Zone 8 to grow it and overwinter it indoors or in a greenhouse. It creates an uncommon and highly scented focal point in the garden. Choose large clay or concrete containers to provide ample room for the roots, planted with a fast-draining, lightweight potting soil mixed with controlled-release fertilizer. Unlike when it is planted in the ground, in a container, Cleveland sage will need to be watered regularly, with a light application of organic fertilizer in the spring. Allow the soil to dry out slightly between waterings.

CULINARY USES

Perhaps no other herb besides rosemary has such immediate scent associations as sage. If just the word brings to mind its well-known scent, multiply that by several times when in the presence of Cleveland sage. As a native herb, it has strong, resinous, menthol, and camphor notes when fresh. Dried, its subtle tones diminish, and the musky character of the herb is more pronounced—of which there can be no doubt in your sage-scented kitchen after you have dried it in the microwave oven. Cleveland sage, as well as other sages, should be used with a light hand because of the strong essential oil in its leaves, thujone. The assertive aroma and scent of Cleveland sage is excellent in rich dishes such as pork roast, stuffed duck with apples and onions, the Christmas goose, and of course the Thanksgiving turkey and its stuffing. Try it in a stuffing with another native, the pecan, along with sausage and dried fruits, or in a plain cornbread stuffing. Grilled squares of polenta are delicious spread with herb butter made with Cleveland sage. In fact, simple preparations like herb butters, cheeses, and honey are an excellent way to experiment with this sage to accommodate your palate. Cheddar cheese mixed with Cleveland sage, shallots, parsley, and a touch of New Mexico ground chile is a tasty spread on toast rounds or crackers, and honey infused with a leaf or two of dried Cleveland sage is excellent with morning English muffins. A spoonful drizzled over fresh raspberries is a study in sweet and savory.

Rock Cornish Game Hens with Cleveland Sage

Small red potatoes smothered in parsley and a bowl of fresh salad greens tossed with a simple vinaigrette are all you need to accompany these sage-fragrant game hens.

4 Cornish game hens, about 1¼ pounds each   *Canola oil*
1 teaspoon finely chopped fresh Cleveland sage   *Mild Hungarian paprika, to taste*
4 tablespoons butter, softened   *Sea salt, to taste*

Preheat the oven to 400 degrees.

Remove the giblets from the hens and save for another use. Wash the hens inside and out. Pat the skin dry with paper towels. Make a paste of the Cleveland sage and butter. Carefully loosen the skin of the breast with your fingers, then spoon a tablespoon of the sage paste into each hen between the skin and the breast. Rub the hens lightly with the canola oil. Dust them with the paprika. Sprinkle them with salt. Truss them, if desired.

Place the hens breast side up in a heat-proof baking dish just large enough to hold them. Bake for 45 minutes, or until the juices run clear when a skewer is inserted into the thickest part of the breast. The hens may be cut in half. Serve immediately.

Serves 4 to 8

'FRIEDA DIXON' PINEAPPLE SAGE

(*Salvia elegans* 'Frieda Dixon')

Tender Perennial   Zones 8–10
Native Habitat   Mexico

"Elegant" is the translation of pineapple sage's botanical name. If "elegant" describes the fire-cracker red–blossomed pineapple sage, the vibrant salmon-pink of its cultivar 'Frieda Dixon' certainly deserves the name "refined." This handsome herb grows slightly lower than the red-flowering pineapple sage, which grows to 4 feet, but its growth habit and culinary uses are identical in every other way to those of its showy parent, whose virtue lies in the unique pineapple scent of its leaves. A native of Mexico, pineapple sage has an upright growth pattern, with dark green, slightly serrated, rough-textured, pointed leaves 3 to 4 inches long and, at the stem's end, tubular, 1-inch-long flowers with a lower lip turned back like a cuff to reveal a contrasting paler hue of pink. Pineapple sage is a classic ornamental culinary herbal shrub for the edible landscape, and its flowers attract the hummingbirds and butterflies and provide a stunning fall show of coral-colored flowers. It is an outstanding focal point in a large herb garden, as well as a spectacular, attention-getting hedge, and an excellent specimen for a container. Not only is this showy herb a beauty in the outdoor garden, it also aims to please as a houseplant for winter bloom indoors.

GROWING YOUR OWN

Plants of pineapple sage should be obtained from specialty herb nurseries or from cuttings from a friend's garden, for the herb rarely sets seed. Plant it outdoors when the weather has thoroughly warmed. It prefers a position in full sun but will accept partial shade, particularly in the hot climate zones. It grows well in a richly amended, fertile soil. Unlike most sages, pineapple sage prefers a moister soil. As with the other sages, however, good drainage is a must. To keep the plant shapely and to encourage branching, prune the tips from the main stem and side branches and cut it back after it blooms. In warm-winter areas, the plant may be cut back to 1 foot after flowering, then mulched. Soon thereafter, the plant resumes its growth anew. It should then be fertilized to get it off to a good start for the new season. In the southern growing regions of Zones 8 and 9, avoid crowding it with other plants, to provide good air circulation around it and to keep it as cool as possible in the humid environment of the long summer months. Provide a mulch of pecan shells or rice hulls to help protect it from soil-borne diseases. During the winter it can be covered with ramie cloth to protect it from the cold.

Pineapple sage is an excellent herb for containers. At the beginning of the growing season, plant it in fast-draining potting soil in a pot at least 12 inches in diameter. Fertilize regularly with a balanced soluble fertilizer at half strength throughout the growing season. In cold-winter climates, where frost bites pineapple sage before it flowers, cuttings may be propagated midsummer, then planted in small pots to be brought indoors for the winter. It may be coaxed into bloom if placed in a very sunny window or conservatory.

CULINARY USES

Use pineapple sage's luscious leaves fresh, for the pineapple scent dissipates upon drying. Steeping the leaves in a hot herb tea is the prime method to savor its subtle, fruity scent. It also goes hand in hand with fruit-based coolers, punches, and iced teas. Mince the leaves and combine them with fruit salad or a mélange of fresh fruit macerated with a fruity young wine for a refreshing dessert. Use its leaves to line a baking pan to subtly flavor génoise, pound cake, or sugar cookies. On the hors d'oeuvre tray, pineapple sage leaf fritters are an unusual snack to nibble while having apéritifs or cocktails. Use its leaves instead of mint to perfume a jar of homemade apple jelly. The flowers are not scented with the same aroma or taste of pineapple, but there is a sweet, tiny burst of honey at the stem end, like honeysuckle flowers. That they are not scented does not prevent you from using them along with their leaves to provide beauty as a garnish for drinks, such as Roselle Rum Fizz (see page 214), and for any dish where the fruit-scented leaves are used. To make one of the prettiest and most elegant desserts using just pineapple sage's blossoms in a simple and artful manner, garnish a pale-green scoop of Japanese green tea ice cream, served in a black lacquered bowl, with rich coral pink pineapple sage flowers for a striking contrast of colors.

Pineapple Sage Tisane with Tart Cherry Garnish

The mild tropical fruit taste of pineapple sage leaves steeped in a cup of hot herb tea is punctuated by a tart cherry or two—just like the traditional garnish of a cherry-punctuated pineapple wedge for frosty tropical fruit drinks.

4 to 6 dried, pitted tart cherries, or to taste
2 cups boiling water
2 tablespoons chopped fresh pineapple
* sage leaves*
Clover honey, to taste

In a small bowl, soften the cherries by pouring boiling water over them just to cover. Set aside. Rinse a small ceramic teapot with boiling water. Place in it the chopped pineapple sage leaves, and pour in two cups boiling water. Cover and allow the pineapple sage leaves to infuse for 5 to 10 minutes. Strain into 2 warmed cups. Add the honey, and garnish each cup with 2 or 3 of the softened cherries. Serve immediately.

Makes 2 cups

SAMPHIRE

(Crithmum maritimum)

Tender Perennial   Zones 8–10
Native Habitat   The rocky seacoasts of Europe

Some years ago while looking for cornichon pickles in the food and delicacies department at Bloomingdale's in Manhattan, I saw on the shelf a pretty glass jar with curious contents and a more curious name, *cristmarine*. I purchased it instead of the cornichons to accompany my pâté, and on the train home, I kept thinking how familiar the "pickles" looked. I knew why when I looked around my herb garden, for there, samphire was growing, the identical herb in the bottle of *cristmarine*. If I had known more about the plant I had obtained earlier that summer as part of a collection of new herbs for my garden, I could have pickled four times the paltry four ounces I had just purchased!

Samphire is no newcomer to the list of culinary herbs, for recipes for pickling it appear in seventeenth- and eighteenth-century cookbooks, including *The Art of Cookery Made Plain and Easy* by Hannah Glasse, and Eliza Smith's *The Compleat Housewife*. In France, it is known as *perce* or *pousse-pierre*, or *herbe de St. Pierre* in reference to the saint's symbol as a rock; in Italy, it's called *finocchio marino*, or sea fennel; and its English name, true, or rock samphire, refers to its growth in precipitous rock crevices in its seaside habitat. Shakespeare has a character in *King Lear*, Edgar, exclaim as he walks along a high cliff above the sea:

> ". . . *halfway down*
> *Hangs one who gathers samphire, dreadful trade!*"

After the perilous harvest of the herb, it was then sold in London streets as a relish for meats with the cry "Crest marine!"

True samphire is often confused with another delicious maritime plant, marsh samphire or glasswort, available in midsummer, and marketed in France as *pousse-pied* and in the United States as "sea bean." The two herbs are actually easily distinguishable: sea beans resemble a flat Christmas tree with jointed, fleshy green beanlike stems, and samphire looks like a lacy, light green succulent seaweed. I can't describe samphire better than did the sixteenth-century herbalist John Gerard:

> Rocke sampier hath many fat and thicke leaves somewhat like those of the lesser Purslane, of a spicie taste, with a certain saltnesse; among which rises up a stalk divided into many smal spraies or sprigs, on the top whereof grow spoky tufts of white floures, like the tufts of Fennell or Dill; after that comes the seed, like the seed of Fennell but greater.

GROWING YOUR OWN

It is not necessary to live by the sea to grow samphire, although it will undoubtedly have a saltier flavor there than when grown elsewhere. The plant grows 1 to 2 feet high, its smooth succulent leaves 1 to 1¼ inches long. In cold growing zones it should be treated as a tender perennial, heavily mulched with pine boughs after the ground freezes or brought indoors to overwinter. It likes a sandy, rocky, well-drained soil, full sun, and moderate water. Fertilize with sea kelp to provide some of the saline conditions of its natural habitat. You can also side-dress samphire with a spoonful of common table salt several times during the growing season. It can be started from seed (but it must be fresh, for the seed is viable for only a short period), rooted cuttings, or by division in the spring. Samphire is an excellent container plant in any climate. Seeds may be hard to locate, but plants are readily available at specialty nurseries. Because of its distinctive lacy and succulent appearance, it lends itself to creative design in the garden by being placed next to other herbs with especially interesting leaves and texture. I grow samphire in a pot placed next to a container collection of ornamental succulents like Vick's plant, rosary vine, and the fleshy, variegated leaves of culinary Cuban oregano. In the ground I surround it with the fat, succulent leaves of golden purslane. If you like to design theme gardens, samphire is a must in the Shakespeare section.

CULINARY USES

Samphire's slightly saline taste is preserved in pickling. It can be pickled alone so only its natural flavor is featured, or it can be combined with other herbs such as thyme, savory, and oregano, and pickling spices such as coriander seeds, peppercorns, and cloves. The pickle is a nice nibble along with Greek, Italian, or niçoise olives served with aperitifs, and is an excellent garnish to accompany pâté. Only the young shoots are used, for the center stem is tough. The tip end of the young stems are a tangy addition to a green salad. Because of its maritime nature, it is a perfect complementary garnish for fish or shellfish. Sprinkle finely chopped samphire over a cold scallop salad, or in the fold of an omelette. The leaves can be steamed as a vegetable, the only adornment a tablespoon or two of butter and some pepper.

Pickled Samphire

The pickled young stems of samphire make a refreshing change in place of or in addition to cornichons and pickled pearl onions to accompany pâtés and cold meat platters.

For another recipe using samphire, see page 199, Good Husbandry Summer Salad with Pear Vinaigrette.

1 cup young samphire shoots
1 cup cider vinegar
1 tablespoon sea salt
¼ teaspoon coriander seeds
8 peppercorns
4 cloves

4 to 5 sprigs fresh French thyme
1 sprig French tarragon
1 small bay leaf
1 small dried red chile
1 clove garlic, peeled

Wash the samphire shoots and drain. In a small saucepan heat the vinegar, then add the salt, stirring to dissolve. Add the coriander seeds, peppercorns, cloves, thyme, tarragon, and bay leaf. Simmer for 2 to 3 minutes, then remove pan from heat and allow to cool. Place the samphire, chile pepper, and garlic in a sterilized 1-cup glass jar with a nonreactive lid. Add the cooled vinegar mixture, then cover the jar and shake it well to blend ingredients. Store in the refrigerator for one week to allow the flavors to blend, then serve. Store any unused portion in the refrigerator.

Makes ½ cup

SILENE

(S. vulgaris, S. inflata)

Perennial   All Zones
Native Habitat   Europe, North Africa, and temperate Asia

In the past, when visitors to my garden were on the "taste, touch, smell, and name-the-herb" tour, I always used to hesitate when asked the common name of *Silene inflata*. Somehow after reciting such pretty words as sweet cicely, chervil, costmary, and calendula, "bladder campion," the only common name I knew for *Silene inflata*, didn't have quite the same charm. Then one day, my friend the Italian chef Celestino walked through the garden with me, and pointed to bladder campion, exclaiming, "Oh, you grow *see-linn-uh*, a great herb!" Not long after, Renée Shepherd, formerly of Shepherd's Garden Seeds, who seeks out quality vegetable and herb seeds worldwide, returned from a European buying trip with seeds of a salad herb that was the rage in Italy. I trialed it in my garden, to discover it was none other than bladder campion. Since then, besides calling it by its name, silene—Italian style—I have learned other curious names for the herb: campion, catchfly, cowbell, bubble poppy, and maiden's tears.

Not only is silene naturalized in Britain, Europe, and the Mediterranean, but it is also one of the most common "roadside and railroad" weeds from northern New England to British Columbia, southward to Virginia and Tennessee, and in some areas of the Pacific Northwest. It is one of about five hundred species of annual, perennial, and biennial herbs in the silene genus. Historically, *Silene vulgaris* is one of those edible weeds that were destined for the pot and cooked as greens, with a flavor reminiscent of spinach and peas. However, as with many herbs, silene eaten in large quantities can be harmful because of the bitter saponin in its leaves. Its qualities shine best when a few of its fresh leaves are tossed in the salad bowl.

GROWING YOUR OWN

Silene is a low-growing perennial about 1 to 1½ feet high, with many-branched stems spreading to 2½ feet or more. Its handsome lance-shaped, smooth opposite leaves are rich gray-green with a matte finish and grow to 4 inches long. When in flower in mid- to late summer, it is one of the most decorative and unusual herbs in the garden, resembling those pictured in books of fairy tales read to young children. Its pale-green-to-white globular-shaped calyx is inflated like a balloon with conspicuous veins over its surface and holds white flowers with five deeply scalloped petals. These can be dried and mixed with other herbs and plants from the garden and field for stunning indoor winter dried-flower arrangements.

Silene is grown from seed or by stem cuttings and division. It grows in ordinary sandy or gravelly soil in full sun, with a minimal amount of water. It can be invasive if you neglect to maintain its spreading habit, but it is easy to keep in check by pulling out the entire root. Its gray-green leaves coordinate handsomely when planted next to gray or silver herbs like rue, sea kale, artemisia, silver thyme, and glossy-green lemon thyme, the herbs that are its companions in my own garden.

CULINARY USES

Silene leaves have a nice grassy taste and a pleasant "tooth," making silene a good herb to provide texture in a salad of many lettuces and herbs, or to be the single attraction in a bowl of lettuce greens. It blends well with sweet herbs and greens such as sweet marjoram, chervil, sweet cicely, mâche, and lemon balm; with young leaves of romaine, bibb, and butterhead lettuces and edible flowers such as dianthus and violets; with tart herbs such as sorrel, and lemon basil; with spicy herbs such as arugula, broadleaf cress, and mizuna and other brassicas; with crunchy herbs such as samphire and leaf celery; and with bitter herbs like dandelion, escarole, frisée, and radicchio. Combined with other sharp-flavored greens, its leaves are particularly suited to a wilted salad with a hot-oil dressing and a few bits of crunchy bacon strewn on top.

For another recipe using silene, see page 199, Good Husbandry Summer Salad with Pear Vinaigrette.

TRUE FRENCH SORREL
(Rumex scutatus)

Perennial   Zones 3–10

Native Habitat   Central and Southern Europe and western Asia and North Africa

"Oh! This is the sorrel that grows in France," my very French friend and epicure exclaimed as she discovered with delight the true French sorrel growing in my garden. Garden sorrel with its large 6-to-8-inch-long leaves was exuberantly growing across the way, but it was this diminutive one with its lobed, arrowhead-shaped leaves that reminded my friend of her homeland.

   True French sorrel, also known as buckler sorrel, is the more elegant relative of its robust cousin, garden sorrel. True French has a more refined and clearer flavor than the more assertive, coarse-tasting garden sorrel (*Rumex acetosa*). Like many small things, it is surprisingly intense, even though its lemon notes are mild. It is listed in garden catalogs as both

French and true French. You will find that some garden catalogs list *Rumex acetosa* as simply "French" sorrel as well, and in some references French sorrel is also listed as garden sorrel, so make sure to identify the herb's botanical name, *Rumex scutatus*, when purchasing seeds or plants. *Scutatus* is Latin for "shield," which is an apt description of its leaves, and the Old French word for "sour," *surele*, the derivation of "sorrel," certainly describes its flavor.

Historically, garden sorrel was the sixteenth- and seventeenth-century sorrel of choice in salads and the green sauce that accompanied cold meats, until French sorrel with its less bitter culinary properties was introduced into the horticultural trade in the eighteenth century. But even today, in the United States, garden sorrel seems to remain the best-known sorrel.

GROWING YOUR OWN

True French sorrel is an herb that is certain to remain in your garden for many seasons, because it has the ability to be invasive. If this is an issue, you can still plant it in a container, for the herb is a must for your sorrel soup or the sauce for your poached salmon. Planted in the ground in the spring, true French sorrel is easily germinated from seed, or by root division from established plants. Feed established plants with a complete fertilizer at the beginning of the season. True French sorrel should be routinely divided every 2 to 3 years so the plant stays in good shape, and so it does not become a spreading garden pest. It grows 6 to 8 inches high and prefers full sun but will accept some shade; it likes moist to average soil, well drained. Harvest the young leaves throughout the growing season, and more tender ones will continue to appear. Slugs relish it. In my Zone 10 garden families of California quail like to nestle in the ground around it, so I only use benign wood ashes for slug control.

CULINARY USES

As popular as sorrel is for its uses, it should only be consumed infrequently and in small amounts, owing to its high oxalic acid content, which is also found in spinach. If you need to reduce the amount of oxalic acid in sorrel, blanch the leaves and discard the cooking water three times before using it. On the beneficial side, its leaves are packed with vitamin C. Shred sorrel just before preparing a dish so the enzymes released upon cutting the leaves don't have time to destroy the vitamin, thereby reducing nutritional value. Herbs to add to sorrel soup with excellent effect are lovage, rosemary, chervil, tarragon, and parsley, or add an equal amount of sweet green peas for a sweet-tart version. Modernize the classic *potage*

Germiny, the elegant French sorrel soup made with a very rich beef stock, egg yolks, and cream, by using less of the latter two ingredients—or splurge. The green sauce that stars sorrel and has such an affinity for salmon is a sublime sauce for other fish as well; it is made with cooked-down, or "melted," sorrel, onions, a touch of cream, and a little olive oil or butter to bind it. An herb butter made with finely chopped sorrel leaves is a tasty way to enjoy small amounts of true French sorrel. The tart butter is especially good melted over potatoes or rice. True French sorrel mayonnaise spices up anything it touches, including cold shrimp and deviled eggs. Nothing could be more complementary than eggs and sorrel in an omelette filled with the julienned herb for a delectable breakfast or luncheon dish. A few sorrel leaves make a tart surprise tossed into an herbal mesclun. A sweet sorbet infused with sorrel's lemony flavor is a refreshing little something with which to end a meal.

True French Sorrel Vichyssoise with 'Golden Rain' Rosemary

The pine scent and flavor of 'Golden Rain' rosemary is a choice foil for lemon-tart sorrel, and leaf celery lends a rich undercurrent of flavor to this tangy vichyssoise, excellent served hot or cold. The variegated yellow-and-green rosemary leaves make an inviting garnish, all the better if the plants are in flower.

For another recipe using true French sorrel, see page 199, Good Husbandry Summer Salad with Pear Vinaigrette.

2 tablespoons olive oil
2 cups finely chopped yellow onions
2 four-inch stems leaf celery (page 72), chopped, or the light green inner heart of stalk celery with leaves attached
4 medium red potatoes, peeled and quartered
4 cups rich chicken stock, preferably home-made

3 cups packed shredded sorrel leaves
1 tablespoon coarsely chopped 'Golden Rain' rosemary leaves (page 217)
1 cup light cream
Sea salt and freshly ground black pepper to taste
Sprigs of 'Golden Rain' rosemary, for garnish

In a 3-quart saucepan, heat the olive oil. Add the onions and leaf celery, and cook over medium heat until soft. Add the potatoes and chicken stock. Bring to a boil, then lower heat, and simmer for 10 minutes. Add the sorrel and rosemary. Stir well, and cook for approximately 15 minutes, or until potatoes are tender. In a food processor fitted with the metal blade, process the soup to a purée in batches, then return to the saucepan. Simmer over low heat for a few minutes, then stir in the cream. Cook for 2 to 3 minutes, then remove from heat. Season to taste. Divide the soup among 6 warmed soup bowls. (If soup is to be served cold, allow to cool to room temperature, then pour into a covered container and refrigerate until well chilled.) Garnish with the fresh 'Golden Rain' rosemary sprigs. Serve immediately.

Serves 6

'ORANGE BALSAM' THYME

(*Thymus vulgaris* 'Orange Balsam')

Perennial   Zones 4–9

Native Habitat   The western Mediterranean to southeastern Italy

Varieties of culinary thyme have other aromas and flavors besides classic thyme's character-istic pungent taste. Lemon-, caraway-, lemon caraway–, and oregano-scented thyme are all available from specialty seed companies. Another citrus-thyme offering is 'Orange Balsam' thyme. "Delightful," "interesting," and "intriguing" to "fantastic" and "sensational" are words used to describe the taste and scent of this thyme, which is a cultivar of common thyme. Flavor is denoted by the taste buds of the taster, and I will add my own adjective to this list: exotic . Basically it is a strong resinous thyme, for it has terpinol in its chemistry, but like rosemary, with resinous qualities that warm a hearty dish and give punch to a delicate one, this thyme imparts a balsam flavor but with notes of orange citrus. One of the seven chemical forms of common thyme, orange balsam thyme will probably have its champions and detractors, as do rosemary and cilantro, but even if the resinous herb doesn't suit your culinary taste, it makes a fine thyme in the herb garden as a fragrant edging.

GROWING YOUR OWN

'Orange Balsam' thyme grows in a shrubby, upright fashion from a compact 6 inches to 1 foot high and has tiny, soft gray-green leaves on twiggy stems. Its little tubular white or pale, pale pink flowers light up a corner of a garden bed. Its appearance, like its good relative 'Narrowleaf French,' could be described as a "scruffy," but typical of Mediterranean herbs, these are among the hardest-working herbs in the garden, as the powerful scent and taste in their little leaves prove. 'Orange Balsam' thyme likes growing conditions that mimic its native habitat—rocky, light, dry soil that is slightly alkaline and well drained. All thymes luxuriate in full sun.

Prune the tips of the wiry little branches to maintain a fuller appearance. In cold-winter areas, mulch with a protective layer of pine boughs after the ground has frozen, to keep the plants from heaving in the continual freeze-and-thaw conditions in winter. In the southeastern U.S. Zones 8 and 9, this thyme, like others, benefits by a mulch of light-colored gravel and builder's or sharp sand to reflect light into the plant's interior, which aids in keeping the roots dry. In the South, keep thyme regularly pruned with a light hand, for severe pruning will result in dieback in hot weather. In other areas, the previous year's growth can be cut back one half.

'Orange Balsam' thyme can be propagated by stem cuttings. It is the perfect plant for a rock garden, or as one of the garlands in a knot garden. The plants spaced 6 to 8 inches apart make a citrus-scented minihedge. Good companions for a bed of other "tough" Mediterranean partners are pink savory (*Satureja thymbra*), conehead thyme (*Coridothymus capitatus*), and the lemon-scented 'Grey Hill' thyme (*Thymus vulgaris* 'Grey Hill'). The bed can be softened with sweet alyssum and Pennsylvania Dutch thyme (*T. pulegioides*) or other mounding thymes. As thyme always thrives where lavender and rosemary do, the low-growing 'Munstead' lavender (*Lavandula angustifolia* 'Munstead') would be an appropriate planting, with prostrate rosemary nearby. To design the bed with a culinary thyme theme, choose from the large variety of interesting thymes such as a white-flowering thyme (*T. serpyllum* var. *albus*), variegated English thyme, 'Golden Lemon' thyme, 'Silver Lemon' thyme, and the beloved herb garden standard that makes a spreading dark green mat, caraway thyme.

CULINARY USES

The orange flavor in 'Orange Balsam' thyme can be highlighted with a drop or two of orange juice and perhaps a little grated orange zest in a savory herb butter for asparagus or beans or for spreading on hot biscuits or dinner rolls. A vinaigrette made with orange juice with a smattering of chopped 'Orange Balsam' leaves is tasty over a salad of mixed green lettuces, or a fresh fruit salad. Minced, the herb can be added to a beurre blanc for fish. Its resinous leaves are good with chicken and game, and are especially tasty with rabbit. An herbal tea, taken "neat," is a soothing hot refreshment with an ever-so-subtle scent of oranges.

Honey-Baked Rabbit in Parchment with 'Orange Balsam' Thyme

Presenting food cooked in parchment somehow lends a meal special flair. When this honeyed packet is opened, the fragrance of the unusual orange-scented thyme escapes to tempt your taste buds. New potatoes rolled in parsley or buttered noodles are good accompaniments.

Marinade

¼ cup freshly squeezed lemon juice

Zest of 1 lemon

¼ cup olive oil

1 dried bay leaf, broken into pieces

½ small onion, sliced

4 whole peppercorns, lightly crushed

A small handful 'Orange Balsam' thyme sprigs

1 rabbit (2½ to 3 pounds), cut up and ready to cook

1 tablespoon butter

1 tablespoon olive oil

1 cup finely chopped onions

4 tablespoons orange juice

4 teaspoons honey

Sea salt and freshly ground white pepper to taste

2 teaspoons finely chopped 'Orange Balsam' thyme

4 sixteen-inch lengths parchment paper

Prepare the marinade 1 day ahead. Place the lemon juice, lemon zest, olive oil, bay leaf, onion, and peppercorns in a large bowl. Add the sprigs of 'Orange Balsam' thyme and bruise them with a wooden pestle. Stir mixture well. Separate the two thighs of the rabbit and bone them at the leg joint. Save the two back legs and the two front leg sections for another use,

such as a small rabbit stew. Add the thighs and the two loin pieces to the marinade, coating well. Cover the bowl containing the marinade and the rabbit and place in the refrigerator for 24 hours. Turn the pieces several times during the marinating period. Remove the rabbit from the marinade. Discard marinade.

Preheat the oven to 350 degrees.

In a large skillet heat the butter and olive oil. Add the rabbit pieces and brown well on all sides over medium high heat, about 15 minutes. Remove to a platter and set aside. Turn the heat to low and cook the onions until soft. Remove from the heat and set aside. In a small bowl, combine the orange juice and honey, and set aside.

Fold a length of parchment paper in half. With scissors, cut the paper as if making a valentine. Open the heart-shaped paper flat, then butter to the edges of the paper. Spoon ¼ of the onions onto the center of one side of the paper. Place a piece of the rabbit on top of the onion "bed." Add salt and pepper to taste. Pour 1 tablespoon of the orange juice and honey mixture over it. Sprinkle ½ teaspoon of the chopped 'Orange Balsam' thyme over the rabbit. Fold the top of the paper over the rabbit. Starting at the large end, fold and crimp the edges to make a tight pleat. When you reach the pointed end, fold the tip several times to close the packet securely. Make the other three packets in this manner.

Place the parchment packets on a baking sheet and bake for 30 minutes. Remove the packets to heated plates, and serve immediately.

Serves 4

AFRICAN VALERIAN
(Fedia cornucopiae)

Annual
Native Habitat   Mediterranean North Africa, Portugal, and Spain

Purple-flowering African valerian surrounded by other exotic herbs (clockwise from right) White-flowering borage, Plectranthus cv variegated Cuban oregano, culantro, 'African Blue' basil, leaf celery, sweet herb (Lippia dulcis), 'Jigsaw' variegated pepper, Greek oregano

Dandelion, red radicchio, chicory frisée, endive, escarole, fenugreek, hyssop, and garland chrysanthemum are all bitter herbs we toss into salads to counterpoint the peppery, lemony, tart, and sweet taste of other herbal greens and lettuces. Add a newcomer to the bitter list—African valerian. Like cilantro and other strong herbs, it is certain to have its followers and its detractors. On taste trips through my herb garden, I watch for either a grimace on my visitor's face when the herb is sampled or a startled reaction followed by a curious second bite. African valerian is a relative of mâche (*Valerianella locusta*), but they are not interchangeable, although they would make good partners, because of the contrast in flavor. The bitter taste of African valerian is complemented by the sweet taste of mâche.

The herb is a decorative, ornamental edible in the culinary herb garden. It grows to about 1 foot, its oval, light-green leaves forming little bouquets on the branched, hollow stems. When African valerian is in flower, the stem forms a short fork, atop which are two flat-topped clusters of delicate, light purple, tubular blossoms. Let run to flower, the herb is very effective in filling out little bare patches of earth in the garden with a splash of vibrant color. African valerian, also known as horn of plenty, grows abundantly in its native habitat, covering pastures, cornfields, and cultivated ground with a rosy carpet when it is in bloom, from spring through early summer.

GROWING YOUR OWN

Sow seed of African valerian indoors in mid- to late winter for transplanting outdoors, or it may be sown direct into the ground when the weather has warmed. Plant in well-amended soil with plenty of compost. Thin seedlings to 1 foot apart. The herb likes full sun or part shade and a well-drained, moist soil, with plentiful water. It can be incorporated in the early-spring-lettuces patch. Succession plantings may be made through early summer to ensure a good supply of young, tender leaves that are not too bitter. Seed can be collected and saved for the future, as they are viable for four years. African valerian is sensitive to the cold, and unlike its relative, mâche, it is not suitable for autumn sowing. It looks attractive planted with Italian or curly parsley, chives, violets, and spring lettuces.

CULINARY USES

In 1841, the French gardening magazine *Bon Jardinier* praised African valerian as "a good salad plant," yet today it remains little known. Because of its bitterness, it is best to include it as the only bitter herb in a mixed salad, and to combine it with other herbal greens such as broadleaf cress, leaf celery, and arugula, along with lettuces that have a character of their own and sweet salad vegetables like beets and carrots. Toss a few of its leaves in the classic *salade Lorette* consisting of mâche, beets, and celery and dressed with a light French vinaigrette of vinegar and oil, sea salt, and freshly ground black pepper. Vinaigrettes made with sweet walnut or hazelnut oil are complementary to African valerian when used in a dressing for mesclun.

For a recipe using African valerian, see page 199, Good Husbandry Summer Salad with Pear Vinaigrette.

VIETNAMESE BALM

(Elsholtzia ciliata)

Annual

Native Habitat   Japan, Korea, China, Taiwan, temperate Asia, and Western Europe

Vietnamese balm joins the refreshing list of lemon-scented herbs—lemon grass, lemon thyme, lemon verbena, and lemon balm, to name a few. Tastewise, its closest kinship is perhaps to lemon balm, although it is not as delicate and has a stronger, flowery scent of mint. It is a handsome, upright, shrubby herb, growing to 3 feet, with serrated, bright green, veined leaves to 3 inches long and square reddish stems. It flowers late in the season, with soft, 2½-inch-long flowerheads sprouting tubular lavender blossoms on one side only, the whole resembling a fuzzy, one-sided purple caterpillar. This citrus-flavored culinary herb is known as *rau kinh gio'i* in Vietnamese.

GROWING YOUR OWN

Seeds of Vietnamese balm are not readily available, so plants should be obtained from specialty nurseries. The herb likes moderately fertile, moist, well-drained soil, and full sun to partial shade. In hot-climate areas, afternoon shade is a must. Fertilize regularly with liquid fish emulsion or balanced soluble feritilzer. In warm-climate areas where Vietnamese balm flowers, cut the spent blossoms to keep the plant full and healthy. Bunches of the cut herb may be obtained from Oriental markets and propagated by rooting the stems in water. To create a separate theme bed of lemon mimics in the herb garden, plant Vietnamese balm with the aforementioned citrus-scented herbs, plus lemon caraway, lemon monarda, lemon nepeta, and the different varieties of lemon-scented geraniums—heavenly on a hot summer day.

CULINARY USES

Though similar in taste to lemon balm, Vietnamese balm stands up better in cooking. The herb can substitute in any recipe calling for mint. In Vietnamese cuisine it is used in soups, noodle dishes, and egg rolls. It lends Oriental dumplings a subtle, sweet nuance of mint. Use it as the refreshing ingredient in an Asian herbal pesto of peanut oil combined with cilantro, Thai or 'Cinnamon' basil, garlic chives, and ginger, to spoon over egg noodles or pasta. A tasty first-course salad to whet the appetite is carrot slaw flecked with chopped Vietnamese balm leaves and tossed with a lemon vinaigrette. A colorful vegetable salad is one composed of thinly sliced white napa cabbage, red bell peppers, and straw mushrooms with a Vietnamese balm dressing. Steeped, its leaves make a soothing hot herbal tea spiced with a slice of fresh ginger, and a tall, ice-cube-filled glass of lemon balm and Vietnamese mint is a departure from regular lemonade for a cooling summer drink. The delicate citrus essence of Vietnamese balm can be captured in herb honey and is delightful drizzled over fresh berries, melons, Asian pears, papaya, and other fruits.

Four Herb Honeys for Berries

When berry season is in full swing, a simple way to enjoy them is coated with herb honey. The golden-lacquered berries are enrobed with honey infused with the cook's choice among four herb flavors complementary to fruit: Vietnamese balm, 'Golden Rain' or 'Majorca Pink' rosemary, East Indian basil, and 'Orange Balsam' thyme. The four honeys can be made at the same time in small ½ cup amounts and stored on the pantry shelf for use according to the cook's whim. A dessert wine such as Bonny Doon Muscat Canelli or Quady Essensia would be the perfect beverage to sip with these simple confections. For other recipes using Vietnamese Balm, see page 83, Asian Pesto; page 204, Fragrant Fish Soup; page 120, Fraises des Bois Compote with Balsamic Vinegar; and page 155, Lemon Grass and Vietnamese Balm Cooler.

½ cup clover honey

2 teaspoons dried Vietnamese balm or 1 teaspoon dried 'Golden Rain' rosemary or East Indian Basil or dried 'Orange Balsam' thyme

2 small cantaloupes, cut into halves and seeded

2 cups fresh raspberries, or berries of your choice

Pour the honey into a small sterilized glass jar. Warm it for ½ to 1 minute in a microwave oven. Add the herbs. Cover tightly with a sterilized lid, then shake the jar to distribute the herbs throughout the honey. Place the jar in a warm spot for several days or up to 1 week.

Uncap the jar. Warm the honey for ½ to 1 minute in a microwave oven, then strain. Discard the herb and immediately return the strained honey to the jar. Cover tightly. (Can be stored at room temperature on a dark shelf for up to a month.)

Pour the raspberries into a large bowl. Add the honey, and gently toss the berries to evenly coat. Spoon equal amounts of the raspberries into the 4 melon halves.

Serves 4

SWEET VIOLET

(Viola odorata)

Perennial   Zones 6–9
Native Habitat   Europe, Africa, and Asia

Courtesy of White Flower Farm; photo by Michael H. Dodge

The ever-constant sweet violet of shady glades, expansive lawns, literature, and song heralds spring each year, offers its familiar nodding royal purple flowers for a while, then forms an ever larger carpet of green—easily taken for granted as just another pretty perennial that will be back again next year for another floral show. What makes sweet violets exotic in my mind is that this faithful garden standard with its heart-shaped, scalloped leaves and nectar-sweet, brilliant amethyst flowers not only fits the dictionary definition for exotic, "intriguingly beautiful," but is also a celebrated herb that has played a regal role in culinary history from ancient times to the present. Quite apart from the lore of its association with Venus; its adoration in Greece, where Athens was known as "the city of the violet crown"; its depiction in the flora seen on the extraordinary medieval unicorn tapestries; and the love for the flower of "Corporal Violet," a.k.a. Napoleon Bonaparte—violet flowers and leaves are deliciously edible. There are myriad ways to prepare them in all manner of food specialties, historic and contemporary. For example, the popular sixteenth-century "violet plates," a picturesque name for a sugared violet confection or "sweetmeat," made a pleasurable little flowery treat, and a seventeenth-century recipe called for a dish of sautéed violet leaves sweetened with sugar and orange or lemon juice. A poetic sweet violet tea had a pragmatic use as a cure for an unpoetic hangover from excessive dining and drinking at the fabled feasts of the early Romans. Some dispensed with the tea and simply followed the "recipe" of placing violet petals directly on their brow to achieve the same results. In the Middle Ages a popular and colorful salad consisted of sweet violets chopped up with onions and lettuce, and another combined a large handful of violet petals, endive, parsley, leaf celery, salt, pepper, a hint of wine vinegar, and an excellent olive oil—doesn't this sound familiar to our fancy contemporary salads? Nor were vinegars left out, for they were enhanced by steeped violets and other flowers such as roses and pinks to intensify salads with their floral character.

For dessert, a lovely old Syrian recipe for a violet sherbet calls for sugar flavored with violet petals, and presumably garnished with violet blossoms. In fourteenth-century England, sweet violet fritters were a choice way to end a meal, and a grand fifteenth-century English custard colored golden with saffron was cooked with velvet purple sweet violet blossoms— another sumptuous use for this unassuming, faithful spring garden perennial. Closer to our century, the chef d'oeuvre that dear Alice B. Toklas served to her illustrious guests was a violet soufflé. In Toulouse, France, called "la cité de la violette," which is the home of those crystallized violets sold in a little hatbox, one can also obtain violet liqueur and other products made from the regally purple flowers. Naturalists who today lead edible wild plant forays will undoubtedly extol the virtues of sweet violet's vitamin C–rich flowers and leaves, the latter with added vitamin A, perhaps cooked as a vegetable (as was also noted in a fifteenth-century recipe for "herbes for potage"), but probably more tasty in a forager's salad along with purslane, sorrel, nasturtium, and cress, garnished, of course, with violet flowers.

GROWING YOUR OWN

In temperate climates, sweet violets can be found growing along fences, hedgerows, woods' edge, roadsides—and certain bowers and "midsummer" banks ("I know a bank whereon the wild thyme blows, where oxlips and the nodding violet grows"—*Midsummer Night's Dream*,

II, i). The sweet violet found growing in the wild is another to-the-manor-born "escapee," so the herb is easily cultivated in a prepared garden bed. It is the perfect front-of-the-border plant for a semishaded spot, growing from 6 to 8 inches high. Given room to naturalize in a larger area, violets make a lovely focal point when the ground is carpeted with flowers. The tide of sweet purple violets that blanketed the front lawn of our family's summer rental Victorian farmhouse in New Jersey (where the violet is the state flower) is etched in my memory—especially as seen from a worm's-eye view while lying in the grass on a spring day.

It is best to purchase plants from specialty nurseries to ensure obtaining fragrant cultivars. There are purple, rose, and white-flowering varieties to choose from. Purple 'Royal Robe', lavender-blue 'Princess of Wales', rose-pink 'Rosina', and white-flowering 'White Czar' are the most popular scented varieties. If you want to plant violets for an herbal lawn, plant the species, as it will grow the fastest. Save the cultivars for a shady border or for a special shady spot in the herb garden. Plant violets in early spring, spaced 6 to 10 inches apart. They like an environment of evenly moist, well-composted soil of rich loam, in part shade and sun. A mulch of well-rotted leaf mold will help keep the soil cool and damp. When established, plants may be divided in spring or autumn. If violets are happy in a well-chosen location they make rapid growth as a ground cover, spreading by long underground runners. Flower production increases as they grow older and begin to spread. Feeding them with a balanced soluble fertilizer applied just before they flower will produce more blooms. They can be sheared in late summer or early fall, and will return ever more vigorously the following spring—true to the tradition whereby the violet is the symbol of constancy.

CULINARY USES

When most people think of edible violets, what probably springs to mind is the little imported boxes of candied purple flowers that seem a bit of an affectation. That violets are paired with brown in classic French pastry seems strange until you see a simple cluster of them atop a silken chocolate-glazed torte. The unexpected color combination works. Most often the boxed candies are unattractive little clumps of sugar, colored with purple food color, their resemblance to genuine violets slight—however, a rewarding project is to candy your own. First, you need patience—then a fine paintbrush, whipped egg white, and superfine sugar. Lovely, delicate food art is the result. Garnish a plate of chocolate madeleines or chocolate truffles with these crystallized treasures. They look pretty decorating a round scoop of ice cream or pastel-colored fruit sorbets, or perhaps an old -fashioned pot de crème.

When cooking with violets, make sure you know they have not been sprayed with any pesticides. When preparing violet jellies, syrups, and drinks, always use distilled water and nonreactive pots such as stainless steel, ceramic, or glass, and wooden spoons for stirring, so the color of the infusion is not altered. The natural blue dye in violets acts like litmus paper: when an acid such as pectin or lemon juice is added, the mixture turns pink.

Violet syrups, jellies, and vinegars have the same beautiful pale lavender color, and are all useful in the contemporary kitchen. Violet syrup is a standard simple syrup infused with sweet violet flowers and strained. It is delightful poured over peach-filled crepes or morning pancakes. It can also be diluted with water and poured into a tall glass of shaved ice for a refreshing summer drink. Violet jelly, made with simple syrup, pectin, and lemon juice, is a jewellike cerise-colored confection to spoon onto fromage blanc and crackers. Sweet violets, borage blossoms, and calendula petals are a colorful, complementary trio to gently press onto plump rounds of goat or other soft cheeses for a decorative cheeseboard or hors d'oeuvre platter. Easiest of all is a spring salad from your own garden with a shower of just-picked sweet violets strewn over a bountiful bowl of fresh green lettuces and herbs. (Add only small amount of violet leaves to salads, for ingesting too many of its leaves can cause an emetic reaction.) Gild the lily and prepare salads with your own violet vinegar, made by steeping the petals in fine white wine vinegar for 1 week. The enticing result is the color of a delicate lavender windowpane. As pretty as violet vinegar is, it shouldn't be on display, but kept in the recesses of a dark cupboard, for bright light dissipates its lovely violet hue.

Sweet Violet Salad

This spring salad makes a very pretty plate. Be sure the flowers and leaves are pesticide-free.

4 cups assorted young lettuces, including
    garden-fresh pea tendrils, if available
1 cup young violet leaves
1 cup miner's lettuce (page 165)
Large handful sweet violet flowers
Several 'Majorca Pink' rosemary blossoms
    (page 219) if available
2 tablespoons tarragon vinegar

Sea salt and freshly ground black pepper to
    taste
¼ teaspoon mustard
⅓ cup walnut oil
½ teaspoon dried thyme
2 teaspoons finely chopped fresh chervil or
    sweet cicely

Wash and dry the lettuces and herbs. Tear them into bite-size pieces and place them in a large bowl. Gently wash the flowers and pat them dry with paper towels. Place them on a fresh paper towel and keep them in the refrigerator while the dressing is being prepared.

In a small bowl, whisk together the vinegar, salt, pepper, and mustard. Slowly whisk in the walnut oil, then add the thyme and the chervil or cicely. In a large bowl, toss the lettuces and herbs lightly with the dressing. Divide among six salad plates, then sprinkle some flowers over each salad. Serve immediately.

Serves 6

The Za'atars

The definition of the group of eastern Mediterranean and Middle Eastern culinary herbs known as za'atar is every bit as puzzling as the confusion that reigns over the identity of "the real oregano." *Za'atar* is an Arabic word whose literal meaning is "thyme," but not all za'atar herbs are thyme. Botanically, za'atar includes species from several genera, all with similar scents and flavor, mainly those of oregano and thyme. To make the mystery muddier, an oregano species is a prominent member of the za'atar herb clan. Perplexingly, meanings for "za'atar" encountered in ethnic cookbooks and markets and herb encyclopedias include the definitions thyme, oregano, marjoram, wild marjoram pickle, and hyssop. To confuse matters further, za'atar is also referred to as a *mixture* or paste, leading one to ask, "Is za'atar a savory mixture or an herb?" The answer is *both*.

The basic za'atar mixture consists of the dried leaves of one of the za'atar herbs combined with the ground tart red berries of a nonpoisonous sumac (*Rhus coriaria*), roasted sesame seeds, and salt to taste. Blends and the choice of za'atar herbs vary from region to region; ground garbanzo beans, coriander seed, cuminseed, cinnamon, and grains are all possible additions. Charmingly crude little paper cornets filled with the dried fragrant mixture to dip warm bagels in or to be sprinkled over bread snacks are sold as street food in Middle Eastern markets. The addition of olive oil can make the blend into a paste to be spread on pita or other flat breads. It can also be dusted over *labneh* (sheep's or goat's milk yogurt cheese), sprinkled with thinly sliced scallions—and eaten for breakfast. In the Middle East it is said that morning would not be morning without za'atar! The modern culinary repertoire contains delicious variations on the use of this classic blend. Mixed with pine nuts, za'atar becomes a robust pesto for pasta; combined with grains it gives spicy flavor to stews. The condiment is an inspired topping for meat and vegetables; a marinade for chicken or fish; a bold herb sprinkle for pizza; the tang in a spicy vinaigrette; and a unique dip, when mixed with extra virgin olive oil or fromage blanc, for fresh crudités.

It is easiest to obtain plants of these za'atar herbs from specialty herb nurseries, as seed is not readily available. However, seed can be collected from established plants. Cuttings can be taken in late summer and brought indoors for the winter, and the herbs can also be propagated by root division.

Trying to sort out the correct botanical names of the za'atar herbs in order to obtain "the real za'atar" to flavor your own cooking can be bewildering. The plants on the following pages can help to clarify the delicious maze of savory herbs.

SYRIAN OREGANO

(Origanum syriacum)

Tender Perennial   Zone 10
Native Habitat   Syria, southern Turkey, Jordan, Libya, and Egypt

We begin with the generally preferred and most common herb used in the za'atar condiment, Syrian oregano, a handsome upright oregano. The herb grows on rocky limestone terrain and between the sides of rocks in the desert and along the roadways in its native habitat. This is not just another pungent oregano. One of its common names is Bible hyssop, the herb that is purported to be the hyssop of the Old Testament—depending upon which scholar you read. "True" or Bible hyssop is the culinary za'atar of choice in the Holy Land. What is indeed true about this za'atar is the rich, concentrated oregano flavor in its 1-inch-long, elliptical, medium green, downy leaves. It is quite decorative in the landscape, with pretty white clusters of tiny flowers on the upper part of the branches; but don't admire too many of these before you clip them back, so the leaves with their true flavor of Syrian oregano can be encouraged.

GROWING YOUR OWN

Syrian oregano has a shrubby growth habit, generally to 2 feet tall, but in my Zone 10 garden, it grows to 3 feet tall and 4 feet wide and is evergreen. It likes average soil, with excellent drainage, full sun, and moderate water. At planting time, it it beneficial to Syrian oregano to add well-rotted manure, preferably chicken manure. During the growing season, keep the tips of the plant pruned to promote bushy growth. In cold winter areas, it must be brought indoors. The herb is an excellent container plant for growing outdoors with its long stems falling attractively over the sides of the pot, but it quickly fills its container, and the plant must be replaced each year unless a greenhouse is available to overwinter it. Syrian oregano is drought-tolerant when established and looks excellent in the landscape planted next to the silver gray of English lavender, curry plant (*Helichrysum italicum*, formerly *Helichrysum angustifolium*), and culinary garden sage (*Salvia officinalis*). Rosemaries 'Majorca Pink' and 'Golden Rain' are also choice companions, as well as prostrate rosemary (*Rosmarinus officinalis* 'Prostratus').

CONEHEAD THYME

(Thymus capitatus, syn. *Coridothymus capitatus)*

Tender Perennial   Zone 9

Native Habitat   Mediterranean Europe and North Africa

Second in preference of the culinary za'atars is said to be conehead thyme, which is found growing on the dry, sunny hills of its native Mediterranean habitat. Upon close inspection, this stiff-branched little domed shrublet, 8 to 10 inches high, has many fascinating features. The reason for its name becomes quite apparent when it comes into flower in midsummer, for its showy purple blossoms sprout from green pinecone-shaped flowerheads; they also resemble hops, hence one of the alternative names for the herb, hophead thyme. Conehead thyme's elongated stems are almost white, with evenly spaced opposite clusters of tiny, needlelike leaves that are a shiny, rich green. The leaves contain a resinous oreganolike flavor that is somewhat hotter than Syrian oregano. From those fragrant leaves is distilled a commercial essential oil known as Spanish origanum oil, which is used in the food industry to flavor a number of products, including baked goods and condiments. The oil is also used in commercial cosmetics and toiletries. The nectar held in the fragrant flowers of conehead thyme has given the herb a claim to fame, for it is said to be the source of the reknowned Hymettus honey of Greece.

GROWING YOUR OWN

Conehead thyme grows best in average soil with excellent drainage, and full sun. In soils where proper drainage is a problem the herb is best served by planting higher than usual, i.e. with its crown slightly above ground level. It needs only moderate water, and is drought-tolerant when established. Cut back the flowering tips after bloom, and tip-prune during the season to encourage growth on the lower stems. In cold climates it can be grown in the ground or in containers and brought indoors to overwinter.

The soft mounds of creeping thyme (*Thymus serpyllum*) are a nice contrast to the sharp leaves of conehead thyme. The silver, pebbly leaves of 'Berggarten' sage look attractive planted adjacent to a little bed of "scruffy" upright thymes such as 'Orange Balsam' thyme, 'Grey Hill' thyme, with its lemon scent, and the unique 'Italian Oregano' thyme. Planted together, these herbs are a perfect combination for a theme bed of Mediterranean plants.

PINK SAVORY

(Satureja thymbra)

Tender Perennial   Zones 8–9

Native Habitat   Sardinia, Greece, Crete, and the eastern Mediterranean

From the garden at Festival Hill, Round Top, Texas

Pink savory is a wiry herb that grows to about 1 foot tall, but its size and unassuming appearance belie the astonishing flavor it packs. The essential oil of savory is foremost, but pink savory's flavor is hotter than that of its relative, summer savory, and is mixed with strong notes of oregano. In spring and summer, small-petaled pink flowers grow in globular whorls at intervals along the erect stems, encircled by small, medium green, pointed leaves slightly folded lengthwise. Like the other za'atars, pink savory grows on dry, stony hillsides in its native habitat. This robust shrublet yields an aromatic nectar that is the source of an excellent fragrant honey in its homeland. Pink savory was known to the seventeenth-century herbalists Gerard and Parkinson, who called it Wild Time of Candy, "time" being thyme, and "candy," the then name for the island of Crete. The herb is also known as goat thyme, and Roman, Greek, and European hyssop, but you will find it listed in nursery catalogs as pink savory and in some instances by another curious name, barrel sweetener. In Crete, a strong infusion of the herb was used to clean and freshen wine barrels in the fall in preparation for the new vintage.

GROWING YOUR OWN

Pink savory likes dry, average to alkaline soil, full sun, and excellent drainage. Where proper drainage is a problem, plant the herb somewhat higher, i.e. with its crown slightly above ground level. It needs very moderate water once established. Cut back the tip growth to maintain its best appearance. In cold-winter climates the herb can be grown in the ground or a pot sunken into the ground in summer, then brought into a greenhouse to overwinter. This otherwise visually unremarkable herb is quite decorative when in flower, with the lavender pink blossoms covering the plant from the middle to the ends of its stems. It is the perfect herb to provide a pale dash of color to brighten up the corner of a garden bed. After its flowering period, if you forget to cut back the spent flowers, the dried calyces look like a string of dark beads on thin, erect branches—although unless you are collecting seed it's best not to see too much of this decor but to remove it in the interest of flavor in pink savory's leaves. It looks best underplanted with a low-growing thyme to soften its scrubby appearance and lower branches. Pink savory is especially effective planted near the nonculinary *Salvia thymoides,* whose vivid, acid-blue flowers complement pink savory's bluish-pink blossoms. Silver patches of the low-growing cut-leaf tansy (*Tanacetum densum amanii*) also complement its sharp green leaves. The dark green leaves and light purple flowers of conehead thyme, and the elongated leaves and deep pink flowers of spiked thyme are two other perfect partners in a theme bed of Mediterranean herbs and za'atars.

SPIKED THYME
(Thymbra spicata)

Tender Perennial   Zones 8–10
Native Habitat   Greece to Israel and the eastern Mediterranean

From the garden at Festival Hill, Round Top, Texas

In the dry, often rocky, scrubby, sunny hillsides and high meadows of its native habitat grows spiked thyme, a pretty little erect-branched za'atar with tubular rose-pink flowers nestled among the dense leaves on its fat flowering heads, or spikes. It has a spicy taste similar to that of pink savory and conehead thyme. Bees feed on its flowers, and make a fragrant honey from the nectar. So fragrant is the plant that historically it has been used as an incense in Greece. This herb with its 1-to-1½-inch-long narrow leaves is the za'atar sometimes pictured in Middle Eastern cookbooks puzzlingly captioned "thyme," though it does not resemble the herb generally considered to be thyme. This may explain the word "thyme" that sometimes appears on labels of imported za'atar sold in Middle Eastern markets. Spiked thyme is also known as wide-leaf hyssop, dessert hyssop, red hyssop, and donkey hyssop—I suppose because donkeys also enjoy za'atar in the wild.

GROWING YOUR OWN

Spiked thyme grows 1 to 2 feet tall. It likes sandy, mildly alkaline soil. It needs only moderate water. Good drainage is a must, and where that is a problem planting the herb in raised beds or in the ground with its crown somewhat higher than ground level will aid the soil in draining quickly . The herb is drought-tolerant when established. In cold climates it can be grown in the ground or in containers, and brought indoors to overwinter. Keep the herb tip-pruned to encourage bushy growth, and cut back the old shoots in the spring. Good companions for spiked thyme for a Mediterranean theme bed include two of the other za'atars, conehead thyme and pink savory, and the low-growing lavender 'Hidcote' or lavender 'Wallers Munstead'.

CULINARY USES

Despite the exotic nature of za'atar, both the fresh herbs and the blend have many uses with familiar foods. When your za'atar plants are established, you can make your own dried condiment.

Nowhere is the dried za'atar blend more popular than when sprinkled on breads lightly coated with olive oil. The mixture is most appropriate on Middle Eastern flatbreads, but it can also be spread on French and Italian breads, focaccia, bread sticks, and country loaves. One of the most eclectic uses of the za'atar condiment is a dip that a fellow herb gardener prepared for me, which is simply the dried blend mixed with Mexican *crema,* or tangy, thickened cream, and served with fresh vegetable crudités. For a dip with a Mediterranean flavor, hummus and dried za'atar are good companions, served with fresh crunchy carrot sticks and celery, or crackly lavash. To prepare a unique condiment to serve with cheeses, paté, or cold meats, make your own version of "wild marjoram pickle": pack fresh branches of conehead thyme in brine and allow them to sit for a week before serving.

An Italian chef friend gave me a recipe for "poor man's parmesan," a savory mixture of bread crumbs, garlic, and extra virgin olive oil that is baked in the oven till crisp and sprinkled over pasta. But it didn't have any herbs in it. Dried Syrian oregano gave the mixture a savory little punch. When you serve pizza, a shaker of your own dried za'atar blend can be put on the table along with the dried chile flakes.

The robust flavor of dried za'atar is excellent with roasted or grilled meat, with shish kebabs of lamb or beef, and in stews. Make your own version of the Middle Eastern meatballs known as *kefta*, typically ground lamb or beef mixed with parsley, onion, and a pinch of cinnamon, then sprinkle the cooked meat with the za'atar condiment. Chicken breasts and game hens can be marinated in the blend before roasting, and a pinch or two can be dusted over a luncheon or supper omelette. Dried za'atar can be added to bean dishes as well, and is considered a digestive aid.

Any one of the fresh za'atar herbs can be used in any dish where the oregano-thyme-savory taste is desired. As they all differ in strength, use small amounts until the taste suits you. They can be chopped and sprinkled over vegetables such as baked eggplant, baked beets, steamed cauliflower, and green beans. Use them in fava beans with sautéed onions and garlic; add them to grated zucchini pancakes; mix them with extra virgin olive oil and lemon juice to drizzle over steamed artichokes; and sprinkle them over a fresh tomato and sliced onion salad, garnished with feta cheese and black olives. Pink savory is a good resinous herb for curing olives, and a healthy pinch added to good-quality canned or bottled Greek olives greatly enhances their flavor.

Nor is za'atar left out of the beverage category, for both pink savory and Syrian oregano are two of the herbs especially enjoyed when prepared as a hot tea, not only to give flavor and refresh, but to soothe an uneasy stomach or to act as a balm for a cold.

Dried Za'atar Condiment

This recipe for a dried za'atar is only a guide. The amounts can be varied according to the personal taste of the cook, and the strength can be varied according to which fresh za'atar herb is used. In the Middle East, recipes for the blend vary from region to region. Some blends are greener with fresh herbs, others are redder with the addition of more sumac, and with the addition of ground chickpeas or wheat grains, the mixture becomes brown.

It should be noted that the species of edible sumac berries grown in the Middle East (*Rhus coriara*) should not be confused with the three poisonous plants that grow wild in North America, poison ivy, poison oak, and poison sumac. Edible sumac is available at Middle Eastern markets and specialty food shops.

½ cup dried Syrian oregano

¼ cup imported edible ground sumac berries

2 tablespoons roasted sesame seeds

¼ teaspoon sea salt

Black pepper to taste

Pita bread

⅔ cup olive oil (optional)

In a small bowl add all the ingredients and stir together to combine. Pour into a glass jar and cover tightly. Store in a cool, dark place. Makes approximately ⅔ cup.

Preheat the oven to 250 degrees.

Brush pita or other flat bread with extra virgin olive oil. Sprinkle the za'atar condiment mixture over the bread, and warm in the oven. Or, equal parts of the olive oil and the za'atar blend can be mixed together and spread over the bread, then warmed.

White Bean Dip with Red Caviar and Pink Savory

Every time I serve this unusual appetizer, my guests play a guessing game as to *what* the dip is, and it is always a surprise to learn that it is made of plebeian beans paired with nonplebeian caviar. There is no need for added salt, as the caviar provides just the right amount.

1 fifteen-ounce can white cannellini beans
2 cloves garlic, finely minced
1 tablespoon freshly squeezed lemon juice
1 tablespoon extra virgin olive oil

1 teaspoon finely chopped fresh pink savory leaves
Red pepper sauce to taste
1 four-ounce jar red lumpfish roe caviar

Strain the cannellini beans, and reserve the liquid. In a medium mixing bowl, combine the beans and garlic. With the back of a large spoon, crush cannellini beans against the sides of the bowl, mixing well with the garlic. Add the lemon juice, olive oil, pink savory, and the red pepper sauce. Combine well. Thin the mixture with some of the reserved bean liquid if a thinner consistency is desired. Gently fold in the caviar, taking care not to crush the caviar eggs. Cover and refrigerate for at least 1 hour to allow the flavors to meld. When ready to serve, spoon mixture into a serving dish. Serve with crackers or petals of Belgian endive. Makes 1 to 1½ cups.

Serves 4 to 6

Sea Green Bean Dip with Black Caviar

The method of preparation of this dip is identical to the preceding White Bean Dip with Red Caviar and Pink Savory. With the substitution of three ingredients—flageolet or lima beans, spiked thyme, and black caviar—the dip becomes sea green, but is just as tasty.

1 fourteen-ounce can flageolet or lima beans
2 cloves garlic, finely minced
1 tablespoon freshly squeezed lemon juice
1 tablespoon extra virgin olive oil

1 teaspoon finely chopped fresh spiked thyme
Red pepper sauce to taste
1 four-ounce jar black lumpfish roe caviar

Follow the directions for the preceding recipe.
Serves 4 to 6

Appetizers and Condiments (from left to right): Roasted Pumpkin Seed Dip with Mexican Oregano, Purple Pickled Turnips, Chèvre Preserved in Spice-Scented Oil, White Bean Dip with Red Caviar and Pink Savory

Purple Pickled Turnips

White turnips stained a rich garnet purple by beets make a deliciously tart pickled vegetable. In the Middle East, these turnips would be part of the *mezze* table, or little appetizers that signal the start of a meal, similar to Italian *antipasti*, Spanish *tapas*, and French (and American) hors d'oeuvre. The recipe may be cut in half, to make a smaller quantity.

2 pounds small white turnips
2 small beets
6 five-inch branches fresh conehead thyme

2½ cups water
1¼ cups apple cider vinegar
1½ tablespoons sea salt

Wash and peel the turnips and beets. Cut them into bite-sized wedges. Place the turnips, with the beets scattered between them, in a sterilized wide-mouthed 2-quart jar with a nonreactive lid. Add the conehead thyme. Pour the water and vinegar into a medium mixing bowl. Add the salt, and stir until dissolved, then pour into the jar to within 1 inch of the top. Cover tightly and refrigerate for 1 week to 10 days.

   Before serving, bring the turnips to room temperature. They can be stored in the refrigerator for up to 1 month.

Makes 2 quarts

Sources

HERB NURSERIES AND SEED SUPPLIERS

Bountiful Gardens
Ecology Action
5798 Ridgewood Road
Willits, California 95490

Brudy's Exotics
P. O. Box 820874
Houston, Texas 77282-0874

Canyon Creek Nursery
3527 Dry Creek Road
Oroville, California 95965

Companion Plants
7247 North Coolville Ridge Road
Athens, Ohio 45701

The Cook's Garden
P. O. Box 535
Londonderry, Vermont 05148

Evergreen Y. H. Enterprises
Oriental Vegetable Seeds
P. O. Box 17538
Anaheim, California 92817

The Flowery Branch
P. O. Box 1330
Flowery Branch, Georgia 30542

Geo. W. Park Seed Co., Inc.
Cokesbury Road
Greenwood, South Carolina 29647-0001

Glasshouse Works
Church Street
Stewart, Ohio 45778-0097

Goodwin Creek Gardens
P. O. Box 83
Williams, Oregon 97544

Graines Baumaux
B. P. 100
54062 Nancy Cedex, France

The Herbfarm
32804 Issaquah–Fall City Road
Fall City, Washington 98024

J. L. Hudson, Seedsman
Star Route 2, Box 337
La Honda, California 94020

It's About Thyme
11726 Manchaca Road
Austin, Texas 78748

Johnny's Selected Seeds
Foss Hill Road
Albion, Maine 04910-9731

Kartuz Greenhouses
1408 Sunset Drive
Vista, California 92083-6531

Logee's Greenhouses
141 North Street
Danielson, Connecticut 06239

McClure & Zimmerman
108 W. Winnebago, P. O. Box 368
Friesland, Wisconsin 53935

Mountain Valley Growers, Inc.
38325 Pepperweed Road
Squaw Valley, California 93675

Native Seeds/SEARCH
2509 N. Campbell Avenue, #325
Tucson, Arizona 85719

The Natural Gardening Company
217 San Anselmo Avenue
San Anselmo, California 94960

Nichols Garden Nursery
1190 North Pacific Highway
Albany, Oregon 97321-4580

Pacific Tree Farm
4301 Lynwood Drive
Chula Vista, California 91910

Pinetree Garden Seeds
Box 300
New Gloucester, Maine 04260

Raintree Nursery
391 Butts Road
Morton, Washington 98356

Rasland Farm
N.C. 82 at U.S. 13
Godwin, North Carolina 28344-9712

The Redwood City Seed Company
P. O. Box 361
Redwood City, California 94064

Richters
Goodwood, Ontario
Canada L0C 1 AO

The Sandy Mush Herb Nursery
316 Surrett Cove Road
Leicester, North Carolina 28748-9622

Seeds for the World
Garden Lane
Fair Haven, Vermont 05743

Seeds of Change
P. O. Box 15700
Santa Fe, New Mexico 87506-5700

Select Seeds Antique Flowers
180 Stickney Road
Union, Connecticut 06076-4617

Shepherd's Garden Seeds
Shipping Office
30 Irene Street
Torrington, Connecticut 06790

Siskiyou Rare Plant Nursery
2825 Cummings Road
Medford, Oregon 97501

Sunnybrook Farms Nursery
9448 Mayfield Road, P. O. Box 6
Chesterland, Ohio 44026

Sunrise Enterprises
P. O. Box 1960
Chesterfield, Virginia 23838

Territorial Seed Company
P. O. Box 157
Cottage Grove, Oregon 97424-0061

Thompson & Morgan, Inc.
P. O. Box 1308
Jackson, New Jersey 08527-0308

Well-Sweep Herb Farm
205 Mt. Bethel Road
Port Murray, New Jersey 07865

White Flower Farm
P. O. Box 50
Litchfield, Connecticut 06759-0050

HERB SOURCES, LISTED BY HERB

ALLIUMS

'Échalote de Jersey'
Graines Baumaux

Egyptian onion
Goodwin Creek Gardens, Nichols Garden Nursery, Richters, Sunnybrook Farms Nursery, The Natural Gardening Company, The Sandy Mush Herb Nursery, Well-Sweep Herb Farm

Allspice
Pacific Tree Farm, Richters, Well-Sweep Herb Farm

Anise hyssop
Companion Plants, Goodwin Creek Gardens, Johnny's Selected Seeds, Logee's Greenhouses Mountain Valley Growers, Nichols Garden Nursery, Pinetree Garden Seeds, Rasland Farm, Richters, The Sandy Mush Herb Nursery, Seeds of Change, Select Seeds Antique Flowers, Shepherd's Garden Seeds, The Cook's Garden, The Flowery Branch, The Herbfarm, Well-Sweep Herb Farm

BASILS

'African Blue' basil
Companion Plants, Rasland Farm, Richters, Shepherd's Garden Seeds, Well-Sweep Herb Farm

'Mrs. Burns' Famous Lemon Basil'
Companion Plants, Native Seeds/ SEARCH, Rasland Farm, Richters, The Flowery Branch, Well-Sweep Herb Farm

'Cinnamon' basil

The Cook's Garden, The Flowery Branch, The Herbfarm, It's About Thyme, Johnny's Selected Seeds, Mountain Valley Growers, Pinetree Garden Seeds, Rasland Farm, The Redwood City Seed Company, Richters, Sandy Mush Herb Nursery, Seeds for the World, Seeds of Change, Shepherd's Garden Seeds, Thompson & Morgan, Well-Sweep Herb Farm

East Indian basil

Companion Plants, The Flowery Branch, Mountain Valley Growers, Rasland Farm, Richters, Well-Sweep Herb Farm

White-flowering borage

The Flowery Branch, The Herbfarm Shepherd's Garden Seeds

Leaf celery

The Cook's Garden, The Flowery Branch, Johnny's Selected Seeds, Geo. W. Park Seed Co., Pinetree Garden Seeds, Richters, Shepherd's Garden Seeds, Sunrise Enterprises, Thompson & Morgan

Garland chrysanthemum

Companion Plants, The Cook's Garden, Evergreen Y. H. Enterprises, The Flowery Branch, Nichols Garden Nursery, Pinetree Garden Seeds, Richters, Seeds for the World, Seeds of Change, Shepherd's Garden Seeds, Sunrise Enterprises, Territorial Seed Company, Well-Sweep Herb Farm

CILANTRO MIMICS

Culantro

Companion Plants, Mountain Valley Growers, Richters, Well-Sweep Herb Farm

Papaloquelite

Richters, Seeds of Change

Rau ram or Vietnamese coriander

Companion Plants, The Herbfarm, Mountain Valley Growers, Richters, Well-Sweep Herb Farm

Broadleaf garden cress

The Cook's Garden, Nichols Garden Nursery, Seeds of Change, Shepherd's Garden Seeds, Thompson & Morgan

Curry leaf

Logee's Greenhouses, Pacific Tree Farm, Well-Sweep Herb Farm

Superb Pink

The Cook's Garden, The Flowery Branch, J. L. Hudson, Select Seeds Antique Flowers, Shepherd's Garden Seeds, Thompson & Morgan, White Flower Farm

Epazote

Bountiful Gardens, The Flowery Branch, The Herbfarm, It's About Thyme, Johnny's, Native Seeds/SEARCH, Nichols Garden Nursery, Mountain Valley Growers, The

Redwood City Seed Company, Richters, The Sandy Mush Herb Nursery, Seeds of Change, Shepherd's Garden Seeds, Sunnybrook Farms Nursery, Well-Sweep Herb Farm

Bronze fennel
Companion Plants, The Flowery Branch, Goodwin Creek Gardens, The Herbfarm, It's About Thyme, Mountain Valley Growers, Geo. W. Park Seed Co., Pinetree Garden Seeds, Rasland Farm, Richters, The Sandy Mush Herb Nursery, Select Seeds, Shepherd's Garden Seeds, The Redwood City Seed Company

FRAISES DES BOIS

Variegated fraises des bois
Logee's Greenhouses, Well-Sweep Herb Farm

White fraises des bois
Shepherd's Garden Seeds, Siskiyou Rare Plant Nursery, Well-Sweep Herb Farm

Yellow fraises des bois
The Flowery Branch, Pacific Tree Farm, Raintree Nursery

'Mabel Grey' scented geranium
Canyon Creek Nursery, Goodwin Creek Gardens, The Herbfarm, Logee's Green-

houses, Rasland Farm, Richters, The Sandy Mush Herb Nursery, Well-Sweep Herb Farm

Herba stella
Shepherd's Garden Seeds

Houttuynia
Canyon Creek Nursery, Companion Plants, Mountain Valley Growers, Rasland Farm, Richters, The Sandy Mush Herb Nursery, Well-Sweep Herb Farm

'Grand Duke of Tuscany' and 'Maid of Orleans' Arabian jasmine
Kartuz Greenhouses, Logee's Greenhouses, Well-Sweep Herb Farm, Kaffir lime, Pacific Tree Farm, Well-Sweep Herb Farm

Kaffir lime
Pacific Tree Farm, Well-Sweep Herb Farm

Magenta lambs-quarter
Bountiful Gardens, Companion Plants, The Flowery Branch, J. L. Hudson, Seeds of Change

Pink lavender
Companion Plants, Rasland Farm, Well-Sweep Herb Farm, White Flower Farm

White lavender
Shepherd's Garden Seeds, Well-Sweep Herb Farm

Dwarf white lavender
Goodwin Creek Gardens, The Herbfarm, Well-Sweep Herb Farm

Lemon grass
Companion Plants, The Herbfarm, It's About Thyme, Logee's Greenhouses, Mountain Valley Growers, Nichols Garden Nursery, Rasland Farm, Richters, The Sandy Mush Herb Nursery, Shepherd's Garden Seeds, Sunrise Enterprises, Sunnybrook Farms Nursery, Well-Sweep Herb Farm, White Flower Farm

Malabar spinach
Evergreen Y. H. Enterprises, Geo. T. Park Seed Co., Nichols Garden Nursery, Sunrise Enterprises

Mexican tarragon
Companion Plants, It's About Thyme, J. L. Hudson, Logee's Greenhouses, Mountain Valley Growers, Nichols Garden Nursery

Miner's lettuce
Bountiful Gardens, The Cook's Garden, Johnny's Selected Seeds, Richters, Shepherd's Garden Seeds

Ginger mint
Goodwin Creek Gardens, The Herbfarm, Richters, The Sandy Mush Herb Nursery, Sunnybrook Farms Nursery, Well-Sweep Herb Farm

Mitsuba
Evergreen Y. H. Enterprises, Goodwin Creek Gardens, Richters, The Sandy Mush Herb Nursery, Seeds for the World, Seeds of Change, Shepherd's Garden Seeds, Sunrise Enterprises

Nigella
The Flowery Branch, Select Seeds, Antique Flowers, Shepherd's Garden Seeds

OREGANO MIMICS

Cuban Oregano
The Herbfarm, Glasshouse Works, It's About Thyme, Logee's Greenhouses, Mountain Valley Growers, Richters, Sunnybrook Farms Nursery, Well-Sweep Herb Farm, White Flower Farm

Mexican oregano I (*Lippia graveolens*)
Companion Plants, The Herbfarm, It's About Thyme, Mountain Valley Growers, Rasland Farm, Richters, The Sandy Mush Herb Nursery, Well-Sweep Herb Farm

Mexican oregano II (*Poliomentha longiflora*)
Companion Plants, It's About Thyme, Logee's Greenhouses, Mountain Valley Growers, Rasland Farm, The Sandy Mush Herb Nursery, Well-Sweep Herb Farm

Perilla

Companion Plants, Richters, The Sandy Mush Herb Nursery, Shepherd's Garden Seeds, Sunrise Enterprises, Well-Sweep Herb Farm

'Bronze' perilla

Companion Plants

Golden purslane

The Cook's Garden, Pinetree Garden Seeds, Shepherd's Garden Seeds

Green purslane

The Herbfarm, Nichols Garden Nursery, Richters, Seeds for the World, Shepherd's Garden Seeds, Territorial Seed Company

Rice paddy herb

Companion Plants, Richters, Well-Sweep Herb Farm

Roman mint

Richters, Well-Sweep Herb Farm

Calamint

Richters (Nepitella)
Companion Plants (Niebita)
Well-Sweep Herb Farm ('Pompeii')

Roselle

Brudy's Exotics

ROSEMARY

'Golden Rain' rosemary

Canyon Creek Nursery, Companion Plants, The Herbfarm, Goodwin Creek Gardens, It's About Thyme, Logee's Greenhouses, Rasland Farm, The Sandy Mush Nursery, Well-Sweep Herb Farm

'Majorca Pink' rosemary

Companion Plants, Goodwin Creek Gardens, Mountain Valley Growers, Rasland Farm, Richters, Sunnybrook Farms Nursery, Well-Sweep Herb Farm

Saffron

The Herbfarm, McClure & Zimmerman (also white saffron), Nichols Garden Nursery, Richters, Shepherd's Garden Seeds

SAGES

Cleveland sage

Canyon Creek Nursery, Companion Plants, The Flowery Branch, Goodwin Creek Gardens, It's About Thyme, J. L. Hudson, Logee's Greenhouses, Mountain Valley Growers, Richters, The Sandy Mush Herb Nursery, Sunnybrook Farms Nursery, Well-Sweep Herb Farm

'Frieda Dixon' pineapple sage
Canyon Creek Nursery, Companion Plants, Goodwin Creek Gardens, The Sandy Mush Herb Nursery

Samphire
Glasshouse Works, Goodwin Creek Gardens, Logee's Greenhouses, Nichols Garden Nursery, The Sandy Mush Herb Nursery, Sunnybrook Farms Nursery, Well-Sweep Herb Farm

Silene
Shepherd's Garden Seeds

True French sorrel
The Herbfarm, Richters, Sunnybrook Farms Nursery

'Orange Balsam' thyme
Companion Plants, Goodwin Creek Gardens, The Herbfarm, Logee's Greenhouses, Mountain Valley Growers, Rasland Farms, Richters, The Sandy Mush Herb Nursery, Well-Sweep Herb Farm

African valerian
The Flowery Branch, Shepherd's Garden Seeds

Vietnamese balm
Richters, The Sandy Mush Herb Nursery, Well-Sweep Herb Farm

Sweet violet
Canyon Creek Nursery, The Flowery Branch, The Herbfarm, It's About Thyme, J. L. Hudson, Logee's Greenhouses, Seeds for the World, The Sandy Mush Herb Nursery, White Flower Farm

ZA'ATARS

Syrian oregano
Mountain Valley Growers, Rasland Farm, Richters, The Sandy Mush Herb Nursery, Well-Sweep Herb Farm

Conehead thyme
Companion Plants, The Sandy Mush Herb Nursery, Well-Sweep Herb Farm

Pink savory
Mountain Valley Growers, The Sandy Mush Herb Nursery, Well-Sweep Herb Farm

Spiked thyme
Companion Plants, Mountain Valley Growers, Well-Sweep Herb Farm

Selected Bibliography

Algar, Ayla. *Classical Turkish Cooking*. New York: HarperCollins, 1991.

Barash, Cathy Wilkinson. *Evening Gardens*. Golden, Colorado: Fulcrum Publishing, 1993.

Barron, Rosemary. *Flavors of Greece*. New York: William Morrow, 1991.

Bayless, Rick, with Deann Groen Bayless. *Authentic Mexican Regional Cooking from the Heart of Mexico*. New York: William Morrow, 1987.

Boisvert, Clotilde, and Annie Hubert. *Herbes et épices*. Paris: Editions Albin Michel, 1977.

Boxer, Arabella. *The Encyclopedia of Herbs, Spices and Flavorings*. London: Crescent Books, 1984.

Bremness, Lesley. *The Complete Book of Herbs*. London: Dorling Kindersley, 1988.

———. *Herbs, Eyewitness Handbooks*. New York: Dorling Kindersley, 1994.

Brown, Deni. *The Herb Society of America Encyclopedia of Herbs and Their Uses*. New York: Dorling Kindersley, 1995.

Buchanan, Rita, ed. *Taylor's Guide to Herbs*. Boston: Houghton Mifflin, 1995.

Burkhill, I. H. *A Dictionary of the Economic Products of the Malay Peninsula*. Vol. 1. Kuala Lumpur: Ministry of Agriculture and Cooperatives, 1966.

Chin, H. F., and H. S. Yong. *Malaysian Fruits in Color*. Tropical Press, SDN, BHD, University of Malaysia, 1982.

Clarkson, Rosetta. *Magic Gardens*. London: Macmillan, 1942.

Clausen, Ruth Rogers, and Nicolas H. Ekstrom. *Perennials for American Gardens*. New York: Random House, 1989.

Cost, Bruce. *Bruce Cost's Asian Ingredients*. New York: William Morrow, 1988.

Craker, Lyle E., and James E. Simon. *Herbs, Spices, and Medicinal Plants: Recent Advances in Botany, Horticulture, and Pharmacology*. Vol. 1. Phoenix, Arizona: Oryx Press, 1986.

Creasy, Rosalind. *Cooking from the Garden*. San Francisco: Sierra Club Books, 1988.

Culpeper, Nicholas. *The English Physician Enlarged*. Printed for A. and J. Churchill, London, 1698.

Davis, P. H., ed. *Flora of Turkey and the East Aegean Islands*. Edinburgh: University Press, 1982.

DeBaggio, Thomas. *Growing Herbs from Seed, Cutting and Root*. Loveland, Colorado: Interweave Press, 1994.

de Gingins-Lassaraz, Baron Fred. *Natural History of the Lavenders*. Trans. the New England Unit of the Herb Society of America. Boston: Herb Society of America, 1967.

Dong, Binh, and Marcia Kiesel. *Simple Art of Vietnamese Cooking*. New York: Simon & Schuster, 1981.

Dugdale, Chester B. *A Modern American Herbal*. Cranbury, N.J.: A. S. Barnes, 1978.

Duke, James. *Handbook of Edible Weeds*. Boca Raton, Fla.: CRC Press, 1985, 1992.

Elbert, George, and Virginie Elbert. *Plants That Really Bloom Indoors*. New York: Simon & Schuster/Fireside, 1974.

Facciola, Steven. *Cornucopia: A Source Book of Edible Plants*. Vista, Calif.: Kampong Publications, 1990.

Fernald, Merritt, and Alfred Charles Kinsey. *Edible Wild Plants of Eastern North America*. Rev. ed. New York: Harper & Row, 1943.

Foster, Gertrude B., and Rosemary Louden. *Success with Herbs*. Greenwood, S.C.: Geo. W. Park Seed Company, 1980.

Foster, Steven. *Herbal Renaissance*. Salt Lake City: Gibb Smith Publisher, 1993.

Ganor, Avi, and Ron Maiberg. *Taste of Israel*. New York: Galahad Books, 1993.

Gray, Patience. *Honey from a Weed*. New York: Harper & Row/Prospect Books, 1987.

Greig, Denise. *The Book of Mint*. Kenthurst, Australia: Kangaroo Press, 1989.

Griffiths, Mark. *Index of Garden Plants*. London and Blassingstoke: Timber Press, 1994.

Halpin, Anne Moyer, ed. *Gourmet Gardening*. Emmaus, Pa.: Rodale Press, 1981.

Hamady, Mary Laird. *Lebanese Mountain Cookery*. Boston: David R. Godine, 1987.

Hansen, Barbara. *Barbara Hansen's Taste of Southeast Asia*. New York: Harper & Row/HPBooks, 1987.

Herklots, G. A. C. *Vegetables in Southeast Asia*. New York: Hafner Press, 1972.

Hill, Madalene, and Gwen Barclay. *Southern Herb Growing*. Fredericksburg, Tex.: Shearer Publishing, 1987.

Hopkinson, Patricia. *Herb Growing*. New York: Pantheon Books, 1994.

HORTUS Third. The Staff of the Liberty Hyde Bailey Hortorium. New York: Macmillan Publishing Co., Inc., 1976.

Howes, F. N. *A Dictionary of Useful and Everyday Plants and Their Common Names*. Cambridge: Cambridge University Press, 1974.

Hutson, Lucinda. *The Herb Garden Cookbook*. Austin, Texas: Texas Monthly Press, 1987.

James, Tina. *Lovely Lavender*. Littlestown, Pa.: Alloway Gardens Print Productions, 1990.

Karaoglan, Aida. *Food for the Vegetarian*. New York: Interlink Books, 1988.

Kennedy, Diana. *The Cuisines of Mexico*. New York: Harper & Row, 1972.

Kindscher, Kelly. *Gardening with Southeast Asian Refugees*. Route 2, Box 394A, Lawrence, Kansas 66044.

Kirkpatrick, Debra. *Using Herbs in the Landscape*. Harrisburg, Pa.: Stackpole Books, 1992.

Kuebel, K. R., and Arthur O. Tucker. "Vietnamese Culinary Herbs in the United States," in *Economic Botany* 42, no. 3 Bronx, New York: New York Botanical Garden, 1988.

Larkcom, Joy. *Oriental Vegetables*. Tokyo: Kodansha International, 1991.

———. *The Salad Garden*. New York: Viking, 1984.

Lathrop, Norma Jean. *Herbs: How to Select, Grow and Enjoy*. Tucson, Arizona: H P Books, 1991.

Leung, Albert. *Encyclopedia of Common and Natural Ingredients Used in Food, Drugs, and Cosmetics*. New York: John Wiley, 1980.

Marcin, Marietta Marshall. *The Complete Book of Herbal Teas*. New York: Congdon & Weed, 1983.

McDermott, Nancie. *Real Thai*. San Francisco: Chronicle Books, 1992.

McLeod, Judyth A. *Lavender, Sweet Lavender*. Kenthurst, Australia: Kangaroo Press, 1989.

McVicar, Jekka. *Herbs for the Home*. New York: Viking Studio Books, 1995.

Moldenke, Harold, and Alma Moldenke. *Plants of the Bible*. New York: Ronald Press, 1952.

Morton, Julia. *Atlas of Medicinal Plants of Middle America, Bahamas to Yucátan*. Springfield, Ill.: Charles C. Thomas, 1981.

Morton, Julia, ed. *Golden Guide to Herbs and Spices*. Racine, Wis.: Western Publishing Company, 1976.

Muenscher, Minnie. *Minnie Muenscher's Herb Cookbook*. Ithaca, N.Y.: Cornell University Press, 1978.

Muenscher, W. C. *Weeds*. New York: Macmillan, 1955.

Norman, Jill. *The Complete Book of Spices*. New York: Viking Studio Books, 1990.

Ochse, J. J. *Fruits and Fruit Culture in the Dutch East Indies*. Batavia, Indonesia: G. Kolff & Co., 1931.

Ortiz, Elisabeth Lambert, and Sheldon Greenberg. *The Spice of Life*. New York: Amaryllis Press, 1983.

Painter, Gillian. *A Garden of Old Fashioned and Unusual Herbs*. Auckland/Sydney/London: Hodder & Stoughton, 1982.

Paterson, Allen. *Herbs in the Garden*. London: J. M. Dent, 1985.

Phillips, Roger. *Wild Food*. London: Pan Books, 1983.

Phillips, Roger, and Nicky Foy. *Herbs*. New York: Random House, 1990.

Poladitmontri, Panurat, and Judy Lew. *Thailand the Beautiful Cookbook*. Text by William Warren. New York: HarperCollins, 1993.

Pond, Barbara. *A Sampler of Wayside Herbs*. New York: Greenwich House, 1974.

Poulin, Oleg, and Audrey Huxley. *Flowers of the Mediterranean*. London: Chatto & Windus, 1965.

Purseglove, J. W. *Tropical Crops: Dicotyledons*. Vol. 2. New York: John Wiley, 1968.

Quintana, Patricia, with Jack Bishop. *Cuisine of the Water Gods*. New York: Simon & Schuster, 1994.

Reuther, Walter, ed. *The Citrus Industry*. Vol. 1: *History, World Distribution, Botany and Varieties*. University of California, Division of Agricultural Sciences, 1967.

Rinzler, Carol. *Herbs, Spices and Condiments*. New York: Henry Holt, 1990.

Rodin, Claudia. *A Book of Middle Eastern Food*. New York: Alfred A. Knopf, 1972.

Root, Waverly. *Herbs and Spices*. New York: Alfred van der Marck Editions, 1985.

Routhier, Nicole. *The Foods of Vietnam*. New York: Stewart, Tabori & Chang, 1987.

Sahni, Julie. *Moghul Microwave*. New York: William Morrow, 1990.

Sanecki, Kay. *The Complete Book of Herbs*. New York: Macmillan, 1974.

Sen Gupta, Pranati. *The Art of Indian Cuisine*. New York: Hawthorne Books, 1974.

Simmons, Adelma. *The Strawberry Book*. Tolland, Conn.: Clinton Press, 1977.

Smaus, Robert. *Planning and Planting the Garden*. New York: Harry N. Abrams, 1989.

Stobart, Tom. *Herbs, Spices, and Flavorings*. Harmondsworth: Penguin Books, 1970.

Sturtevant, E. L. *Sturtevant's Notes on Edible Plants*, ed. U. P. Hedrick. Albany: J. B. Lyon State Printers, 1919.

Tanaka, T. *Tanaka's Cyclopedia of Edible Plants of the World*. Tokyo: Keigaku Publishing Co., 1984.

Tindall, H. D. *Vegetables in the Tropics,* Westport, Conn.: AVI Publishing Company, Inc., 1983.

Tutin, T. G., ed. *Flora Europaea.* Vol. 3. Cambridge: Cambridge University Press, 1972.

Tyler, Varro E. *The Honest Herbal.* Binghamton, N.Y.: Pharmaceutical Products Press, 1982.

Uphof, J. C. Th. *Dictionary of Economic Plants.* New York: Verlag von J. Cramer, Stechert-Hafner Services Agency, Inc., 1968.

Vilmorin-Andrieux, MM. *The Vegetable Garden.* London: John Murray Ltd., 1885; Berkeley, Calif.: Ten Speed Press, 1993, facsimile reprint.

Wrensch, Ruth. *The Essence of Herbs.* Oxford: University of Mississippi Press, 1992.

Zohary, Michael. *Plant Life of Palestine.* New York: Ronald Press, 1962.

Index